CARROTS, STICKS & SERMONS

EDITED BY

Marie-Louise
Bemelmans-Videc

Ray C. Rist

Evert Vedung

CARROTS, STICKS & SERMONS

Policy Instruments & Their Evaluation

Transaction Publishers
New Brunswick (U.S.A.) and London (U.K.)

Fourth paperback printing 2007
Copyright © 1998 by Transaction Publishers, New Brunswick, New Jersey.

This book is printed on acid-free paper that meets the American National Standard for Permanence of Paper for Printed Library Materials.

Library of Congress Catalog Number: 97-45617
ISBN: 978-1-56000-338-0 (cloth); 978-0-7658-0546-1 (paper)
Printed in the United States of America

Library of Congress Cataloging-in-Publication Data

Carrots, sticks, and sermons : policy instruments and their evaluation / edited
  by Marie-Louise Bemelmans-Videc, Ray C. Rist, Evert Vedung.
       p. cm.—(Comparative policy analysis series)
  Includes bibliographical references and index.
  ISBN 0-7658-0546-4 (alk. paper)
    1. Policy sciences—Cross-cultural studies. 2. Evaluation research (Social
  action programs) I. Bemelmans-Videc, Marie-Louise. II. Rist, Ray C.
  III. Vedung, Evert, 1938-. IV. Series.

H97.C37 1998
320'.6—dc21   97-45617
                                                                      CIP

Contents

Introduction

Policy Instrument Choice and Evaluation

Marie-Louise Bemelmans-Videc

This book aims at offering its readers insights into the process of policy instrument choice and the role assigned to and actually played by evaluation in this process. The literature on policy strategies, instruments, and styles is quite impressive, both in quantitative and qualitative terms. The student of the field faces a complex variety of theoretical and conceptual approaches and analytical tools which hamper a good overview. Overview and insight presupposes an enlightening structuring of the field. The ambitious objective of this book is to propose such a structure.

It sets out to do so by offering a comprehensive analysis of categories and typologies in the literature, and a reasoned choice for a general typology of policy instruments which then is tested for its theoretical value and, to the degree a book's size allows, for its empirical value. It looks at policy instrument choice from two angles: cross-policy sector, concentrating on one type of instrument, as well as context-bound by offering case studies of choice-processes where the institutional context is taken into consideration.

To the degree the studies are situated in different nations, the book also offers a comparative perspective. These nations are Sweden, The Netherlands, Belgium, England, Canada, the United States, and the Republic of Korea. The variety offered represents rather different histories and political cultures; the nations are alike insofar that, given their differing historical starting points, they represent forms of mixed economies, democratic political structures, and a high level of economic development.

This book's first emphasis is on choice and evaluation; the comparative outlook should help to explain differences and similarities in those processes. The concept of policy style may be of some help in this regard as we shall see. As such, the book is a contribution to the literature on comparative public policy, which Heidenheimer et al. defined as "the study of how, why, and to what effect different governments pursue particular courses of action or inaction" (1990: 3). This definition implies knowledge of structures and processes through which government decisions are reached and of political cultures of nations and the nations' relevant subsections as well as the multitude of actors engaged in public tasks. Should government inaction be considered a policy? Heidenheimer et al. suggest that government inaction, or nondecision, becomes a policy when it is pursued over time in a fairly consistent way against pressures to the contrary (1990: 5).

Heidenheimer et al. point at the diverse theoretical approaches in the literature on comparative public policies which offer varying explanations for policy choice (1990: 7–9):

- the socioeconomic theories that mainly argue that nations respond to the general processes of economic growth and social modernization with basically similar policies;
- the cultural values approach with special emphasis on the deeply embedded cultural ideas arising from the distinctive historical experiences of nations, such as the tradition of laissez-faire liberalism of Anglo-Saxon nations, the statist paternalism of Continental European countries, or the familial quality of organizational life in Japan;
- the political class struggle model where the fundamental dynamic of policy development is seen to lie in the contest between business forces driven by the imperatives of capitalist accumulation on the one hand, and workers and their representatives on the other;
- the neo-corporatist framework emphasizing the broader system of interest representation and its linkages to government through institutionalized bargaining. The capacity to frame, coordinate, and successfully implement policy is seen to be dependent on strongly organized interest blocs (labor, employer, professional, and so on) that are continually engaged in centralized negotiations with government on policy matters of mutual interest; and,
- the institutional-political process perspective: while other frameworks tend to treat policy as the result of outside pressures (socioeconomic, party demands, interest blocs, and so on) on government, institutional analysts put the state at center stage, paying particular attention to distinctive historical patterns in the formation of the nation-state, the way structures and capacities interact with other social actors and the feedback effects of policy on political alliances, party competition and other features of the policy-making landscape.

The theory of comparative public policies should offer understanding and, from that, guidance in designing better policies. Heidenheimer et al. rightly point to a third raison d'être, of growing relevance: increasing interdependencies between nations. The international dimension in public-policy choice is in need of further exploration. The "mosaic pieced together by government authorities at different levels and by private sector actors with public policy responsibilities" (pp. 4–5) has been extended by supranational liaisons and commitments. Recent changes in international political and economic relations clearly influence national sovereignty especially in the social, economic and environmental policy fields. Thus, for example, problems of implementation and evaluation are a factor of growing gravity in policy choices in the European Community (EC) context (Andersen and Eliassen 1993).

This book is not on policy-instrument choice only. Given the shared interest of the members of the IIAS Working Group on Program and Policy Evaluation, it also pays attention to the role of evaluation processes and results as they are used in the choice process. With that, it provides insights into the tradition and actual practice of policy and program evaluation in various countries. It stands in the tradition of the Working Group's publishing activities: it aspires to offer insights into the evaluation practice in countries and to help cross language barriers which all too often stand in the way of dispersing research results among the international community of theoreticians and practitioners (Rist 1990; Mayne et al. 1992; Gray et al. 1993; Leeuw et al. 1994; Toulemonde and Rieper 1996; Mayne and Zapico-Goñi 1996).

Matters of Definition: Our Choices

Any research project faces the challenge of making choices where definitional problems present themselves. A chapter could be dedicated to national and disciplinary variations in definitions of the seemingly clear concepts of "policy," "program," "instrument," and "evaluation." In comparative research one faces the additional linguistic and concomitant cultural differences in conceptual traditions. There needs to be a choice made on the basics.

In line with the definition offered by Vedung in chapter 1, we limit our study to *public policy instruments*. Public policy instruments are the set of techniques by which governmental authorities wield their power in attempting to ensure support and effect social change. In this book, we concentrate (but not exclusively) on instruments of external policies which aim at the behavior of citizens, and therefore imply mechanisms of social influence in society. There are also instruments of internal policies which aim at the social conduct of administrative actors in the public sector such as personnel policies, budget policies, and organizational reform.

The definition indicates a crucial choice. In the words of Vedung: the discourse on public policy instruments is a discourse on political *power.* In modern theories on responsive government, the power factor on which governments may act, also to encourage democratic governance processes, seems to remain out of view, and sometimes even seems to have become a taboo. Central government is pictured as a mediator between interests, a client-oriented manager, responsive and consultative to all relevant actors and stakeholders. Talk is less frequently about the government as being entitled to wielding power, to mediate—if necessary through decisive force—on the basis of a "final" authority. In this book, the government is what it is first and foremost—a democratically legitimized power factor, acting upon its power, and being held accountable for the way that power was wielded.

By our definition we also make clear that policy instruments are understood to be concrete and specified operational forms of intervention by public authorities. They indicate in what concrete action-forms policy is being interpreted and implemented. Policy instrument choices will reflect more general political or administrative *strategies* which are main lines of political and administrative action reflecting general aims and dominant means of action. They are often indicative of either a certain period in the political and administrative history of states or of a dominant political and administrative culture. They vary along a line indicating the degree of intervention: from reserved, cautious, minimalistic, and subsidiary intervention, to more intrusive, active, and developmental forms of intervention, and from repressive forms of intervention (ex- post corrective action regarding deviant behavior) to preventive action, implying the creation of conditions that favor preferred behavior (Van Braam and Bemelmans-Videc 1988: 124–126).

Depending on the governing arrangements in a nation or policy sector, various *actors* (stakeholders) are involved in the actual formulation and choice of policy instruments. They may be consulted in the phase of policy design, they may be involved in implementing a policy and consequently in the actual handling of a policy instrument. Their discretion in interpreting the instrument will shape its actual contents and effects. Government instruments are co-owned by many actors.

In currently published research, the role of the so-called policy networks is emphasized and often presented in a normative fashion, that is, as something basically good or desirable. Abstracting from this ideological connotation, the typology which Vedung will offer stresses the fact that government still has the power (and the ensuing responsibility and accountability) to dictate, to a large degree, the structure and culture (rules of the game) of its varying "partnerships" with other actors in designing and implementing policy programs. As Mayntz asserts, Max Weber's *Verantwortungsethik* (ethics of responsibility) is also highly functional for modern, strongly differentiated societies. The complex interdependencies which result from functional differentiation may pose the problem of indifference of actors to the negative externalities they are producing in the pursuit of their own interests (1993: 12). This illustrates the lasting need for coordination, which requires actualization of power of the more centrally and hierarchically higher positioned governmental actor, who represents larger governmental units. Our conclusion here is that in a multi-actor context, our typology of policy instruments will still provide basic insights.

As for policy-instrument *choice*: the choice between two or more alternatives is the essence of decision making. It is, in the end, an individual activity, a mental or cognitive activity. This is Linder and Peters' main starting point in analyzing the choice of policy instruments: "We will need to move beyond the abstract analytical schemes concerning policy instruments to a more complete understanding of the manner in which they are conceptualized by the individuals who must make policy decisions, and contextualized to meet the demands of particular situations. It may well be that those policymakers do not, in fact, have very complete conceptualizations of policy instruments" (1989: 41). They therefore expect that design and choice of instruments will vary with the background, roles, and cognitive orientations of policymakers, as well as with the contextual factors that have historically influenced their views of instruments. Consequently, what is needed is an understanding of the cognitive mapping of the basic features of instruments that underlie choice.

The literature on the specifics of policy fields and policy characteristics in various countries and sectors sometimes employs the concept of *policy style*. The leading question here is: why is it that in some countries, or policy sectors, certain policy instruments seem to be favored? One example is the economic instrument of subsidies, widely used in Western European countries like Sweden and The Netherlands, but scarcely used in the United States. There are similar examples for information (exhortation) policy tools (see e.g., Freeman 1985 and

Howlett 1991). Howlett even identifies national styles in the way "theories of policy instruments which purport to be 'general theories' appear to differ on a national basis" (1991: 13).

Richardson defines policy style as the reflection of the characteristics of a government's approach to problem solving (active or reactive) and its relationship to other actors in the policy-making and implementing process (consensual or impositional) (1982: 13). The identification of a policy style is often based on the observed preference of national governments, or sectoral policy networks and communities, for certain types of instruments, given the nature of the state-society relations existing in nation or sector. Freeman points at the need to differentiate between (elite) preferences and outcomes in a policy typology, therefore a subjective and an objective dimension. Preferences would then be a cultural dimension (norms). As such, policy-making style would be little more than an aspect of the political culture of elites. "The educational and occupational background of elites may shape their approach to public problems in ways that lend a distinctive style to national decisionmaking" (1985: 474)—which brings us back to the Linder and Peters' understanding of the choice concept along cognitive dimensions! They relate style to political culture using that term "to capture the values of a statist tradition in different countries, and hence the acceptability of centralized governmental intervention into the economy and society. We hypothesize that, other things being equal, countries with a more statist tradition, such as in Germany and Scandinavian nations, will accept more intrusive policy instruments more readily than in less statist countries" (1989: 49–50).

To enlighten the decision-makers in the instrument choice, *evaluation* becomes germane. Evaluation is understood as "the systematic application of social research procedures for assessing the conceptualization, design, implementation, and utility of social intervention programs" (Rossi 1993: 5; Fischer 1995: 2). "Utility" in this definition refers to both effectiveness and efficiency.

Evaluations may focus on the *product* (the policy or program)—called output or outcome (impact) evaluations—as well as on the *process* of designing and implementing the policy or program (the policy process): process evaluations. As we shall see, the policy (or program) as well as the policy process may be evaluated in terms of effectiveness and efficiency; for the process there are the additional criteria of legality and democracy.

"Evaluation" in these definitions may relate to all phases of the policy process: from problem analysis and forecasting policy outcomes—*ex-*

ante evaluation—through monitoring the implementation, to the appraisal of actual results of government intervention—*ex-post* evaluation.

Policy Instrument Choice and Central Criteria of "Good Governance"

In pointing at their problems with classificatory schemes of policy instruments, Linder and Peters maintain that these schemes remain just that. They see relatively little attempt at utilization of these schemes as mechanisms for policy analysis and point out that this could be done in one of at least two ways. The first would be to develop evaluative mechanisms related to the instruments, or to the entire range of instruments. "What do we expect in a 'good' policy instrument, and what sort of mixes of criteria does each instrument imply?.... To the extent that there are evaluative criteria associated with policy instruments they tend to be unidimensional (political or economic) rather than sufficiently multidimensional to reflect the reality of policymaking situations" (1989: 41). Indeed, various evaluative criteria are involved, which all too often clash. We are not only looking at (mixes of) policy instruments but should also look for evaluative criteria by which to judge their adequacy: the criteria of "good governance."

The search for insights into the process of instrument choice is ultimately inspired by the quest for the rationale of that choice in view of four central values by which government action is appraised: effectiveness, efficiency, legality, and democracy. These are the dominant criteria of "good governance," of policies (product) and of administrative action in devising and enacting policies (process) in democratic societies. Policy instrument choice is based on the choice between these often competing and most often conflicting values.

1. *Effectiveness* stands for the degree of goal-realization due to the use of certain policy instruments; evaluation should also include (positive and negative) side-effects of the instrument;

2. *Efficiency* refers to the input-output/outcome ratio of policy instrumentation; evaluation includes problems of implementation of programs through the devised means (evaluation of the administrative process); and two additional process criteria:

3. *Legality*, which refers to the degree of correspondence of administrative action in designing and implementing policies with the relevant formal rules as well as with the principles of proper (administrative) process. These last principles may entail values like equity and motivation (of administrative decisions); and

4. *Democracy*, referring to the degree to which administrative action in designing and implementing policies correspond with accepted norms as to government-citizen relationships in a democratic political order.

Usually, this democratic quality is understood to refer to the degree citizens may influence the process of policy formulation and implementation: their participation, consultation, and information. The concept of "democracy" may also refer to the degree to which political representative organs (parliament, community councils, etc.) are actually in a position to exert effective political control.

Often, one finds a fifth central criterion by which to judge instrument choice: *legitimacy.*

The concept has various meanings: it may refer to the degree to which government choices are perceived as "just" and "lawful" in the eyes of the involved actors (subjective lawfulness).

Legitimacy should be discerned from "legality" (objective lawfulness) which we defined earlier and which is one of the grounds for legitimacy. Legitimacy may also have a broader meaning in referring to the degree of actual support a government may realize for its choices, because the actors involved perceive them as in correspondence with their own views, feelings, or objectives. In this book, the latter meaning is used in the definition of "policy instrument." Legitimacy represents a political criterion which stresses that acceptance is crucial for actual effectiveness of a policy or program. It is then regarded as a "conditio sine qua non" for effectiveness; without it, the governee will look for behavior alternative to the one prescribed or induced by government, and will thus frustrate the intended effects.

Now, one might speculate about the relation between this value of legitimacy and the four values mentioned before. The hypothesis here is that an effective and efficient policy instrument, that can be handled in a legal and democratic way, will enhance its legitimacy. This reasoning is in line with the Weberian conception of legitimacy as conditional for the acceptance of power. In either case, legitimacy would be a necessary, but not sufficient condition for effective government action.

The four values are related to the disparate approaches to the basic question of what public administration is in contemporary public administration theory: the managerial approach, emphasizing effectiveness and efficiency (and economy); the political approach, stressing representativeness, political responsiveness, and accountability through elected officials to the citizenry; and the legal approach, with its procedural norms of due process, individual substantive rights and equity (Rosenbloom 1983).

These central criteria of good governance need to be combined, while at the same time they compete or conflict, e.g., instruments that score high on the democracy criterion often have a price tag in terms of their efficiency. Therefore, the choice of policy instruments is a search for optimum solutions, a prioritizing process, a balancing act.

A Typology of Instruments

The aim of Vedung's chapter is to suggest a "parsimonious and fruitful classification of policy instruments." He offers an extensive analysis of the variety of instruments in use and of the available theories on policy instrument choice. The resulting typology should answer the usual taxonomic requirements: the categories should be mutually exclusive and exhaustive of the domain of discourse. He subscribes to a categorization that brings out the crucial characteristic of public policy instruments: their representation of the authoritative force or degree of constraint involved in the governance efforts. Other authors have done this before (see, for an overview, Linder and Peters 1989: 46–48), and have, for instance, indicated that decision makers will always choose first the least coercive instrument, moving over time from least coercive to most coercive in any given policy area.

Vedung defines a tripartite instrument configuration: *regulation* (the stick), *economic means* (the carrot), and *information* (the sermon). Any of them may vary among criteria like resource intensiveness, targeting (precision and selectivity), or political risk (the legitimacy criterion) (see e.g., Linder and Peters 1989: 47). The choice of the coerciveness criterion provides a link to a nation's dominant ideological position with regard to the degree of intervention in societal processes (its political culture). It relates policy instrument choice to the general political and administrative strategies that we identified earlier.

Given the values of "good governance," policy-instrument choice involves a necessary "give-and-take strategy" to mediate between them. Various instruments will have varying effects in terms of their effectiveness, efficiency, legality, and democracy. This once more underlines the character of policy-instrument choice as being a search for the optimal combination of various instruments. The question therefore becomes: what is, or ought to be, the logic of combining instruments, given the effects on the criteria mentioned? How can the mixing of instruments enlarge their combined optimal scores on the criteria mentioned? This question is tackled by Van der Doelen in his chapter on the "give-and-take strategy" as a logic of packaging policy instruments.

Stick, Carrot, and Sermon and the Logic of Packaging

The chapters by Lemaire, Leeuw, and Vedung and van der Doelen first of all offer examples of studies of the three categories of instruments: regulation (the stick), subsidies (the carrot), and information campaigns (the sermon). In this part of the book, these examples are offered without systematic consideration for the structural or cultural specifics of a policy context. They are presented as cross-sector examples of instrument choice and evaluation, although illustrations will refer to national experiences.

Vedung defines *regulations* as measures taken by governmental units to influence people by means of formulated rules and directives which mandate receivers to act in accordance with what is ordered in these rules and directives. The defining property of regulation is that the relationship is authoritative, meaning that the controlled persons or groups are obligated to act in the way stated by the controllers. The delimitation of the concept, however, is in stark contrast with several American definitions, which equate regulation with government intervention in general. (see e.g., Almond and Powell 1978: 307 and Francis 1993: 5).

Although in our book we concentrate on regulation by public bodies, Siegel and Weinberg rightly state that:

> "in complex, industrialized societies the state or the political system need not be the sole source of extensive and intensive control. In the United States, for example, decisions made by private institutions, such as large business corporations and trade unions, will frequently have as constraining an effect on individual conduct as many authoritative allocations made in the political system" (1977: 5).

Regulation is the traditional instrument of government. The deregulation movement's main point was that the growing amount and complexity of regulation was a burden on national economies. Lemaire shows how it highlighted some of the regulation's side effects, real costs, and lack of effectiveness in specific policy contexts. In the 1990s there is a move back from deregulation to reregulation or improved regulation. Canadian practice illustrates this change of moods very well. Thus the 1992 regulatory policy prescribes a review for selecting the regulation instrument. At least in Canada, regulation is the only instrument subject to such policy requirements. This new policy aims, essentially, at better ex-ante assessment of the need for regulation by using cost-benefit analysis, increased consultation to ensure a more responsive regulatory process, and finally more ex-post evaluation of regulatory programs. The policy complements earlier formal requirements for program evaluation by departments of the Canadian federal government and therefore offers an extra enforcement of the existing requirements of evaluation policy. From 1986 to 1991, the Office of the Comptroller General provided summaries of evaluation studies on regulatory programs to the government agency responsible for overseeing the regulatory policy. Lemaire answers the question of the actual use of these available evaluations and the lessons learned about regulation from evaluation.

Economic policy instruments are characterized by Vedung as involving the handing out or the taking away of material resources while the addressees are not obligated to take the measures involved. Subsidies are an example of this type of instrument. In Western European countries, subsidies and grants are popular policy instruments: Leeuw shows in chapter 3 that public expenditure on behalf of these tools in countries like Germany, Belgium, The Netherlands, France, and Denmark, vary between 20 and 35 percent of the Gross National Product (GNP). The Netherlands Court of Audit carried out a government-wide audit in the late 1980s which provided rich material to compensate for the lack of empirical knowledge on the management, goals, costs, and effects of subsidies. The study fits well in this chapter on "institution-free" consideration of types of instruments, where attention is not being paid to the specifics of the political, legal, and social contexts, but general criteria of good management of this policy instrument are being stressed. One of these criteria, of direct relevance to our study, relates to the role of ex-ante and ex-post evaluation in the management process.

As for our third category of instruments, the popularity of *information (or exhortation) instruments* has grown. They are regarded as modern forms of intervention, with an emphasis on prevention of wrong or stimulation of the right conduct by offering insights into consequences of behavior. Vedung defines them as attempts at influencing people through the transfer of knowledge, the communication of reasoned argument, and persuasion. They represent voluntary appeals to the electorate as a whole or to particular parts of it. "In this sense many would properly view exhortation as democratic government in its highest and most ideal form. It would be equated with the essence of leadership

and of democratic consent, of legitimate government in its most pris-
tine form. The concept would be equated even more broadly to governing based on an appeal to common values" (Doern and Phidd 1983:
124).

Evaluation research results of this instrument type are available. Thus
Weiss and Tschirhart (1994) reviewed 100 public information campaigns, and they point at the considerable controversy surrounding this
instrument: government-directed and sponsored efforts to communi-
cate to large numbers of citizens in order to achieve a policy result, or
what might be called government propaganda. They analyzed the campaigns from the perspectives of their effectiveness, political benefits
for public officials, and consequences for democratic processes (see
our criteria of effectiveness, democracy, and legitimacy). They conclude that the advantages of public-information campaigns justify their
use as policy instruments when used appropriately and with care to
mitigate the disadvantages.

Vedung and van der Doelen's chapter on the sermon (ch. 4) also
deals with information programs. They ask themselves why information programs are chosen as a policy instrument, and in line with that
question they offer an intriguing overview of theories on the use of
information programs, what their effects are, and in which ways this
policy instrument is being evaluated. Evaluation of information programs faces specific problems since they do not contain automatic feedback mechanisms. This chapter offers comparative material on the role
of information programs and of their evaluation in Dutch and Swedish
energy conservation policies after the 1973 Oil Crisis.

In chapter 5, on the "give-and-take" packaging of policy instruments,
van der Doelen looks for an optimal combination of instruments, as
indicated by their effects (effectiveness) and actual acceptance (legitimacy). Commenting on that crucial division criterion in the stick-car-
rot-sermon typology, the degree of constraint, his assertion is that the
regulatory, economic, and communicative control models have a
stimulative and a repressive mode of their own. Consequently, there is
a need to search for an optimal combination of stimulating and repress-
ing policy instruments.

Contextual Variables

When studying policy styles in different contexts, both in terms of
nation and policy sector, complication grows. The literature offers an

interesting variety of hypotheses but not enough results, if we understand result to be normative indications for good choices given a specific context.

The policy context is, again, a complex concept. It may refer to:

- characteristics of a general nature (systemic context) of nation or sector under consideration: its history, physical environment, the relevant social, political, economic, and cultural factors. Linder and Peters, for instance, attribute a high explanatory potential to these factors:

  "To the extent that social cleavages based in language, religion, region, and so on, are present in a country and have substantial political salience, governments may prefer less visible policy instruments. For example, varieties of tax and regulatory instruments would be preferred over direct expenditures or governmental provision of services. Presumably, the gains and losses conferred on different social groups by regulatory controls or tax breaks are less readily calculable than those associated with expenditure and service programs, and hence are less likely to raise objections based on inequity among competing groups. Similarly, governance in divided societies may require more coercive instruments, while in well-integrated, more homogeneous societies, instruments such as public promotion and information may be sufficient for the same purposes" (1989: 50).

- characteristics of the government-arrangements (structure): relation patterns among the relevant (co)actors in government in nation and sector: policy networks, relations among the relevant national, regional or local (non/para) governmental institutions involved in consultation, choice, implementation, and evaluation of policies and policy instruments;

- the dimension of *culture*: the rules of the governing game that significantly relate to policy choice such as the dominant political, administrative, or professional approaches (ideologies, paradigms, beliefs, and attitudes) that influence perceptions in the choice process. Particular organizations within the public sector also have their cultures and value systems; "they also have both a mission and an institutional memory shaping the course of their intervention in a particular policy domain" (Linder and Peters 1989: 50).

The policy-sector approach means at least two things. First it predicts that the style of policymaking and the nature of political conflict in a country will vary significantly from sector to sector and secondly the "policy-sector approach implies that there should be crossnational similarities in the way issues are treated, whatever the styles particular nations adopt" (Freeman 1985: 485). For our study this might mean, that within an individual sector, there are crossnational similarities in the choice of instruments. Our empirical material does not suffice to test this hypothesis but does give some illustrative evidence, for in-

stance, on energy conservation policies in Sweden and The Netherlands and radiation protection policies in Belgium, The Netherlands,
and the United Kingdom. Freeman gives a critical review of the two
important analytical perspectives, the national styles approach and the
policy-sector approach. They lead to sharply different conclusions about
the relative importance of politics, and the likelihood of policy convergence. The idea that distinctive and durable national policymaking
styles are causally linked to the policies of states asserts that "politics
determines policy."

The policy-sector approach argues, in contrast, that the nature of the
problem is fundamentally connected to the kind of politics that emerges
as well as the policy outcomes that result. The policy-sector approach
shifts our attention away from political inputs to categories of issues
and outputs of the political system; it suggests that "policy determines
politics." His conclusion must, however, be "that there are significant
trends toward the convergence of public policies within particular issue
sectors across Western democracies, although these are by no means
uniform and it is not obvious that they will continue. The two concepts
of style and sector need to be integrated in an approximately complementary manner" (1985: 469).

Our book offers four case studies from a variety of nations and sectors which should help:

- to test the policy instrument typology devised and our conjectures on the
  logic of combining instruments;
- to gather indications for the presence of a policy "style", whether nation-
  or sector-bound;
- and, of course, to understand more about the role of evaluation in the instrument choice process and in a particular context.

The case studies discuss policy instruments of the economic and
information type in fields that have had limited attention n the empirical literature: contracting out of social services, sponsoring of government enterprises, radiation policy, and privatization in a former "statist"
country (the Republic of Korea).

Chapter 7, by Hudson, Nutter, and Galaway, offers two case studies
of the purchase of service contracting for a particular type of social
service—treatment foster care—in the American state of Minnesota
and the Canadian province of Alberta. This economic policy instrument amounts to a decision by government to buy from private agencies rather than make or deliver goods and services. It implies the

involvement of government and private agencies as well as service recipients and individual service providers. Child welfare policy in the United States and Canada was originally in the hands of private agencies, then government, then there was the more recent shift to relying on private agencies in a movement back to "privatization." The authors discuss the rationale for this contracting out. They also reflect on the actual and potential evaluations in an environment in which many actors have a stake in the implementation of the policy.

DeMarco and Rist look at government-sponsored enterprises (GSEs) as a credit allocation tool in the United States (ch. 8). Their reason for doing so is that federal credit programs are among the least understood areas of government involvement in the economy, while at the same time of substantial impact within the economy. They link what is known of GSEs via evaluation efforts to the current thinking on the future of GSEs as a policy tool. GSEs are privately owned, federally chartered financial institutions with nationwide scope and specialized lending powers that benefit from an implicit federal guarantee to enhance its ability to borrow money. Thus the 1991 Congressional Budget Office (CBO) report states "The objective of federal supervision of the safety and soundness of GSEs is most similar to the objective of the supervision of depository institutions. In both cases the government is protecting itself as the ultimate guarantor of the institution's liabilities" (cited in Stanton 1991: 572). Several institutes have reported on GSEs: the Treasury Department, the U.S. General Accounting Office (GAO), and the CBO. These reports mainly discussed ways to improve financial accountability of government sponsored enterprises (Stanton 1991). Six GSE's were subject of the GAO report that forms the basis of DeMarco and Rist's study; together they represent a contingent liability of over one trillion dollars for U.S. taxpayers. An important lesson from the various evaluations was that effective federal supervision and meaningful capital standards must accompany federal credit support such as deposit insurance and the implicit guarantee of enterprise obligations (Stanton 1991: 574).

Arentsen (ch. 9) discusses the regulatory approach of radiation protection policy in The Netherlands, the United Kingdom, and Belgium. Is there a case for analyzing policy styles in devising and implementing this policy program? Are there interesting combinations with other types of instruments? Arentsen sets out to answer two questions in his chapter:

- To what extent did contextual factors condition the policy style in radiation protection policy in the three countries?

- What has been the impact of policy evaluation on the policy style in radiation protection policy in the three countries? What can be the role of policy evaluation in a technologically (problem) driven policy environment such as radiation policy?

A culturally different national context is offered by the case study on privatization in Korea by Nam-Kee Lee (ch. 10). In Vedung's analysis of instruments, privatization is not so much a policy instrument as a general organizational strategy. Earlier in this introduction we have stated, that policy-instrument choice is linked to the general strategies in a nation or sector. This is certainly true for privatization in Korea where it has acquired a status that, at least in the perception of the country's elite, is an instrument of governance that created basic conditions for the impressive economic upswing. The literature on privatization is quite large; the meanings and implications of privatization are generally less clear than its apparent popularity these last two decades. The concept has many definitions which makes evaluation of its practice difficult; they range from selling of public assets, payment for or production of goods/services by private organizations (e.g., a mandate from government to private companies to take care of public tasks, planning, and budgeting being still in the hands of the government), to mandating an internal government agency to work in a market-like fashion.

During the 1980s, with the trends towards internationalization and liberalization, the Korean government committed itself to realigning Korea's social and economic systems according to free-market principles in order to strengthen the economy. It was believed that the best way to increase efficiency is through privatization and competition. It involved a new management system including the introduction of structures and procedures for performance evaluation.

Let us now face a primary challenge: the development of a classification of policy instruments that brings out their crucial characteristics and consequently enlightens the choice between values of good governance.

References

Almond, G.A. and G.B. Powell, Jr. 1978. *Comparative Politics: System, Process and Policy.* Boston and Toronto: Little, Brown and Company.

Andersen, S.S. and K.A. Eliassen, eds. 1993. *Making Policy in Europe: The Europeification of National Policy-making,* London, Thousand Oaks, New Delhi: Sage.

Braam, A. van, and M.L. Bemelmans-Videc. 1988. *Leerboek Bestuurskunde: A Tekstboek.* Muiderberg: Dick Coutinho.

Bressers, J.Th.A., and P.J. Klok. 1988. "Fundamentals for a Theory of Policy Instruments," *International Journal of Social Economics* 15: 22–41.

Bressers, J.Th.A. et al. 1993. *Beleidsinstrumenten bestuurskundig beschouwd.* Assen/Maastricht: Van Gorcum.

Doern, G.B. and R.W. Phidd. 1983. *Canadian Public Policy: Ideas, Structure, Process.* Toronto: Methuen.

Fischer, F. 1995. *Evaluating Public Policy.* Chicago: Nelson-Hall.

Francis, J.G. 1993. *The Politics of Regulation; A Comparative Perspective.* Oxford and Cambridge, MA: Blackwell.

Freeman, G.P. 1985. "National Styles and Policy Sectors: Explaining Structured Variation," *Journal of Public Policy* 5(4): 467–496.

Gray, A., B. Jenkins, and B. Segsworth. 1993. *Budgeting, Auditing and & Evaluation; Functions & Integration in Seven Governments.* New Brunswick, NJ: Transaction Publishers.

Heidenheimer, A.J., H. Heclo, and C.T. Adams. 1990. *Comparative Public Policy: The Politics of Social Choice in America, Europe, and Japan.* New York: St. Martin's Press.

Hood, C.C. 1986. *The Tools of Government.* Chatham, NJ: Chatham House.

Howlett, M. 1991. "Policy Instruments, Policy Styles, and Policy Implementation: National Approaches to Theories of Instrument Choice," *Policy Studies Journal* 19(2): 1–21.

Lane, J.-E. 1993. *The Public Sector; Concepts, Models and Approaches.* London: Sage.

Leeuw, F.L., R.C. Rist, and R.C. Sonnichsen, eds. 1994. *Can Governments Learn? Comparative Perspectives on Evaluation & Organizational Learning.* New Brunswick, NJ: Transaction Publishers.

Linder, S.H. and B.G. Peters. 1989. "Instruments of Government: Perceptions and Contexts," *Journal of Public Policy* 9(1): 35–58.

Mayne, J., M.L. Bemelmans-Videc, J. Hudson, and R. Conner, eds. 1992. *Advancing Public Policy Evaluation: Learning from International Experiences.* Amsterdam: North Holland/Elsevier.

Mayne, J. and E. Zapico-Goñi, eds. 1996. *Performance Monitoring for Effective Public Sector Reform: Future Directions from International Experience.* New Brunswick, NJ: Transaction Publishers.

Mayntz, R. 1993. "Modernization and the Logic of Inter-organizational Networks," *Knowledge and Policy: The International Journal of Knowledge Transfer and Utilization* 6(1): 3–16.

Richardson, J., ed. 1982. *Policy Styles in Western Europe,* London: George Allen and Unwin.

Rist, R.C., ed. 1990. *Program Evaluation and the Management of Government: Patterns & Prospects across Eight Nations.* New Brunswick, NJ: Transaction Publishers.

Rosenbloom, D.H. 1983. "Public Administration Theory and the Separation of Powers," *Public Administration Review* 3: 219–227.

Rossi, P.H. and H.E. Freeman. 1993. *Evaluation: A Systematic Approach.* Newbury Park, CA: Sage.

Salamon, L.S., ed. 1989. *Beyond Privatization: The Tools of Government Action.* Washington, DC: The Urban Institute Press.

Siegel, L.S. and L.B. Weinberg. 1977. *Comparing Public Policies; United States, Soviet Union and Europe.* Homewood, IL: The Dorsey Press.

Stanton, T.H. 1991. "Increasing the Accountability of Government-Sponsored Enterprises," *Public Administration Review* 51(6): 572–575.

Toulemonde, J. and O. Rieper. 1996. *Policies and Practices of Intergovernmental Evaluation*. New Brunswick, NJ: Transaction Publishers.

Trebilcock, M.J. et al. 1982. *The Choice of Governing Instrument*. Ottawa: Canadian Government Publishing Center.

Weiss, J.A. and M. Tschirhart. 1994. "Public Information Campaigns as Policy Instruments," *Journal of Policy Analysis and Management* 13(1): 82–119.

Part I
Typology of Instruments

1

Policy Instruments: Typologies and Theories

Evert Vedung

The major shortcoming of current implementation research is that it focuses on the wrong unit of analysis, and that the most important theoretical breakthrough would be to identify a more fruitful unit on which to focus analysis and research. In particular, rather than focusing on individual programs, as is now done, or even collections of programs grouped according to major "purpose," as is frequently proposed, the suggestion here is that we should concentrate instead on the generic tools of government action...that come to be used, in varying combinations, in particular public programs...[T]he development of...a systematic body of knowledge about the alternative tools of public action is the real "missing link" in the theory and practice of public management.

—Lester M. Salamon, *Rethinking Public Management*, 1981

Conceptions of Policy Instruments

Public policy instruments are the set of techniques by which governmental authorities wield their power in attempting to ensure support and effect or prevent social change. It has been rightly asserted that policy instruments should be carefully selected and honed to become the finely tuned means which are needed to achieve those very ends that the public authorities are pursuing. Effective and legitimate programs for environmental protection, housing, and agriculture will probably involve unique mixes of several policy instruments. For policymakers it is crucial to have a good overview of the generic forms of these instruments, because the issue of choosing the appropriate combination is one of the most intricate and important in strategic political planning.

Nowhere in the international literature on policy analysis and public administration is to be found a uniform, generally embraced classification of policy instruments. There are presently a plethora of classifications of policy instruments.

In this chapter, I shall illustrate this conceptual diversity by providing a few samples from the ample smorgasbord of classifications. Yet the purpose is more far-reaching. The chapter aims to suggest a parsimonious and fruitful classification of policy instruments. There cannot, however, be one universal categorical scheme on any topic. The search for universality is futile, even counterproductive. There must be numerous classifications varying with theoretical and practical perspective. In this chapter, however, I shall choose only one scheme and explore it from various angles.

The Choice Versus Resource Approach

Basically, there are two pairs of fundamental approaches to taxonomy in the literature: the "choice versus resource approach" and the "maximalist versus minimalist approach." In the choice versus resource approach, the question is whether instruments ought to be classified from the viewpoint of the basic choices that government can make (the choice of "doing nothing" included), or whether classification ought to be predicated on the situation that government has already decided to do something, and that the categories are categories for the resources that the government can then use. This distinction was noted in an interesting paper by Michael Howlett (1991: 3f.), although I have substituted "choice approach" for his "continuum approach." In the maximalist versus minimalist approach, the controversy is whether to provide a long list of all possible policy instruments or to create two or three fundamental types under which all specific kinds of policy instruments can be categorized.

The *choice approach* can be illustrated by a fourfold classification drawn from Charles W. Anderson's textbook *Statecraft*. His categorization departs from a common theme in the literature: the degree of coercion exercised by government toward the subjects of control. In talking about moving along "the continuum from freedom to control" or deciding upon "how much events will be controlled and regulated by government authority, and how much they will be left up to the voluntary initiatives of individuals and their spontaneous adaption to the acts of others," Anderson himself seems to imply that there is a voluntary-mandatory principle of sorts underlying his scheme. However, his classification is a categorization of broad government choices more than a categorization of government tools, because one of the alternatives is doing nothing. Writes Anderson:

> When we face a public problem, there are really only four sorts of things that we can do about it... Which we will decide to employ depends largely on how much freedom and how much compulsion we think as appropriate in the particular situations.
>
> 1. *Market mechanisms.* We can let the outcome depend on what individuals decide to do, without any interference or direction from government.
> 2. *Structured options.* We can create government programs...that individuals are free to use or not as they see fit.
> 3. *Biased options.* We can devise incentives and deterrents, so that individuals will be guided, voluntarily, toward the desired ends of public policy.
> 4. *Regulation.* We can directly control, setting up constraints and imperatives for individual action, backed by the coercive powers of government.

These four possibilities, in their many permutations and combinations, are the basic tools of the trade of statecraft.

Anderson's classes appear to run the gamut from complete freedom from government intervention to complete government coercion. The freedom extreme of the continuum suggests that government does not interfere at all, but leaves all decisions to the consumers in the marketplace. The next position implies that policymakers provide options which did not previously exist. In this case, the outcome will depend on the voluntary choices of individuals. However, policymakers specify what the alternatives will be. Third, in a program of biased options, the policymaker structures incitements and impediments to guide individuals in the direction of the objectives of the public policy. The individual is still free to defy the wishes of the policymakers, but does so at a price. The fourth possibility reflects the other extremity of the scale. Government decides which actions will be permitted to or required from the individual and which will not. Freedom of choice is defined and delimited by statutes, rules, and regulations (Anderson 1977: 56–71).

Undeniably, Anderson's classification taps something important as far as government choices goes. Since Max Weber, the degree of compulsion to be used in a control situation has been heralded as the crucial issue in decisions on public policy. It is an indisputable strength in Anderson's typology that it pays heed to this idea.

Yet his typology does create problems, of which I shall address just one: market mechanisms. The problem of market mechanisms is equated with government noninterference, but do-nothing is not identical to leaving everything to the market. There are other alternatives to public intervention than markets, the most important of which are civil society and households. The family is the paradigm case of households. Typical cases of civil society are the neighborhood, social networks, and voluntary associations. Such communities fulfill numerous roles in every society. They make cooperation on an informal basis possible outside the market and the households, and they provide the foundation for the emergence and maintenance of social norms (Karlsson 1993: 76ff).

Most importantly, however: is governmental noninterference really a government tool? It is a policy choice that governments have, and of course a very important choice at that. We can also refer to it as a public policy strategy. But is it reasonable to call it a tool or an instrument? At this point I shall reserve the tool concept for the situation when governments have decided to actively take action. And before tools can be used, governments have a choice between intervention and nonintervention, and the latter may be divided into "market mechanisms," "civil society," and "households." This approach would neither make nonintervention identical to "market mechanisms" nor make market mechanisms a choice on a par with the government interventionist alternatives. The suggested elaboration of the Anderson typology is illustrated in figure 1.1.

FIGURE 1.1
The Amended Anderson Typology of Basic Policy Choices

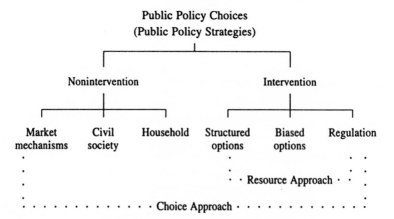

Source: Adapted from Charles W. Anderson, *Statecraft*, 1977, pp. 56 ff.

The choice approach would comprise the government- nonintervention as well as the government-intervention branch of the classification tree whereas the resource approach would include only the options within the government-intervention branch.[1]

The Maximalist Approach

While maximalist and minimalist approaches might be applied within both the choice and the resource approach, the present discussion will be limited to their application within the resource approach. The subsequent sections will then be predicated upon the situation that government has decided to intervene.

The minimalist approach engenders the search for a few, preferably two or three categories, into which all available instruments could be pigeonholed. In the maximalist approach long lists of instruments are provided, but little effort is made to arrange the instruments into smaller or larger groups. Figure 1.2 provides two cases of the maximalist approach, one with sixteen and the other with fourteen instruments.[2]

FIGURE 1.2

Examples of the Maximalist Approach to the Classification of Policy Instruments

Catalog of Federal Domestic Assistance (1981)[a]	Carl P. Chelf, Public Policy-making in America (1981)[b]
Formula grants	Expenditures
Project grants	Grants
Direct payments–unrestricted	Welfare
Direct payments–restricted	Loans
Direct loans	Legal sanctions
Loan guarantees	Self-regulation
Insurance	Inspection and testing
Sale, exchange of property	Taxation
Use of property facilities	Service contracts
Provision of specialized services	Government ownership & operation
Advisory services and counseling	Publicity and investigation
Dissemination of technical information	Certificates
Training	Licenses
Investigation of complaints	Franchises
Federal employment	
Property management	

Sources: [a] U.S. Office of Management and Budget, *Catalog of Federal Domestic Assistance* (1981), Washington, D.C.; [b] Carl P. Chelf, *Public Policymaking in America* (1981), Santa Monica, CA: Goodyear Publishing Company.

The most comprehensive list I have come across in the literature is the one compiled by E.S. Kirschen and his associates (1964). In his famous nine-country comparative study of economic policies, he came up with sixty-three different instruments (see Howlett 1991). Lists like Kirschen's provide extensive overviews of a wide range of possible options. (Please see Appendix I at the end of this chapter.) The major problem with them is their lack of structure and organization. However, Kirschen and his associates did apply their scheme to a vast amount of comparative data. Their list is also more sophisticated than usually quoted, because they divided the instruments into several subgroups.

The Minimalist Approach

The simplest classification is the twofold classification into affirmative-negative or promoting-restraining policy tools. Policy tools, it is maintained, might be formulated either in the negative to prohibit or deter an action, or in the positive to prescribe or encourage an action. They could be used to promote something that the controller deems desirable or restrain or inhibit something undesirable (Bernard 1939: 13f.8).

An example of this is the dual categorization of penalties and incentives proffered by Brigham and Brown in *Political Implementation: Penalties or Incentives?* (1980: 7, 9ff.) This distinction, they argue, has its roots in conventional dual divisions between the carrot and the stick, rewards and punishments, and benefits and costs. Incentives include grants, tax exemptions, and facilitative measures (not just those based on money). Penalties, on the other hand, are sanctions that involve unpleasant consequences imposed by a legally constituted authority for violation of the law. In figure 1.3, their and other unadorned minimalist dichotomies are portrayed.

FIGURE 1.3
The Minimalist Approach—Twofold Classifications of Governance Tools

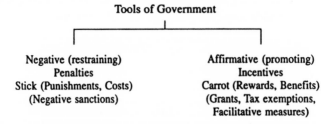

Tools of Government

Negative (restraining)	Affirmative (promoting)
Penalties	Incentives
Stick (Punishments, Costs)	Carrot (Rewards, Benefits)
(Negative sanctions)	(Grants, Tax exemptions, Facilitative measures)

Sources: L.L. Bernard, *Social Control in Its Sociological Aspects* (1939), pp. 13ff.; J. Brigham and D.W. Brown, *Political Implementation* (1980), pp. 9ff.

A major merit of this and similar twofold schemes is their outstanding simplicity and parsimony.[3] Another virtue is their supposedly theoretical fruitfulness. We might assume that addressees react differently to penalties and incentives. The use of penalties represses the energies of the persons controlled and creates a spirit of alienation in their relationship to the controller. The use of incentives, on the other hand, offers the persons controlled an objective which they are made to believe worth achieving, which may produce a mood of cooperation and mutual trust. Negative controls decrease policy legitimacy and acceptability while positive controls increase it (see ch. 5).

Yet these frugal schemes also generate some persistent difficulties. The Brigham and Brown categorization provides no explicit pigeonhole for the transfer of knowledge, education, counselling, persuasion, propaganda, and other techniques based on argumentation and persuasion. Yet, we all know that provision of information is a major concern of governments in post-industrial societies. And by itself, information seems to involve neither penalties nor incentives. It accommodates plain knowledge, normative appeals, emotional persuasion, or recommendations for action.

On the other hand, communication programs could be either against something or for something, that is, they might be either negative or affirmative. They might propagate that something should not be done or that something should be done. From this angle, it seems that moral suasion with some difficulties might fit into the twofold schemes. However, it does not seem entirely appropriate to squeeze moral suasion to the effect that the receivers ought to refrain from doing something under the "penalty" heading.

There is a second problem with these dichotomies. We may very well ask whether it is justified to place economic costs in the same category as punishments and negative sanctions. Regulatees are punished or subjected to negative sanctions because they have broken a government rule, but economic costs such as taxes on oil, perfume, and tobacco are inflicted upon consumers just because they buy these products, although no violation of a rule is involved. Third, while costs and grants are referred to different categories, we may very well maintain that they should belong to the same, involving the taking away or giving out of material assets of various kinds. It might be argued, then, that each of the two classes contain elements that are too different. On the other hand, this argument might be countered by making divisions within the two major categories. Here it will be argued, however, that a threefold classification is more fruitful.

The Etzioni Threefold Classification

An appropriate starting point for the elaboration of a threefold classification can be found in Amitai Etzioni's widely acclaimed work *A
Comparative Analysis of Complex Organizations*. Having initially defined power as "an actor's ability to induce or influence another actor
to carry out his directives or any other norms he supports," Etzioni sets
out to differentiate between three kinds of power, referred to as coercive, remunerative, and normative. States Etzioni (1975: 5ff.):

> Power differs according to the means employed to make the subjects comply.
> These means may be physical, material, or symbolic.
>
> *Coercive* power rests on the application, or the threat of application, of physical
> sanctions such as infliction of pain, deformity, or death; generation of frustration
> through restriction of movement; or controlling through force the satisfaction of
> needs such as those for food, sex, comfort, and the like.
>
> *Remunerative* power is based on control over material resources and rewards
> through allocation of salaries and wages, commissions and contributions, "fringe
> benefits," services and commodities.
>
> *Normative* power rests on the allocation and manipulation of symbolic rewards
> and deprivations through employment of leaders, manipulation of mass media,
> allocation of esteem and prestige symbols, administration of ritual, and influence
> over the distribution of "acceptance" and "positive response." (A more eloquent
> name for this power would be persuasive, or manipulative, or suggestive power.
> But all these terms have negative value connotations which we wish to avoid.)

The main thrust of Etzioni's argument is summarized in figure 1.4.
It should be emphasized that Etzioni's arrangement is a typology of
power. His is a classification of means to make the subjects comply.
However, throughout his book he also refers to coercive, remunerative,
and normative power as means of control. Actually, in his earlier work
Modern Organizations (1964: 59ff.; Gross and Etzioni 1985: 108ff.),
he argues that it is a classification of means of control. He also maintains that control (or controls) is synonymous with power ("the use of
various classes of means for control purposes—for power, in short—
has different consequences..."). This elucidates the significant though
often overlooked and blurred fact that the employment of policy instruments involves the wielding of political power. It also underscores the
fact that power is much more than the use of brute force.
     Second, a crucial difference between Brigham and Brown's scheme
and Etzioni's is found in the latter's third category, designated *normative power*. It seems to cover the transfer of knowledge, moral suasion,

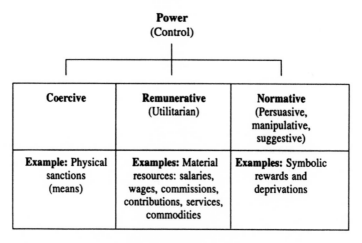

FIGURE 1.4
Etzioni's Threefold Classification of Power

Coercive	Remunerative (Utilitarian)	Normative (Persuasive, manipulative, suggestive)
Example: Physical sanctions (means)	Examples: Material resources: salaries, wages, commissions, contributions, services, commodities	Examples: Symbolic rewards and deprivations

Source: A. Etzioni, A Comparative Analysis of Complex Organizations, pp. 5ff.

exhortation, and other persuasive action as well as nonverbal symbolic performances. This is an important and largely overlooked category in the debate on governing instruments. While coercion is the central aspect of government, exhortation is a means that is more and more used.

Another tenet worth highlighting is that remunerative power concerns the allocation not only of money but material resources in general. Thus, government provision of services and commodities is included in this category. Consequently, the remunerative category covers rewards and incentives in cash as well as in kind.

A legitimate question concerning the Etzioni scheme is whether disincentives are covered. Where do taxes, duties, and fees belong? Are they included in the remunerative category? In the later edition of his work, Etzioni talks of "material rewards" only. Disincentives do not seem to be included in the remunerative category.

A Basic Scheme: Regulations, Economic Means, and Information

Here, the Etzioni taxonomy will be chosen as a point of departure and an attempt will be made to probe it a little deeper. The three classes will be called regulations, economic means, and information. The popular expressions used in this context are the stick, the carrot, and the sermon. The government may either force us, pay us or have us pay, or persuade us.[4]

First, an attempt will be made to define the three classes of the tripartite instrument configuration and consider what its basis of division is. Then, I shall discuss whether the categories are mutually exclusive and exhaustive of the domain of discourse. Thirdly, I shall provide some examples of theories that have been suggested in relation to the scheme. Finally, a few alternative classifications will be discussed and some subcategories to the three basic ones will be suggested.

This threefold taxonomy is based on the resource approach to policy instruments' classification, not the choice approach. It starts from the assumption that a decision has been made that some form of government intervention is justified. The question is what kinds of instruments might be used in such situations.

A parsimonious and comprehensive taxonomy of policy controls should distinguish between those policy instruments that imply (1) coercion, (2) the use of remuneration or deprivation of material resources, and (3) intellectual and moral appeals. It is particularly important that intellectual and moral appeals are singled out as a separate category, since argumentation and suasion, while more and more used, are largely overlooked by the scholarly community.[5] The instruments are classed as regulation, economic means, and information. The contention here is that all other types of policy instruments advanced in the literature can be reduced to these fundamental three. It is also contended that this trichotomy cannot be further reduced; it cannot be collapsed into any twofold scheme without an irretrievable loss of insight.

Although this threefold scheme is not an original creation, it should be stressed that twofold, fourfold, fivefold, or even sixfold constellations are much more common in the literature (Doern and Phidd 1983: 110ff.; Martin 1977).

The basic threefold arrangement of policy instruments is presented in figure 1.5.

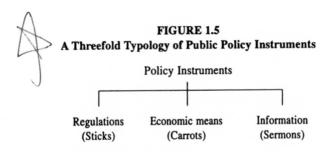

FIGURE 1.5
A Threefold Typology of Public Policy Instruments

Policy Instruments

| Regulations | Economic means | Information |
| (Sticks) | (Carrots) | (Sermons) |

As to the relationship between governor and governee, the typology takes three basic possibilities into consideration. In the regulatory case, the governee is obligated to do what the governor tells her to do. In the second instance, the governee is not obligated to perform an action, but the governor may make action easier or more difficult by adduction or deprivation of material resources. Thirdly, the relationship may be persuasive, to wit, involving only the communication of claims and reasons but neither material resources nor obligatory directives. These three relationships are the defining properties of the classes of regulatory, economic, and informative policy instruments.

Regulations are measures undertaken by governmental units to influence people by means of formulated rules and directives which mandate receivers to act in accordance with what is ordered in these rules and directives.

This conceptualization deviates somewhat from standard English usage, where "regulation" refers to the issuance of rules, orders, directives, norms, standards, and statutory provisions of an obligatory nature, backed by negative sanctions or threats of negative sanctions by government. A case of this usage is provided by Alan Stone in his *Regulation and Its Alternatives* (1982: 10), when he suggests that "[r]egulation is best defined as a state-imposed limitation on the discretion that may be exercised by individuals or organizations, which is supported by the threat of sanction."

True, regulations are often associated with threats of negative sanctions such as fines, imprisonment, and other types of punishment. However, this is not always the case. There are regulations intentionally not coupled with threats of negative sanctions. In jurisprudence, there is a classic term for these nonsanctioned rules: *lex imperfecta*. This justifies the resistance here in defining regulation with respect to negative sanctions. Rather, the defining property of regulation is that the relationship is authoritative, meaning that the controlled persons or groups are obligated to act in the way stated by the controllers. In this usage then an authoritative rule followed by the threat of negative sanctions is just one type of a regulation, authoritative rules not followed by such threats being the other.

The delimitation of the concept, however, is in stark contrast with several American definitions, which equate regulation with government intervention in general. In the latter cases, "regulation" is an all-embracing category, covering all forms of political control. A quotation from K.J. Meier's book *Regulation: Politics, Bureaucracy, and Economics* (1985: 1) may illustrate this wider usage:

> Regulation is any attempt by the government to control the behavior of citizens, corporations or sub-governments. In a sense, regulation is nothing more than the government's effort to limit the choices available to individuals within society.

Practically everything that governments undertake would then be "regulation." However, this is not the way the term is used in the present context where regulation is regarded as just *one* of a wider variety of the tools that governments have at their disposal to exert power over the actions of their citizens.

Economic policy instruments involve either the handing out or the taking away of material resources, be they in cash or in kind. Economic instruments make it cheaper or more expensive in terms of money, time, effort, and other valuables to pursue certain actions. However, addressees are not obligated to take the measures involved, a fact that makes economic instruments principally different from regulations. Economic tools always leave the subjects of governance a certain leeway within which to choose by themselves whether to take an action or not.

The addressees may decide not to make use of a government incentive—a particular grant, for instance—because they hesitate to take the measures required to get it. Or they may prefer to apply for a grant because they feel that the strings attached to it are perfectly worthwhile, even in their own interest. The point is that economic incentives neither prescribe nor prohibit the actions involved, but make them less expensive. The same goes for disincentives. A tax levied on tobacco purchase does not prohibit ingrained smokers from purchasing and enjoying their Ritmeesters and Camels. It only makes the indulgence of their habit more expensive.

Taxes certainly entail coercive traits. In performing the action the tax is levied upon—tobacco purchasing—the agent has to pay the tax. With Linder and Peters (1989: 40) we may justifiably ask where the authoritative element of a tax program ends and the economic element begins. What is really the difference between a tax and a prohibition? Both of them seem to involve a measure of authority or obligatory force.

The difference is that a prohibition forbids the action proper—tobacco purchasing—while the obligation in the tax example applies to the payment of the tax when you purchase cigars, not the purchasing itself. There is an obvious principal difference between banning the purchasing of cigars and levying a tax on the purchasing of them.

It ought to be stressed that economic instruments include non-monetary as well as monetary material resources. The delivery of free medical services at public hospitals and clinics, and the provision of free medicine from pharmacies are economic instruments to the same extent as the disbursement of child allowances in cash is. A bump in the road to prevent motorists from speeding is an economic instrument just as a tax levied on gasoline is.

Information, the third class, also referred to as "moral suasion," or exhortation, covers attempts at influencing people through the transfer of knowledge, the communication of reasoned argument, and persuasion. The information dispensed may concern the nature of the problem at hand, how people are actually handling the problem, measures that can be taken to change the prevailing situation, and reasons why these measures ought to be adopted by the addressees. However, no more than transfer of knowledge or persuasive reasoning is offered to influence people to do what the government deems desirable.

The information category is used here as catch-all terms for all communication campaigns; for the diffusion of printed materials like brochures, pamphlets, booklets, folders, fliers, bulletins, handbills, and posters; for advertising, labeling, audits, inspections, demonstration programs, custom-made personal advice, training programs, and educational efforts; and for other forms of amassing, packaging, and diffusing of knowledge and recommendations.

In ordinary language as well as in information theory, "informing" is identical with providing objective and correct facts about states of affairs. Naturally, this basic meaning has been retained in the language of public policy analysis. Yet, in public policy, government can also "inform" the citizenry about what is good or bad, right or wrong. Moreover, government can "provide information about" what people are allowed to do, or how they should act and behave. The information category covers, in other words, not only objective and correct knowledge, but also judgments about which phenomena and measures are good or bad, and recommendations about how citizens should act and behave. In the policy science literature, information has come to embrace much more than just the transmission of knowledge.

As with the economic tools of statecraft, no government obligation or coercion is involved. Under no circumstances are addressees mandated to act in the way suggested in the information. Whether or not to follow the recommendations is entirely up to the citizens because, by definition, information includes no stronger means of influence than plain recommendation and concomitant reasoning. This absence of obligation makes information different from regulation, which by definition contains mandatory rules of conduct.

Yet, information is also different from economic policy instruments in that no handing out or taking away of material resources is involved. The information diffused may very well include arguments to the effect that addressees will actually benefit materially from taking the measures recommended. However, government neither materially rewards people who take the action, nor materially deprives people who do not do anything. The only thing offered are data, facts, knowledge, arguments, and moral appeals.

The Basis of Division: Degree of Authoritative Force

The basis of division inherent in the threefold classificatory scheme is technique of governance, or more specifically, the authoritative force involved in the governance efforts.

Let me try to develop some implications of this. In principle, policy instruments have two constituent parts. They have a certain *action content*, telling the target population what to do or how not to behave. They also have a certain *authoritative force*, that is, they state the degree of power which the government is prepared to use in order to achieve compliance (Sandahl 1986).

The basic scheme presented here is based on the authoritative force, not the action content. The substantive action content of policy instruments differs enormously. We might classify them into social policy instruments, research policy instruments, cultural policy instruments, land-use policy instruments, and so on. The substantive action content of a regulation is the material rules contained in it. If a regulation includes a stipulation to the effect that owners and operators of nuclear power plants must show that radioactive waste from reactors can be stored in a safe way, then this requirement is the action content of the regulation. If it contains a directive saying that municipalities in their planning must work for a safe energy supply and promote the conservation of energy in their geographic area, then this is the content of the regulation.

In a similar vein, an economic means of government might tell members of the prospective audience that provided they meet certain provisions, for instance, earn incomes below a certain level or promise to perform some specified actions, they will be eligible for certain material rewards. These eligibility provisions constitute the substantive action content of the economic instruments.

But the authoritative force—upon which the threefold classification is based—is something quite different from the action content. The authoritative force concerns the degree of *constraint*, or even better, degree of power, that the governing body has invested in the governance attempt. In principle, regulation is more constraining for addressees than economic means, and the latter are more constraining than information. A *ban* on the production of cigars is more constraining than a tax levied on the production of them, which is in turn more constraining than information to the effect that these means of sensual gratification should not be produced.

The Categories are Mutually Exclusive

One presumably damaging objection to the idea of organizing policy instruments according to the degree of constraint in the relationship between the governor and the governed would be that, on several occasions, economic means seem to be much more constraining than regulation (see ch. 5). Compare the case where a particular line of action is forbidden but the concomitant fines for not complying are very low, to the case where an enormous excise tax is levied on the same line of action. The regulation is far less "prohibitive" than the excise tax, because the fine for violating the prohibition is so low. Since the economic instrument in this case is more constraining than the regulation, the threefold scheme crumbles and breaks down.

This argument is true, of course, but slightly beside the point. In principle regulation is more constraining than taxes, however high, because in the prohibition case above you are not allowed to take the action, whereas in the tax case, the action is allowed although it will cost a considerable amount of money to perform it. You are a lawbreaker if you violate a regulation, but a law-abiding citizen if you take an action in spite of the fact that you must pay a tax if you do it. It is in this sense that regulations are more constraining than economic means.

Another disputed case concerns the difference between penalties like a fine and taxes like a sales tax. Is there really any difference between paying a sales tax on the purchase of some service and paying a fine? In both cases, material deprivation is all that seems to be involved. Would it not be reasonable to regard both as economic tools of government, since both make some courses of action more expensive for those affected? From the point of view advocated here, this is a misclassification. Penalties are married to mandatory prescriptions and prohibitions. Fines are penalties for not complying with authoritative rules and belong to the appropriate regulatory system. While paying a fine is a consequence of a breaking of an authoritative rule, the paying of a sales tax is not.

Another seemingly strong objection concerns the difficulty of drawing a line between information and, for instance, *threats* of imposing a regulation or *promises* of introducing a grants system. In a negotiation, would it not be reasonable to view, for instance, threats of enacting some regulatory measure as a form of information? Because it is not yet enacted, it does not seem to be a regulation. Still, in the present scheme, it would be a regulatory measure.

The three means of governance can be *employed* in various ways. They may be employed in the sense that they are formally enacted by the proper institution. But they can also be used in the way that government officials threaten to impose them (Baldwin 1985: 41), or promise to do so. During the course of an information campaign, government officials may threaten to resort to unilateral compulsory measures, should information not lead to the desired behavior. A taxation system may also be used as a threat. Thus, threats of regulation or taxation are not persuasive tools of government, as defined here, but are one conceivable way of using the devices of regulation or economic means.

In reasoning about policy instruments it is important to keep in mind the *level* in the chain of implementation to which the policy instruments are primarily and secondarily directed. The government uses policy instruments to control the central civil service, the central civil service employs instruments to control the local civil service, and the local administrators use instruments to ensure compliance on the part of the citizens. Furthermore, central, regional, and local units may direct instruments toward producers and sellers in order to influence the consumers. The instruments directed at the various levels may also be of different kinds. To illustrate the idea of vertical levels, consider this example.

In the contemporary Western world, informative *labeling* is a widely used technique of government to narrow the information disparity between sellers and buyers. Susan Hadden, whose *Read the Label* is an important contribution to our knowledge about this particular technique, talks interchangeably about "regulation by label" or "information provision" (1986: 1ff). And she is perfectly right in doing so. For in relation to sellers, who are required by government to provide with their merchandise certain information on labels, labeling is regulation. However, in relation to consumers, who are supposed to read the labels, learn something, and maybe also act in some way or another, labeling is a tool of information. And of course the real point of labeling is to inform consumers.

Labeling, and many other strategies of government control, is constructed as a combination of regulation and information, in that intermediaries—in this case sellers—are required to provide something—information—whereas the proper addressees of the particular control system—the consumers—are only supposed to read, learn, and act, should they find it appropriate to do so. Labeling is information mandated by regulation. But information is the major component, because regulation is used only as a means of having the information displayed to the consumers.

Again, in determining the type of policy instrument, it is important to keep in mind to which vertical stage in the chain of implementation the instrument is directed. Cases of vertical packaging of various policy instruments will be provided by Lemaire, Joe Hudson and his associates, and DeMarco and Rist in the present volume. For the sake of simplicity, the issue of vertical packaging will be disregarded in the rest of this chapter, and the reasoning will be predicated on the simplifying assumption that policy instruments are directed at consumers and other end-users.

We may also wonder whether the threefold classification is truly exhaustive. Consider, for example, *negotiations* between public authorities and some private party and the ensuing agreement. Is this not a policy instrument in its own right? The answer here is no. Pursued in calm and civilized forms, negotiations are cases of governing through persuasion. The public authority confines itself to informing, arguing, and persuading. At a certain point, however, a threat of regulating the matter may be enunciated. But not even this would constitute a new, separate means of governance but only a threat of regulation.

Organizational Strategy is Different from Policy-Instruments Choice

Several important means of government seem to be excluded from the present scheme. One obvious case is organization. If, for instance, the government chooses to establish an organization of its own for direct *government provision of goods and services*, would that not be a policy instrument? Or, by analogy, if the government chooses to privatize a service formerly provided by the public sector by transferring the service organization to some private owner, is that not also a policy instrument? Socialization and privatization should be treated as policy instruments, should they not?

This is the road taken by several authors, for instance Doern and Phidd (1983: 134), who among "instruments of governing" distinguish between public ownership, exhortation, expenditure, and regulation. Public ownership is a category on the same level as the other three. Also Christopher Hood in his *Tools of Government* (1983: 4ff., 72ff.) provides a fourfold scheme in which "organization" is placed on a par with nodality, treasure, and authority. Nodality, treasure, and authority—like exhortation, expenditure, and regulation—seem quite similar to the categories of information, economic means, and regulation in the threefold scheme. Organization on the other hand "denotes the possession of a stock of people with whatever skills they may have (soldiers, workers, bureaucrats), land, buildings, materials and equipment, somehow arranged.... Organization gives government the physical ability to act directly, using its own forces rather than mercenaries."

Organizing, reorganizing, and deorganizing are no doubt crucial tenets in every administrative policy. Governments constantly change their organizations to cover new issue-areas, ensure public confidence and increase functional effectiveness. Organization is necessary for the provision of regulatory, economic, and exhortatory policy instruments. Policy instruments cannot be applied if there is no government organization or government mercenary to do the job. The view taken here, however, is that organization is a prerequisite for the application of policy instruments, not a policy instrument in itself. In the present context I prefer to regard organization as an important public governance strategy, not a policy instrument in the narrow sense.

One type of organizational change is privatization. A minimum meaning of privatization is transformation of the ownership or the operation of an activity from the public to the private sector. The opposite is socialization, meaning that ownership or the operation of an activity is transferred from the private to the public. Privatization and socialization are important government organizational strategies that for analytical purposes should be kept apart from what we here call policy instruments, that is, regulation, economic means, and exhortation. For this reason they are referred to as government *organizational strategies*, not policy *instruments*.

Policy-Instruments Theories

A final test of a good classification is that it proves empirically and theoretically fruitful. Will the threefold classification deliberated here pass this test? This must be left for future evaluations. In the present context, consider a few arguments in favor of the scheme.

While ex-ante studies of the effectiveness of governing instruments are important, emphasis here will be placed on other issues. The following list of important research questions concerning policy instruments suggests the width of theoretical issues to be addressed:

1. With few exceptions, policy instruments come in packages. How are various policy instruments horizontally and vertically packaged into overall programs or comprehensive policies? How are policy instruments time-sequenced?

2. Policy instruments must be wielded by some organizational arrangement. Is there any covariation between choice of policy instrument and choice of institutional arrangement for the implementation of the policy instrument?

3. What contingencies and motivations account for the choice of policy instruments? Why are some instruments preferred to others for particular purposes in particular contexts? What balance is struck between effectiveness/efficiency, legitimacy, legality, democratic participation, and symbolic or token considerations?

4. Is it the case that different countries consistently prefer some instrument or instrument package to others in solving similar problems? Are there national policy styles?

5. Political parties quarrel not only about ends but also about means. Means are never politically neutral, instrumental devices to reach accepted policy goals. To what extent do political parties differ with respect to policy instrument choices? Do decision makers choose the same instruments regardless of the problem under consideration or do they prefer different instruments to match a given situation (Linder and Peters 1989: 37f.)?

6. To what extent does an outcome regarded as successful by the initiating policymakers lead in the future to repeated and increased use of the instrument(s) originally employed (Hermann 1982: 159)?

7. To what extent do political processes vary in accordance with different policy instruments? In which ways does the choice of policy instruments affect the political processes? Is it the case that different policy processes surround the various policy instruments (Woodside 1986: 780)?

8. What consequences—intended, unintended, expected, unexpected—does the choice of policy instrument have for the effectiveness and efficiency of government programs?

9. What consequences—intended, unintended, expected, unexpected—does the choice of policy instrument have for public acceptance of the program and for the legitimacy of government in general?

10. Which criteria and standards on these criteria should be applied in the ex-post evaluation of various policy instruments?

11. What consequences—intended, unintended, expected, unexpected—does the choice of policy instruments have for the politics of program implementation?

Within the confines of a short chapter, it is impossible to illuminate in depth all of these questions (Bressers and Klok 1988). May it suffice here to shed some light on the effectiveness (8) and legitimacy (9) issues.

The use of various policy instruments for governance purposes will probably have different consequences on the nature of addressee responses. All other things being equal, in most cultures at least, the use of coercive power is more alienating to those subject to it than is the use of economic power, and the use of economic power is more alienating than the use of information and exhortation. Or, to put it the other way around, exhortation and information tend to generate more commitment than economic instruments, and economic instruments more than regulatory instruments. In other words, the application of an informative means of control tends to convince people; that of a material means tends to build up their self-oriented interest in conforming, and that of a regulatory means tends to force them to comply.

The three types of policy instruments might be politically linked together in a particular sequence. Doern and Wilson (1974: 339, Doern and Phidd 1983: 128ff.) have suggested that "politicians have a strong tendency to respond to policy issues (any issue) by moving successively from the least coercive governing instrument to the most coercive." The idea is that over time a policy problem is tackled in three different ways: first by the provision of information such as uttering a broad statement of intent, subsequently by the application of selective incentives, and lastly by the establishment of regulations accompanied by the threat of sanction. The underlying notion is that in solving social problems the authorities employ instruments of increasing strength in successive stages (see again, ch. 5).

Why are policy instruments applied in this particular order? One explanation for this is the legitimacy of and the public confidence in the program. The least coercive instruments are introduced first in order to gradually weaken the resistance of certain groups of individuals and adjust them to government intervention in the area. After some time, the authorities feel entitled to regulate the matters definitively by employing their most powerful instrument.

A certain preference of order among the instruments may also be deduced from a liberal political philosophy. The first principle of classic liberals is to avoid government intervention altogether. And if government intervention is deemed necessary, they would ideally adhere to a minimal constraint principle. Minimal constraint means to visit on the populace the least possible amount of "trouble, vexation and oppression" as Adam Smith put it (Hood 1986: 190ff). The minimal constraint principle would dictate that lower constraint instruments such as moral suasion and financial incentives be preferred to higher constraint instruments like regulation, where all else is equal (Doern and Phidd 1983: 112).

This shows that policy instruments should not be regarded only as means through which the ends of political life are achieved. Instruments are ends in themselves. They are an object of political dispute because they fundamentally affect the process and content of policy-making. Often, then, there is a politics of policy-instruments selection. Actually, political parties quite often disagree on means while they agree on ends. While broad policy objectives are at best something to be achieved far into the future, instrument choice is real and will have immediate consequences (Doern and Phidd 1983: 111).

Varieties of Regulation

The basis underlying the tripartition into regulatory, economic, and information instruments is the degree of constraint intended to be imposed upon the addressees. The general idea of constraint can also be employed to discern and order subcategories within each of the three main types. Following Woodside (1986: 787ff.), within each major grouping there are subtypes that differ with respect to the degree of constraint involved. Actually, these differences within each of the three broad classes may be almost as interesting as the differences between the classes themselves (van der Doelen 1989, and ch. 5 of this volume).

Regulations, to start with, encompass numerous varieties (Mitnick 1980; West 1985). First, they can be phrased in the negative, expressly proscribing certain phenomena or actions. Also, they may be formulated in affirmative terms, prescribing what has to be done (see figure 1.3 above). Leaving out prescriptions and concentrating on proscriptions, we may discern four types: unconditional (absolute) prohibitions, prohibitions with exemptions, prohibition with permissions (enabling legislation), and obligations to notify. This is illustrated in figure 1.6.

Unconditional prohibitions are absolutely binding for the addressees and valid without exception. The basic idea is that the activity should

FIGURE 1.6
Prohibitions Ordered According to Their Strength

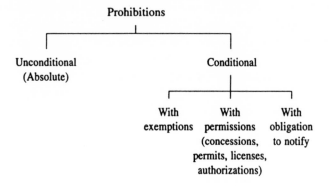

not exist at all. There are numerous such absolute proscriptions, for instance, against manslaughter, murder, child abuse, and driving on the left. In general, however, regulations are reminiscent of colanders; they are perforated—by exceptions and exemptions. Most constraining among these conditional proscriptions are rules combined with exemptions in exceptional cases, *prohibition with exemptions*. In such situations, the proscription is, to be sure, meant to be the normal course followed, but to prevent authorities from ending up in distinctly absurd situations, the exemption option is offered as a safety valve.

In *enabling legislation*, the prohibition does not aim to obliterate but to control, or raise demands on the activity involved. Permissions are granted on a regular basis, provided the applicant can show that the activity will satisfy certain specified requirements. The permissions granted can be described as permits, concessions, warrants, quotas, certificates, licenses, or authorizations. An operator of a restaurant in Sweden must apply for permission to be granted the right to serve alcoholic beverages. A moose hunter must have a weapon's license to be allowed to carry a rifle. A building permit is necessary to be granted the right to build a house in the city.

A third possibility is that proscriptions are combined with an *obligation to notify*. The planned course of action is plainly forbidden, as long as the authorities are not informed about it. Once the practitioner has notified the proper authority, however, he can start. The point with the notification requirement is that under normal circumstances the notifier can start his undertaking, but the notification can in a few, rare cases trigger a process of investigation, which can lead to permission or continued prohibition (see ch. 9).

Another rationale is to defend customers against fraud. The authorities want the name and the whereabouts of the notifier in the event that he may deceive some of his customers. Obviously, this is the rationale with registrations of taxi drivers. They are supposed to register and have a sign on their cars carrying a number and a name. In case of deception, the customers can contact the authorities, get the identity of the deceiver, and seek redress.

Types of Economic Instruments

Economic instruments cover enormous ranges of activities (Baldwin 1985; Mosher 1980: 543). Like regulations, they vary along the positive-negative dimension (see figure 1.3 above). In the positive case, a material resource is handed over to the agent, whereas in the negative case the individual or organization is deprived of some material resource. Programs of financial incentives are enacted to improve the conditions of some agents or reduce the costs and risks of taking some particular action. Financial disincentives carry the opposite significance: to worsen the condition of target actors or to increase the costs and risks of their taking some action in order to discourage it.

Economic instruments may also be arranged according to the in-cash–in-kind dichotomy. Governments can choose between transfer payments in money or in kind. Grants, subsidies, charges, fees, credit guarantees, and interest subsidies are all economic instruments in cash, while free health care, free medicine, free dental care, and free meals for school children are instruments in kind. In-kind instruments are more constraining to recipients than in-cash instruments. There are also considerable differences with respect to the constraint involved within both of these categories.

The merits of cash versus goods and services as a form of public assistance have long been debated. The cash principle would entail that all people deemed eligible, for instance those below a certain level of income, would receive disposable cash from the state. This would give the receivers the freedom to choose to do whatever they like with their money. Personal integrity would not be encroached upon and social stigmatization would be avoided. Against this, some people have argued that cash payments are ineffective in alleviating social problems, because recipients are often unable to manage their household economy. They fall prey to advertising which encourages them to spend money for nonessential items and to overlook the food and clothing needs of themselves and their children. Therefore, social welfare should take the form of government-produced goods and services, offered to the people through publicly owned and operated organizations. In this vein, the state would ensure that recipient citizens do not waste their resources on less desirable consumption but enjoy those goods and services decided on by the authorities in cooperation with scientific expertise. However, the recipients themselves often resent the goods and services approach, charging that it is overly paternalistic. From this it is obvious that the in-cash approach is less constraining to the recipients than the in-kind approach.

In figure 1.7, economic means of control are organized first according to the cash-kind idea and then along the incentives-disincentives dimension. Only a few examples of each are provided.

To start with cash incentives, *cash transfers* are unilateral payments by a government to a person or a firm, which do not form part of any exchange of goods or services. Social security benefits are cases in point; they form part of the redistribution of an economy's output.

FIGURE 1.7
Economic Means of Control

Economic means in cash:
Incentives (affirmative, promoting, encouraging):
    Cash transfers
    Cash grants
    Subsidies
    Reduced-interest loans
    Loan guarantees
    Tax expenditures (exemptions, write-offs, credits)
    Insurances of loans, crops, investments
Disincentives (negative, restraining, discouraging):
    Taxes
    Charges
    Fees
    Customs duties
    Tariffs

Economic means in kind:
Incentives:
    Government provision of goods and services
    Private provision of goods and services under government contracts
    Vouchers

Cash grants are also funds provided by a government to individuals or collective bodies which represent a one-way transfer of payments. One such type is grants-in-aid. A grant-in-aid is a payment by a central government to assist smaller governmental units. While general grants are available for any type of expenditure, selective grants are tied to specific uses. Selective—or categorical grants—can be based on a formula, for example, reflecting the size and age distribution of the population or on a project such as introducing a new educational curriculum.

The common characteristic of all grants-in-aid is that the larger governmental unit provides financial assistance without supplanting the smaller units that actually provide the public service. Grants-in-aid have been used primarily to achieve specific objectives rather than to offer general financial assistance. Such objectives have included the construction of roads, day-care centers, schools, apartment buildings, and homes for the elderly.

A *subsidy* is a conditional payment to individuals or businesses by a government for which it receives no products or services in return. The purpose of such payments is to make available a particular service or product at a price that the public can readily afford, when the service or product cannot otherwise be profitably supplied at this price. The particular service or product is considered essential to the public welfare, and the government therefore finds it necessary to subsidize the enterprise in order to keep it operating and producing the service or product (see ch. 3).

Reduced-interest loans are disbursed to people at a rate lower than ordinary bank interest rates. In Sweden, this tool is used particularly in housing policy. During the 1970s, for instance, Swedish municipalities and counties could apply for reduced-interest loans from the National Board of Housing for energy conserving measures in their own buildings.

Government could issue *loan guarantees* to people who purchase equipment which meets defined standards, e.g., for energy conservation. Under such a program, addressees would borrow money from a traditional lending source, and government would guarantee repayment of the principal and the interest. The idea of loan guarantees is to reduce the risk of loss to lending organizations and to encourage them to lend to certain borrowers at a low interest rate (Friedrich 1978: 19ff.).

Tax expenditures are revenues foregone by the treasury. They constitute departures from the normal tax structure. The most common forms include tax exemptions, tax write-offs, and tax credits (Rutherford 1992: 454; Surrey and McDaniel 1985).

Tax exemption means that some part of an income or fortune or action is exempted from taxation. The idea underlying a tax exemption scheme is to impede certain types of action deemed valuable by government from resulting in higher taxation in the future. Tax exemption will reduce the effective cost of taking the actions.

Tax exemptions come in as many forms as there are varieties of taxes. Consider exemptions from income tax. Some categories of income may be exempted from income tax. In Sweden, an example is income derived from selling wild berries collected in the vast forests. This means that people, when filing their tax returns, do not indicate the revenue from berry collection as part of their income. Examples from other countries include old-age pensions, maternity allowances, sickness allowances paid until employees have recovered from their illness, and disability allowances paid to employees totally or partially disabled by illness or accident.

Popularly referred to as "loopholes," *tax write-offs* mean that some expenditures can be deducted from taxable income. The difference between tax exemptions and tax write-offs is that the former engenders no taxes on some income whereas the latter implies that some expenditures are allowed to reduce taxable income. Tax deduction can take the form of accelerated depreciation. In many countries, business people who purchase capital equipment for the production of income are permitted to deduct from their taxable income an amount attributable to the value of the equipment lost annually because of wear and tear. Typically, industrialists, farmers, and other business people use standard depreciation tables to calculate the percentage that may be depreciated for tax purposes. If the government allows businessmen to shorten the time period over which an item may be depreciated, the value of the deduction will be greater because the deductions are larger and their benefit more immediate.

A third form of tax expenditure takes the form of a *tax credit*. This means that the treasury gives a sum of money to those taxpayers who contribute to some cause deemed worthwhile by the government. We may imagine, for instance, that taxpayers would receive a fixed rebate for each franc, mark, or schilling they give to charity. This credit would work through the income tax system by returning to each charitable donor an amount equal to a percentage of his or her contribution. Contrary to a tax-deduction program, the individuals' marginal tax rates would no longer dictate the size of the government subsidies they would receive.

Among *cash disincentives*, consider taxes, charges, fees, customs duties, and tariffs. There is an interesting semantic difference between taxes and charges (fees). While a *charge* is the price of a discernible service, a *tax* is not (Rutherford 1992: 68). A charge is a levy, which requires a direct and discernible service on the part of the government. An entrance fee to a public museum is a charge, since as a service, the payer is offered a view of the wonders of the museum. On the other hand, taxes must be paid with no discernible service. Taxes include income taxes, corporate taxes, property taxes, inheritance taxes, excise taxes, and sales taxes, to mention just a few. User charges have been inaugurated as environmental policy instruments. An emission charge is a fee related to the quantity of a discharged pollutant, for instance, a noxious liquid, and imposed on the firm causing the pollution. *Customs duties* and *tariffs* are both taxes levied on imported products. While tariffs are used as a means to protect domestic producers from foreign competition, customs duties are levied for the purpose of raising revenue for the government.

The *in-kind (non-cash) approach* to public assistance includes municipal childcare centers, municipal homes for the elderly, hospitals operated by regional public bodies, military forces, police forces, government-operated universities, and government-operated facilities for solid waste disposal. The latter, for instance, may comprise landfill sites, garbage incinerators, and storage facilities for hazardous radioactive wastes from nuclear power plants. Sometimes, governments contract-out these functions to private entrepreneurs, who in turn provide the in-kind services to the citizens.

A more indirect and less constraining in-kind government assistance device is the *voucher*. A voucher system is a method for consumers of government-provided goods and services to choose between alternatives. Instead of a government agency deciding who gets what, individuals are given vouchers which entitle them to make purchases up to a particular cash amount. This has been used in the United States under the food stamp scheme.

Vouchers have also been discussed as a means of providing a choice of health care and parental choice between schools. In the education case, vouchers would be distributed to parents to spend at any school they choose for their children. Municipalities, and in the final analysis, the national government, would redeem the vouchers submitted by schools by paying specified amounts. All schools would compete equally for students and government education funds would flow to the schools in proportion to their being selected by the students (Rutherford 1992: 485).

Kinds of Information Instruments

The category of information includes measures undertaken to influence addressees through the transfer of knowledge, communication of reasoned argument, persuasion, advice, moral appeals, and so on. Exhortation would be another generic term for this category.

As with regulations and economic means, information may be phrased in the affirmative or the negative. Information may attempt to persuade the agent to perform an action or dissuade the same agent from performing it (see figure 1.3 above).

Information is either a policy instrument in its own right or a metapolicy instrument in the sense that it is used to disseminate knowledge of the existence, meaning, and availability of other policy instruments. The latter case is an example of vertical packaging of instruments. Information is a necessary condition for the functioning of all other policy instruments. Seriously designed public programs require that intended beneficiaries are informed about the programs' existence and meaning. Such information may be called information *on* policy instruments as opposed to information *as* a policy instrument.

If a regulation—such as a law or a statute—is to be effective, individuals in the target group must be aware of its existence and contents; otherwise, they cannot abide by it. In many cases, the national government must convey information to citizens about the meaning and existence of recently imposed regulatory instruments. A good example of this is the campaign in connection with the 1967 transition to right-side driving in Sweden. Extensive state funds were allocated to informing motorists about the new, positively coercive legislation (Björkman 1971).

Economic instruments also require concomitant information to function. It is almost a truism to maintain that prospective recipients must know that there is a grant program, and under what conditions economic help might be given, in order to be able to apply for it. The dissemination of such knowledge *on* other programs will often require specific information measures from the authorities responsible.

Sometimes, government also has to inform people about information programs. After new information material has been developed, the administrative body concerned has to decide whether the material should

be disseminated immediately to the target population or whether information-dispensing tools should be used to tell people about the
existence of the material, pointing out how valuable it is as well as
encouraging people to order it. In the latter case, the potential users of
information will be informed about the availability of the material, that
it is important, and that prospective addressees should make an effort
to order it.

Our three cases highlight the importance of making a sharp distinction
between information as an independent policy instrument—information *as*—and information as a metapolicy instrument—information *on*.

Leaving out information on other policy instruments, we may distinguish between several forms of information transfer proper. An overview is provided in figure 1.8.

Mass-mediated versus interpersonal transmission of information is
taken as the major basis of division. The meaning of the distinction is
quite obvious. Mass media channels are all those means of disseminat-
ing messages that enable a source of one or a few individuals to reach
an audience of many without meeting them in person. Interpersonal
dissemination involves face-to-face exchanges between individuals.
Mass media channels are usually divided into television, radio, film,
newspapers, and other printed matter such as books, brochures, fold-

FIGURE 1.8
Forms of Information according to Mode of Transmission

Mediated transmission:
Television, radio, film
Newspapers
Printed matter (books, brochures, booklets, leaflets, folders)
Labels
Posters

Interpersonal transmission:
Direct, personal advice
Classroom or on-site education
Workshops
Conferences
Demonstrations
Government example
Exhibitions
Investigation and publicity

ers, and so forth. To this, we may also add labels and posters. Most of these categories are self-explanatory.

Among *interpersonal channels of transmission*, consider just a few of those mentioned in figure 1.8. The idea underlying a *demonstration* is that if a particular technology, material, program or process can be viewed in actual operation, the probability of its adoption and use will increase. In addition, a demonstration project allows the innovation to be evaluated in practical operation (Hastings 1982: 40ff).

A very special tool in the information tool kit is *investigation and publicity*. One effect of an investigation—for instance, in the field of environmental policy—could be to push the management of an industrial plant, under the spur of public opinion, to make changes in, for instance, polluting practices, in advance of or without recourse to regulatory schemes.

Effective as this means of control may be in some cases, certain drawbacks associated with it make it one to be used sparingly. It is inquisitorial and therefore less pleasant to use. The practices of all property owners or industries in a field can seldom be publicized. Often small businesses and small property owners escape attention, while a few large companies are forced by public outcry to abstain from certain polluting practices (Koontz and Gable 1956: 49ff.).

Summary and Conclusions

Discourse on public policy instruments is discourse on power. This fact, often overlooked, is the point of departure for the article. Public policy instruments are a set of techniques by which governmental authorities—or proxies acting on behalf of governmental authorities—wield their power in attempting to ensure support and effect social change.

Yet, policy instruments are persistently neglected in the research and discourse of political science and public administration. When political scientists take interest in what happens after authoritative decisions have been made, they tend to focus on comprehensive policies or individual programs, not on the specific governing instrument or specific package of governing instruments involved in the policies or programs. The systematic, empirical study of policy instruments still has hardly got off the ground (Salamon 1981: 262).

Four approaches to policy instruments categorization have been framed in this chapter. The *choice approach* is very comprehensive. It classifies instruments from the point of view of the basic options that governments have, the option of doing nothing and leaving the matter to the civil society included. Because doing nothing cannot be regarded as an instrument, the choice approach is put aside in favor of the *resource approach*. The latter is less comprehensive and starts from the assumption that government has decided to intervene and that the categories concern the resources that the government then can use. Within both of these approaches we can apply either the maximalist or the minimalist approach. The *minimalist approach*, which attempts to create a small number of basic types into which individual policy instruments can be pigeonholed, is deemed more fruitful than the *maximalist approach*, which only provides a long list of all possible policy instruments without any particular ordering. In choosing a combination of the resource and the minimalist approach, this chapter has suggested a *trifold scheme of regulation, economic means, and information*. The tripartition is very much in line with Amitai Etzioni's classification of the dimensions of power. The tripartition is discussed in the chapter from various angles.

Regulations are measures undertaken by governmental units to influence people by means of verbally formulated rules and directives which mandate receivers to act in accordance with what is ordered in these rules and directives. Economic instruments involve either the handing out or the taking away of material resources, in-kind as well as in cash. Information (moral suasion, exhortation, public communication) covers attempts at influencing people through the transfer of knowledge, the communication of reasoned argument, and persuasion. No more than the plain transfer of knowledge or persuasive reasoning is offered to influence people to do what the government deems desirable.

The dimension underlying this division into sticks, carrots, and sermons is the degree of constraint intended by the policymakers. Regulation is thought to be more constraining than economic means, and economic means more constraining than information.

Several, if not most, authors also include organization as a policy instrument on a par with the others. This classification is rejected. In order to use all three kinds of policy instruments toward the general public, government needs organizations to handle them. Actually, devising appropriate organizational structures for the implementation of policy instruments is a key task in public policy. However, it seems more logical to regard organization as a *prerequisite* for the handling of regulatory, economic, and informational means than as a policy instrument by itself on a par with the others. Organization, it is argued, belongs to the broader category of policy strategies. It is also argued that socialization of entities which earlier belonged to the private sector and privatization of governmental organizations are very important policy strategies, but, to repeat, they are not referred to as policy instruments in the present chapter.

The degree-of-constraint idea is also used within the trifold scheme to discern subclasses of regulation, economic means, and information. This idea is applied, for instance, in the classification of regulation into unconditional and conditional and the latter into regulations with exemptions, with permissions, and with obligation to notify. It is also argued that economic instruments in-kind are more restraining in principle than instruments in-cash.

In real life, policy instruments come in packages. In vertical packaging, one policy instrument is used to promote or restrain another. Horizontal packaging implies the use of two or more instruments for the same purpose.

In part 1 of this book there are chapters on the stick, the carrot, and the sermon, respectively. Donald Lemaire (ch. 2) explores the formation, application, evaluation, and efficiency of regulatory tools. Among other things, the author argues that the selection of government tools are largely determined by the nature of the policy area. He further maintains that regulation can be used to regulate regulation, as when the Canadian government instituted a policy that directs federal departments and agencies on how and when to use regulation—a case of vertical packaging of regulations.

Difficulties and possibilities with subsidies as a case of economic tools of government is the subject of Frans L. Leeuw's contribution (ch. 3). After a general discussion of the merits and drawbacks of this economic incentive, he tells us about a Dutch government-wide empirical investigation of subsidies dealing with questions like: (1) How many subsidies in which functional policy areas where issued by The Netherlands government? (2) Which information did the government possess with regard to the goal-directedness, implementation, and ex-post evaluation of these subsidies? and (3) Were there differences between types of subsidies on the one hand and coverage by ex-post evaluations on the other? One of his findings is that only 40 out of 718 subsidies (6 percent) were covered by both ex-ante and ex-post evaluations.

Types, choice, effects, and evaluation of information programs is the subject of chapter 4, by myself and Frans C. J. van der Doelen. A typology of information instruments is presented and some theories on the use of information-dispensing tools are sketched. In general, information programs have effect when they strengthen the well-reasoned self interest. The authors conclude with an evaluation paradox: the policy instrument most in need of intensive evaluation due to its almost invisible character is little evaluated because of its cheapness.

Part 1 ends with a more general chapter by Frans C.J. van der Doelen (ch. 5) where he argues that sermons, carrots, and sticks—the communicative, economic, and juridical control models—have a stimulative and repressive mode of their own. He further maintains that the stimulative, rewarding modes of these three control models (information programs, subsidies, and covenants) enlarge the alternatives of behavior and promote the legitimacy of the intervention. The repressive, punishing modes (propaganda, levies, and directives) limit the alternatives of behavior, contribute to the change of behavior in the desired way, and enhance the effectiveness of the intervention. The author's conclusion: in order to pursue legitimacy as well as effectiveness, governments should combine stimulative and repressive policy instruments.

Appendix I

The Maximalist Approach to Policy Instruments: K.S. Kirschen's Scheme

    1.   Manipulation of current balance of expenditures
    2.   Manipulation of overall balance of expenditures
A. Expenditure instruments
    3.   Government investment
    4.   Subsidies and capital transfers to enterprises
    5.   Transfers to households
    6.   Government stock changes
    7.   Current purchases of goods and services
    8.   Wages and salaries
    9.   Transfers in the rest of the world
B. Revenue instruments
    10. Direct taxes on household incomes
    11. Direct taxes on enterprise incomes
    12. Indirect taxes on internal transactions
    13. Customs duties
    14. Social security contributions
    15. Taxes on property
    16. Succession duties
    17. Transfers from the rest of the world

C. Government new borrowing and lending
  18. Lending abroad
  19. Lending to households and enterprises
  20. Borrowing from abroad
  21. Borrowing from households and enterprises
D. Government operations in existing debts
  22. Open-market operations in short-term securities
  23. Other open-market operations in existing debt
E. Interest rate instruments
  24. Bank rate
  25. Legal imposition of maximum rates
  26. Government guarantees of loans
F. Instruments acting on credit ???
  27. Reserve ratios, etc.
  28. Quantitative stops on advances
  29. Approval of individual loans
  30. Other directives, recommendations, and persuasion
G. Instruments acting on lending or borrowing by other agents
  31. Control of local authorities and nationalized enterprise borrowing
  32. Control of private companies' borrowing new issues
  33. Control of hire-purchase transactions
  34. Control of other financial institutions
H. Instrument of the exchange rate
  35. Devaluations
  36. Revaluations
I. Instruments of direct control
(i.) Control of foreign trade, exchange and immigration
  37. Control of private imports
  38. State import trading
  39. Control of private imports
  40. Exchange control
  41. Control of immigration
(ii.) Control of prices
  42. Price controls of goods and services
  43. Rent control
  44. Dividend control
  45. Control of wages
(iii.) Other controls on the internal economy
  46. Control of investment
  47. Raw material allocation
  48. Control of operations
  49. Regulation of conditions of work
  50. Control of exploitation of natural resources
  51. Rationing of consumer goods
  52. Quality controls and standards
  53. Changes in the system of transfer to households
  54. Changes in the system of subsidies to enterprises

55. Changes in the tax system
56. Changes in the credit system
57. Changes in the system of direct control
58. Agricultural land reforms
59. Changes in the conditions of competition
60. Changes increasing labor's influence on management
61. Changes in the extent of public ownership of industry
62. Creation of national institutions
63. Creation of international institutions

Source: E. S. Kirschen et al., *Economic Policy in Our Time* (1964), Amsterdam: North Holland Publishing Co.

Notes

1. Another case of the choice approach is provided by Doern and Phidd (1983: 111) who distinguish between self-regulation, exhortation, expenditure, regulation (including taxation), and public ownership. It is the "self-regulation" category which makes their taxonomy a case of the choice approach.
2. For an overview of existing American classification schemes, see Salamon and Lund 1989: 32f.
3. There are several other dichotomies in the literature, for instance, general-selective instruments, and statutory- administrative, one-way-reciprocal, and detecting-effecting instruments. These dichotomies will be covered later in the chapter.
4. I have used this threefold scheme in two earlier publications in Swedish, Vedung 1991 and 1993.
5. Karlsson (1993: 141), for instance, writes: "I shall define...'interventions' as deliberate and planned attempts by the state, or by organizations authorized by the state, to create particular results or end-states for certain groups or individuals in society by commanding the actors what to do or not to do." This formal definition seems to exclude both information and economic instruments, because neither a subsidy nor a piece of advice involves commands. However, Karlsson continues in the following fashion: "In general three different methods of intervention are used by the state: provision of some good or service, tax or subsidy of some good or service, and regulation of the quantity, quality or price of some good or service, or of the market or even of the social structure itself." Obviously, government information campaigns, while omnipresent, are not included in government intervention.

References

Anderson, Charles W. 1977. *Statecraft: An Introduction to Political Choice and Judgement.* New York: John Wiley and Sons.
Baldwin, David A. 1985. *Economic Statecraft.* Princeton, NJ: Princeton University Press.
Bernard, L.L. 1939. *Social Control in Its Sociological Aspects.* New York: Macmillan.
Björkman, Johan. 1971. *Kortsiktiga effekter av trafikinformation.* Stockholm: Stockholm School of Economics. Mimeo.
Bressers, Hans and P.J. Klok. 1988. "Fundamentals for a Theory of Policy Instruments," *International Journal of Social Economics* 15: 22–41.

Brigham, John and Don W. Brown. 1980. "Introduction," in John Brigham and Don W. Brown (eds.), *Policy Implementation: Penalties or Incentives?*, pp. 7–17. Beverly Hills, CA.: Sage.

Chelf, Carl P. 1981. *Public Policy-making in America*. Santa Monica, CA: Goodyear Publishing Company.

Doelen, Frans C.J. van der. 1989. *Beleidsinstrumenten en energiebesparing*. Enschede: Universiteit Twente, Faculteit der Bestuurskunde (with an English summary).

Doern, G., Bruce and Richard W. Phidd. 1983. *Canadian Public Policy: Ideas, Structure, Process*. Toronto: Methuen.

Doern, G., Bruce and V. Seymour Wilson, eds. 1974. *Issues in Canadian Public Policy*. Toronto: Macmillan of Canada.

Elmore, Richard F. 1987. "Instruments and Strategy in Public Policy," *Policy Studies Review* 7: 174–186.

Etzioni, Amitai. 1964. *Modern Organizations*. Englewood Cliffs, NJ: Prentice-Hall.

———. 1975. *A Comparative Analysis of Complex Organizations: On Power, Involvement, and their Correlates*, rev. ed. New York: Free Press.

Friedrich, Robert A. 1978. *Energy Conservation for American Agriculture*. Cambridge, MA: Ballinger.

Gross, Edward and Amitai Etzioni. 1985. *Organizations in Society*. Englewood Cliffs, NJ: Prentice-Hall.

Hadden, Susan. 1986. *Read the Label: Reducing Risk by Providing Information*. Boulder, CO: Westview.

Hastings, Anne H. 1982. *The Strategies of Government Intervention: An Analysis of Federal Education and Health Care Policy*. Ph.D. diss. Charlottesville, VA: University of Virginia. Mimeo.

Hermann, Charles F. 1982. "Instruments of Foreign Policy," in P. Callahan, L.P. Brady, and M.G. Hermann (eds.), *Describing Foreign Policy Behavior*, pp. 153–174. Beverly Hills, CA: Sage.

Hood, Christopher C. 1983. *The Tools of Government*. London: Macmillan.

Howlett, Michael. 1991. "Policy Instruments: Policy Styles, and Policy Implementation: National Approaches to Theories of Instrument Choice," *Policy Studies Journal* 19: 1–21.

Karlsson, Nils. 1993. *The State of State: An Inquiry Concerning the Role of Invisible Hands in Politics and Civil Society*. Stockholm: Almqvist & Wiksell International.

Kirschen, E.S. et al. 1964. *Economic Policy in Our Time*. Amsterdam: North Holland.

Koontz, Harold and Richard W. Gable. 1956. *Public Control of Economic Enterprise*. New York: McGraw-Hill.

Linder, Stephen and B. Guy Peters. 1989. "Instruments of Government: Perceptions and Contexts," *Journal of Public Policy* 9: 35–58.

———. 1990. "The Design of Instruments for Public Policy: Groundwork for Empirical Research," in Stuart Nagel (ed.), *Policy Theory and Policy Evaluation: Concepts, Knowledge, Causes, and Norms*, pp. 103–119. London: Greenwood Press.

Martin, Laurence H. 1977. "The Role of Government in Causing Energy End Use Efficiency—An Overview," in Rocco A. Fazzolare and Craig B. Smith (eds.), *Energy Use Management: Proceedings of the International Conference*, vol. 2, pp. 475–519. New York: Pergamon Press.

Meier, Kenneth J. 1985. *Regulation: Politics, Bureaucracy, and Economics*. New York: St. Martin's Press.

Mitnick, Barry M. 1980. *The Political Economy of Regulation: Creating, Designing, and Removing Regulatory Forms*. New York: Columbia University Press.

Mosher, Frederick C. 1980. "The Changing Responsibilities and Tactics of the Federal Government," *Public Administration Review* 40: 541–548.

Neiman, M. 1980. "The Virtues of Heavy-Handedness in Government" in John Brigham and Don W. Brown (eds.), *Policy Implementation: Penalties or Incentives?*, pp. 19–42, Beverly Hills, CA.: Sage.

Redford, Emmette S. 1952. *Administration of National Economic Control*. New York: Macmillan.

Rutherford, Donald. 1992. *Dictionary of Economics*. London: Routledge.

Salamon, Lester M. 1981. "Rethinking Public Management: Third-Party Government and the Changing Forms of Government Action," *Public Policy* 29: 256–275.

Salamon, Lester M. and Michael S. Lund. 1989. "The Tools Approach: Basic Analytics," in L.M. Salamon (ed.), *Beyond Privatization: The Tools of Government Action*, pp. 23–49, Washington, DC: Urban Institute Press.

Sandahl, Rolf. 1986. *Offentlig styrning: en fråga om alternativ* (Governance: A Question of Alternatives). Stockholm: The General Accounting Office. Mimeo.

Stone, Alan. 1982. *Regulation and Its Alternatives*. Washington, DC: Congressional Quarterly Press.

Surrey, Stanley S. and Paul R. McDaniel. 1985. *Tax Expenditures*. Cambridge, MA: Harvard University Press.

U.S. Office of Management and Budget. 1981. *Catalog of Federal Domestic Assistance*. Washington, DC.

Vedung, Evert. 1991. *Utvärdering i politik och förvaltning* (Evaluation in Public Policy and Public Administration). Lund: Studentlitteratur. English version forthcoming.

———. 1993. *Statens markpolitik, kommunerna och historiens ironi* (Land Use Policies, the Municipalities, and the Irony of History). Stockholm: SNS Förlag.

West, William F. 1985. *Administrative Rulemaking: Politics and Processes*. Westport, CT: Greenwood Press.

Woodside, Kenneth. 1986. "Policy Instruments and the Study of Public Policy," *Canadian Journal of Political Science* 19: 775–794.

Acknowledgements

The following people have offered valuable comments and criticisms: Marie-Louise Bemelmans-Videc, Frans van der Doelen, who wrote me a letter full of penetrating insights, Frans L. Leeuw, and Ray C. Rist, all of the Working Group on Policy and Program Evaluation; Emmette S. Redford, L.B.J. School of Public Affairs, University of Texas (Austin), Palle Svensson, Aarhus University, Lennart J. Lundqvist, Göteborg University, my present and former Uppsala colleagues Stefan Björklund, Axel Hadenius, Lennart Nordfors, and Sverker Gustavsson, Rolf Sandahl, the National Audit Bureau, Stockholm, and Tage Klingberg, the National Institute for Building Research, Gävle. Alexander Davidson, then at Uppsala, has rectified my English, and Laila Grandin and Pour Mitrahi-Bijän, Uppsala, have made copies, labeled letters, and sent faxes.

Financially, I wish to acknowledge the contributions of the Swedish Council for the Humanities and the Social Sciences (HSFR) where I occupied a special research position for evaluation research from 1986 to 1991; the Swedish Council for Building Research (BFR) through Sture Blomgren and the so-called NOGA Project, headed by Ola Nyquist; the IIAS, Brussels; the Algemene Rekenkamer in The Hague through Marie-Louise Bemelmans-Videc and Frans L. Leeuw (the 1991 Bruges meeting where the subgroup on policy instruments was established); the Office of the Comptroller General in Ottawa through John Mayne (the 1992 meeting); the *Statskonsult* in Oslo through Bjarne Eriksen (the 1993 meeting); the CEOPS-ENTPE in Vaulx-en-Velin through Jacques Toulemonde (the 1994 meeting); and finally the Knute and Alice Wallenberg Foundation at my alma mater Uppsala University through Stig Strömholm.

To the above mentioned people and institutions—and particularly to the HSFR—I extend my warm thanks. In order not to embarrass anybody, I want to stress most emphatically that the responsibility for the content and form of the chapter rests entirely with me.

2

The Stick:
Regulation as a Tool of Government

Donald Lemaire

Regulation is commonly referred to as the government's "stick." Regulatory instruments are used to define norms, acceptable behavior, or to limit activities in a given society. The law, backed up with the threat of sanction, represents the "stick" used to prescribe or prevent certain types of human behavior. Any infringement of the rules brings the specter of sanction. In other words, the government uses the "stick" to force the recalcitrant to obey the rules.

The instrument of regulation as a mode of intervention can be traced back to the beginning of history. Its weakness and strength as a policy instrument have been subject to extensive review (Bartlett 1992; Hancher and Moran 1989; Hangrove 1976; McGarity 1991; Salamon 1989; Stanbury 1986). Bartlett (1992) has even attributed the decline of civilizations to the interventions of governments and their regulations. A review of the literature tends to show that many regulatory interventions prove to be ineffective and excessively costly because they address situations reasonably well managed by the forces of the marketplace and liability law. And those interventions that, in principle, could usefully supplement market forces and the threat of litigation, indeed do so up to a point; but they also tend to be pushed to a point beyond which marginal costs exceed marginal benefits.

Over the last twenty years, there have been many calls for reducing the regulatory burden on national economies (House of Commons 1991–92; Seidman and Gilmour 1980). Economists have led the charge by demonstrating the inefficiency generated by economic regulation. They have argued that government regulatory intervention cause more harm to the economy than the shortfall of market forces that they are intended to rectify.

The deregulation movement in the 1980s resulted in some success and horror stories. One thing is clear: once a regulation has been in place for some time, a return to the pre-regulation situation is often not feasible. More generally, regulation modifies the policy context in which it is implemented and deregulation signals a redefinition of that policy context, not always with predictable results.

The 1990s is the decade focused on competitiveness: government interventions are assessed from the perspective of their impact on the competitiveness of national economies. It would seem that the lesson learned from the 1980s is that deregulation, by itself, will not cure all economic malaise. Each case deserves a closer look and sometimes reregulation is the order of the day. In the 1990s, we are moving from a position of deregulation to reregulation or improved regulation to ensure competitiveness.

In this chapter, I explore the morphogenesis of the tool of regulation. In the following sections, I will explore the formation, application, effectiveness and efficiency of regulatory tools.

Formation of Regulation

Regulation is often seen as the sole accomplishment and initiative of government. In the popular press, we read headlines calling for the end of excessive government red tape and unnecessary regulations. Although the authority to sanction and give force to a government intervention through regulation rests within the exclusive domain of that government, the initiation, even the production and actualization, is not in practice so exclusive as the perception seems to be in the popular press.

Public choice theory suggests that quite often the role of government is like an arbitrator between competing stakeholders on various issues. In those cases, the resulting regulation is the outcome of debates and negotiation among the interests involved. Thus, the government is not always a proactive proponent of regulation, but frequently functions as a mediator where regulation defines the competition and conflict between other parties.

This could be said for any government intervention. After all, government is elected to manage the public affairs of the country which incorporates the interests and well-being of all its citizens. When government decides to intervene on an issue or particular problem, it is always as a result of some demand or pressure, real or perceived, from its constituencies and from its bureaucracy. The literature in political science is abundant with how particular issues or problems find their way on to the government agenda. What is not so evident and well understood is how government is led to use regulation as intervention.

The "garbage-can approach" is used to suggest, by analogy, how a particular policy instrument is selected. In a nutshell, this analogy suggests that decision-makers pick whatever is accessible and known to them. What is known and accessible to them depends on their own history, professional characteristics of the analysts preparing the proposals, and precedent government interventions on similar issues and problems. This approach is too simplistic in explaining the selection of policy instruments: if this was actually the case, it would only be necessary to change policy instruments by changing the people involved in the decision-making process. The experience, knowledge, and skills of people involved in the process have some explanatory power concerning the ultimate choice of instruments. However, the nature of the issue and the institutional context also play important roles.

Elected officials have the final say in most government interventions; but they are not alone. The process takes place within a particular institutional context with multiple actors offering their version of the problem and action to be taken. Hence, the definition of the problem is influential in the decision of elected officials to have specific types of government intervention.

These dimensions of policy instruments could be captured and analyzed by using the concept of policy context (Hancher and Moran 1989). This concept refers to the historical, political and legal settings, organizational structure, the character of markets, and the nature of issues. By this, we include the rule of admission, the relations between occupants, and the variations introduced by differences in markets, and issue for government intervention in a particular national context.

The hypothesis here is that the nature of the issue and the institutional context largely determine the policy context in which particular policy instruments are acceptable and possible, and largely determine the formation of tools. In other words, not all instruments are equally acceptable for specific government interventions. Each policy instrument has a policy context in which it occupies a predominant position in relation to other policy instruments. That policy context will also define the configuration and application that tools will take.

For example, in the current Canadian context, if a problem is presented as one of health and safety, the government feels compelled to intervene. In addition, regulatory instruments usually have a head start as ways of responding to issues related to health and safety.

The government decision to intervene, and how it plans to do so, on issues of health and safety depends, to a large extent, on the nature of the policy context. A key dimension of any health and safety issue is to determine if the potentially affected citizens are sufficiently capable and knowledgeable to assume certain risks to health and safety associated with an activity, behavior, product, or service. Another is to determine when government should supplement the normal institutional framework of responsibility present in the market economy with a specific regulatory intervention. The generic answer to the latter question is "yes" when the situation is such that it would serve the "common good" or "public interest." For this idea to be useful, one needs to look at how common good and public interest are defined and who benefits from them. This is true for all government instruments.

Health and safety in the workplace is a good example to illustrate the concept. The historical, political, legal settings, organizational structure, the character of markets and the nature of issues are all dimensions that determine how and when the regulatory instrument will be selected. The capacity of workers to make health and safety at work the object of government intervention is dependant on the capacity of workers to organize themselves, which is still dependant on the legal setting in which their organizations can take form. The legal setting is dependant on the historical relationship between government, industry, and workers. In addition, the preference for the regulatory instrument also is related to the issue, namely health and safety. This is a sphere of human life in which the directive power of government and law is perceived to be necessary in furthering the common good.

In Canada, with every announcement of a reduction in government spending, there is a statement to the effect that it will be achieved in such a way that the health and safety of citizens will not be jeopardized. Therefore, any issue presented as one of health and safety, with enough profile to raise public concern, has a good chance of bringing government intervention. More often than not, a regulatory instrument will be selected.

This is not surprising when we consider the categorization given by Vedung earlier in this book to regulatory instruments as being the "stick" of government. On health and safety issues, governments want to give a clear signal of no compromise and strong action. Regulatory instruments have an advantage over other policy instruments on that front. This is not to say that regulatory instruments are the only ones selected and used. For example, economic instruments (taxes) and information (labeling) are used for health-issues related to smoking.

Application of Regulation

There are at least two aspects of the application question: (1) Where is the tool applied and (2) How is it applied?

Where Regulation Is Applied

The Sub-Committee on Regulation and Competitiveness of the Standing Committee on Finance in the Canadian government (House of Commons 1991–92) makes the affirmation that regulation is by far the preferred instrument of government intervention in the private sector. This, despite the fact that regulation is not always superior in terms of efficiency and effectiveness. Reasons for the bias towards the regulatory instrument according to the Committee are the following:

- Relative to other means of changing incentives and affecting behavior, regulation appears more certain and effective.
- For governments, the regulatory instrument is relatively costless, with most of the costs falling on the private sector. With cash-strapped governments, facing increasing demands for public services, to resort to regulation is particularly tempting.
- Most of the costs of regulation are hidden. They are reflected in higher prices for the things we buy or lower returns on labor or capital owing to lower productivity. While the benefits of regulation tend to be visible and known, the costs are often unseen or underestimated.

It must be noted that only the regulatory instrument was examined by this Committee. It would have been interesting to see if they would have reached the same conclusion had they compared regulation with other instruments.

It is true that regulation is extensively applied in Western economies. Unfortunately, there is no distinction as to the domain of application of the regulation. For example, reference to market economies suggests private initiatives and minimum government intervention; however, in this context there is a need for an institutional arrangement in which the rule of law plays a crucial role. Market economies require basic infrastructure to function efficiently. They need basic rules of the game which include, for example, trade, incorporation, competition, intellectual property, weights and measures, money supply and financial institutions.

The point is that some applications of the regulatory instrument have little to do with the discretion of government to intervene or not. There is a sphere of activities that needs some institutional arrangements to allow the orderly functioning of markets. A good example of difficulties generated by deficient institutional arrangements can be found in the current Russian experience.

In the literature, reference is made to economic and social regulations to capture the different domains of application (Hancher et al. 1989; Law Reform of Canada 1985, 1986; McGarity 1991). Social regulation refers to health, safety, fairness, and equity issues. Economic regulation deals with some aspect of "market imperfection." This classification is too general to be useful in assessing regulatory tools in comparison to other instruments. We need a classification that permits drawing conclusions and making comparisons with other instruments.

Broadly, regulation can be grouped as general or specific. The latter can be further divided as industry-specific, product-specific, or consumer-specific. These specific-purpose regulations can be subdivided into regulations with economic or social objectives. However, it may be best to classify regulations in terms of three distinct objectives, that is, (1) to internalize externalities; (2) to seek market stabilization or control; and (3) to establish an appropriate infrastructure.

Externality-targeted regulation aims at correcting some market failure. Despite the advantages of the market system, it sometimes leads to results which may not be the "best" from society's point of view. These results occur when there is a divergence between the private and the social costs or benefits of activities. Three types of such failure are environmental, safety, and informational. In the case of safety, the competitive markets do not provide enough correct information on the nature and extent of hazardous activities and products. For example, occupational safety, transportation safety, and product safety are areas of concern for governments. The informational problems arise from asymmetric availability of knowledge of products to buyers and sellers. The seller of a new commodity often knows more about its quality than does the buyer. This provides justification for consumer protection legislation, such as "truth-in-packaging" or "truth-in-advertising."

The latter case could be interpreted as a form of packaging of instruments: regulation is used to force producer to provide information to consumers. Vedung states that the real point of labeling is to inform consumers and that regulation is used only as a means of having information displayed to the consumers. Information is the "end" policy instrument.

Regulation aimed at market stabilization is essentially aimed at non-renewable resources, market structure, or natural monopolies. The overall thrust of these types of regulation is to ensure market stability and maintenance of appropriate control in certain areas of the economy. Regulation is used where demand is relatively inelastic, supply responses are slow, and storage costs are high. In these situations, a form of "destructive" competition may occur (e.g., agriculture). Regulation as an instrument in these cases could be assimilated as a form of packaging with economic instruments. As in the case of labeling, it depends on how the distinction between "ends" and "means" is made. The regulation ensures a minimum price for agricultural products and, as a consequence, farmers are guaranteed a certain level of income. From the addressees' (farmers') perspective the end result is income maintenance which is an economic instrument. From the governees' perspective, it is more a regulatory instrument, considering the authoritative force applied to regulate prices.

For non-renewable resources (minerals, petroleum, natural gas, etc.), the economic rationale generally suggested for regulation relates to common-property externality problems. It has been shown that in a market setting, common- property resources tend to be overused. Regulation of market structures or natural monopolies target situations in which firms, either through design or necessity, act in a manner which tends to reduce competitive pressures.

Finally, some regulation aims to create certain institutions which facilitate exchange and production, and which, among other things, define property rights. This provides the rules of the game within which institutions may develop. Social regulation is best thought of as an infrastructure regulation promoting fairness, equity, and justice.

How Regulation Is Applied : Regulation of Regulation

In the introduction, I referred to a claim that the intrusiveness of government through regulation is associated with the decline of some civilizations. I mentioned also that the literature tends to suggest that many regulatory interventions are ineffective or excessively costly. If this is the case then government intervention, based on the regulatory instrument, should be like any toxic substance: it should be banned completely or at least subject to strict control. As we will see below, this seems to be the approach taken in Canada.

The deregulation movement has highlighted some of regulation's side effects, real costs, and lack of effectiveness in specific policy contexts. It has generated enough momentum to force governments to review their approach for selecting this instrument. At least in Canada, regulation is the only instrument subject to such policy requirements. For other instruments there are administrative requirements for implementation; however, there is nothing about when and how a particular instrument should be selected.

For the government of Canada, there is a new regulatory policy (October 1992) which directs federal departments and agencies on how and when to use regulation. The stated objective of the policy is to ensure that use of the government's regulatory powers results in the greatest net benefit to Canadians. Departments and agencies are required to justify the need for regulation; weigh the benefits of the regulations against their cost; establish the framework (compliance and enforcement policies, management systems and resources) needed to implement regulatory programs; determine the relevance, success and cost-effectiveness of existing regulatory programs; and provide for an open regulatory process.

For existing regulatory programs and for substantive new or amended regulations, departments, and agencies *must* demonstrate that:

1. A problem or risk exists, government intervention is justified, and regulation is the best alternative.
2. Canadians have been consulted and have had an opportunity to participate in developing or modifying regulations and regulatory programs.
3. The benefits of regulation outweigh the costs, and the regulatory program is "structured" to maximize the gains to beneficiaries in relation to the costs to Canadian:
   • governments,
   • business, and
   • individuals.
4. Steps have been taken to ensure that the regulatory activity impedes Canada's competitiveness as little as possible.
5. The regulatory burden on Canadians has been minimized through such methods as cooperation with other governments.

6. Systems are in place to manage regulatory resources effectively. In particular:
   • compliance and enforcement policies are articulated, as appropriate; and,
   • resources have been approved and are adequate to discharge enforcement responsibilities effectively, and to ensure compliance where the regulation binds the government.

This new policy is on the continuum of government's efforts to improve the use of regulation. So far, the success with these efforts is mixed. The Subcommittee on Regulation and Competitiveness of the Standing Committee on Finance (House of Commons 1991–92: 102) mention in their report that:

> significant reforms to the regulatory process were introduced in 1986...These reforms were designed to improve the management of federal regulatory programs, give ministers more effective control of the regulatory process and facilitate greater public access and involvement in federal regulatory activities. On the whole, they have resulted in a much improved process...Yet significant problems with the way we regulate remain; problems related to design as well as application.

The 1992 policy aims essentially at better ex-ante assessment of the need for regulation by using cost-benefit analysis, increased consultation to ensure a more responsive regulatory process, and finally more ex-post evaluation of regulatory programs. However, the emphasis of the Committee recommendations is really on the ex-ante assessment and the regulatory process necessary to introduce and implement the regulatory instruments. It is an interesting case of vertical instrument packaging. The government uses its authoritative force on itself. In other words, the addressee and the government are the same.

The assumption seems to be that, by tightening the regulatory process by which new regulations are introduced, the apparent bias for that instrument can be eliminated. Consequently, only "good" or "justified" regulation will be implemented. On the other hand, there is also an expectation that the process of introducing or amending regulation should be more responsive and less time consuming. This implies not only rigorous ex-ante evaluation of proposed regulations, but also in as short a time-frame as possible.

The implementation of the regulatory policy should lead to the selection of the regulatory instrument only when it is the most cost-effective means for implementing the policy. The Committee (House of Commons 1991–92: 102) has hinted at the difficulties departments and agencies will face in fulfilling the requirements of the policy when mention is made of the fact that:

regulations represent the tool by which an Act of Parliament's policy is conducted. The fault may not lay so much with the regulation but with the inherent policy of the legislation. It is our opinion that reviewers should not fear to delve deep into the source of the regulatory problem, and we suggest that the future reviews look beyond the specific regulatory instruments...

The Committee is right in saying that the policy underlying the regulation is quite often the "source of the problem" and not the regulatory instrument per se. In fact, if the government decides not to intervene, then there is no need for any policy instrument. There is no choice to be made.

It is very difficult for the management of departments and agencies to challenge the goal which elected government decides it wants to pursue by adopting policies to respond to a problem. On many occasions, I have witnessed debates in departments on the issue of how to determine if the government should intervene or not and who should answer this question. The option was not perceived to be regulation vis-à-vis other policy instruments; it was perceived to be *no* government intervention vis-à-vis intervention by means of regulation. Other alternatives were simply not considered. There were two perceived options: regulation or no intervention.

For existing government activity, we must distinguish between possibilities where the presence of government has been (1) non-existent or marginal, or (2) significant. In the latter case, we have the emergence of a new problem and an issue within a well-occupied policy context that may require repositioning and offer possibilities for redefining the government's role. I believe this is the dominant situation. However, the current fiscal constraint forces government to reexamine its current functions. This implies a reexamination of policy instruments used to implement policies within these functions. In the case of a new policy context, the selection of policy instruments can be anticipated to be more free from these contextual influences.

Effectiveness of Regulation

There is a formal requirement for program evaluation by departments of the Canadian federal government since 1977 that includes regulatory programs. Regulatory programs typically involve multiple regulations, and within such programs, other instruments might also be used. The 1992 regulatory policy refers to the evaluation policy. In other words, the requirements of the regulatory policy to determine the relevance, success and cost-effectiveness of existing regulatory programs are the same as the requirements of the evaluation policy.

In the rational decision-making model underlying the 1992 Canadian government regulatory policy, the regulation instrument is supposedly applied when available evidence supports the choice of regulation as the most effective instrument, and the implementation or its design is the most efficient. Evaluation plays a role both at the selection phase and at the effectiveness-assessment phase. Retrospective evaluation provides good information on the actual effectiveness of different government interventions. From 1986 to 1991, the Office of the Comptroller General provided summaries of evaluation studies on regulatory programs to the government agency responsible for overseeing the regulatory policy. This information was expected to be used by the agency in reviewing regulatory proposals from departments.

In this context, there are two pertinent questions: (1) What contribution has evaluation made in the selection or review of regulatory programs?; and (b) What have we learned about regulation from evaluation?

How Evaluation Was Used

From 1987 to 1992, thirty-eight ex-post evaluations of regulatory programs were completed by departments of the Canadian government. Completed evaluations are classified into six categories according to type of use. The first category is "confirmation" where new evidence shows that the program is working well, and design and delivery are sound. Evaluations that provide better information to managers on the programs, without leading to modifications, are classified under "understanding." Evaluations that lead to modest operational changes are classified under "modification." "Reform" best describes evaluations that lead to more substantial changes that are visible to the clients. The "termination" category is self-explanatory, and the "no-results" category best fits those evaluations that have not improved understanding or from which no changes have resulted.

The thirty-eight studies were used as follows: confirmation (8 percent), understanding (13 percent), modification (34 percent), reform (8 percent), termination (5 percent), no results (3 percent), and no information available as to utilization as of October 1992 (29 percent).

The ex-ante evaluation has a different perspective. It is expected to provide rational analysis to substantiate the selection of the regulation instrument. This requirement has different names. For example, in

Canada it is called Regulatory Impact Analysis Statement (RIAS); in the United States it is the Regulatory Impact Analysis (RIA). Nevertheless, expectations are essentially the same: "regulatory departments are supposed to formally define the problem motivating the regulatory initiative, consider alternative forms of intervention, and provide an economic evaluation of the draft regulation(s)" (House of Commons 1991–92: 117). The functions of the RIAS are essentially to disclose information to the public at a stage in the policy-making process where it can be used effectively to improve the quality of new regulations. The second function is designed to structure the analytic work leading to proposed regulations. The Canadian Committee states that "Unfortunately, the RIAS requirement concerning the economic assessment of proposed regulations has not been implemented very well" (House of Commons 1991–92: 119).

The same situation seems to prevail in the U.S. government. McGarity (1991), in his book *Reinventing Rationality: The Role of Regulatory Analysis in the Federal Bureaucracy*, presents a series of case studies on the ex-ante evaluation, which he calls regulatory analysis, and the role it has played in the introduction of regulation. One of his main conclusions is that

> The regulatory analysis is currently in a state of awkward adolescence. It has emerged from its infancy, but it has not yet matured. It is often noisy and clumsy, and it generally commands little respect. Yet despite its considerable shortcomings, it has important virtue. (McGarity 1991: 303)

He also makes an interesting remark about retrospective evaluation:

> Retrospective assessment of the predictions made in previous regulatory analysis documents can provide feedback on the accuracy of agency predictions and thereby enable agencies to enhance the accuracy of future predictions. Retrospective analysis can also be useful in evaluating the value of regulatory analysis to an agency's regulatory effort. (McGarity 1991: 307)

This highlights the importance of evaluation as a continuous process to monitor how an instrument performs in achieving policy objectives.

The need to improve the link between ex-ante and ex-post evaluation has been recognized by the Canadian Standing Committee and works are under way to examine the best approach to achieve this. As mentioned earlier, the approach from 1986 to 1992 was to submit summaries of ex-post evaluation studies to the agency responsible for reviewing regulatory analysis and it was up to this agency to use it or not.

The results of that approach were not satisfactory. The agency reviewed the regulatory analysis as they were submitted and they did not necessarily match with the evaluation study that was coming in at the same time.

What Have We Learned from Evaluations
of the Regulation Instrument?

The literature is quite substantial on the theory of the design and expected effectiveness and impacts of regulation. The deregulation fervor of the 1980s was based on the argument that regulation was ineffective in some cases and had negative impacts on national economies. The attack was directed specifically to regulation aimed at remedying externalities and market stabilization or control. The transport sector was at the leading edge of deregulation. A multitude of studies were done demonstrating that these regulations had a net cost on the economy (Winston 1993).

It is argued that regulation is effective in changing behavior as long as there is social consensus around the government policy underlying the regulatory instrument. The effectiveness of a regulatory instrument is associated with its legitimacy. The difficulty is that we might have legitimacy and still have an ineffective regulatory instrument. There is also the situation where a regulatory instrument is used to obtain a change in behavior even though the legitimacy is openly challenged.

Effectiveness also greatly depends on the nature of the policy context, which also determines the capacity of government organization to ensure compliance. Actually, the capacity to ensure compliance is a necessary condition for effectiveness of a specific government intervention by regulatory instruments.

The capacity to ensure compliance is different if we deal with economic regulation versus social regulation. The configuration of the policy context is normally quite different between these two types of application of the regulatory instrument. Not only is the selection process that leads to the adoption of economic regulation and social regulation different because the configuration of the policy context is different, but also effectiveness measurement is different.

In the case of economic regulation, we usually can estimate the direction of the benefits or at least determine who receives the "rent" associated with economic regulation. The actual value is always subject to extensive debates. Nevertheless, it is possible to estimate who pays and who receives part of the economic rent. This was the main focus of the debates surrounding economic deregulation of the 1980s. We must remember that economic regulation is usually justified on the grounds that it corrects some deficiencies and imperfections in the functioning of the market. The proponents of deregulation were arguing that the economic regulation was not only ineffective at correcting the imperfection of the market, but was also having effects actually worse than the market imperfections it was designed to correct.

In the case of social regulation, the benefits are of a different nature, for example, the antidiscrimination regulation in the labor market. The effectiveness here is not measured in terms of monetary value. The intervention is based on the grounds of fairness and equity. There is a growing field of interdisciplinary research involving sociology, political science, and law that are addressing the role of "law" as a policy instrument (Rocher and Vandycke 1986). However, as of yet there seems to be no consensus on the measurement of the results of social regulation—in contrast to that achieved by economists on the theme of economic deregulation.

Conclusion

Policy instruments should not be regarded only as means through which the ends of political life are achieved. Instruments are ends in themselves (see ch. 1). The DeMarco and Rist analysis (ch. 8) of government-sponsored enterprises as a credit allocation tool in the United States is a good illustration:

> Abolishing a GSE once markets are sufficiently developed to be served by fully private entities, or redirecting a GSE to serve segments perceived to be in greatest need is very difficult to accomplish. These enterprises owe their existence to the federal government, and they benefit from numerous federal ties. At the same time, they have proven that they can be so powerful that the government loses much of its ability to control or redirect their resources to meet changing priorities.

In the case of the regulatory instrument, attempts are made in most Western countries to improve the process of how and when to use this instrument. The underlying assumption is that by improving the process of how we choose policy instruments, the "politics of policy instrument choice" will be better managed and lead to rational choices. It recognizes the fact that, once instruments are used in a policy context, they tend to become irreversible. Even though we had deregulation in the 1980s and pressures are still strong to refrain from the use of the regulatory instrument, the changes were more related to how regulation is used than to a total withdrawal of the use of this instrument in a specific policy context.

The corollary of the non-neutrality of policy instruments is that policy context is not neutral either. The historical, political and legal settings, organizational structure, the character of markets, and the nature of the issue in a policy context will influence how the regulatory instrument is implemented and adjusted with time. Chapter 9, by M.J. Arentsen is a good example of how the specific circumstances of policy context impacted on the policy choice.

Policy evaluation has been identified, in Canada and the United States, as an important mechanism for deciding when to choose regulatory instruments or not, and to assess the effectiveness of regulatory instruments in achieving policy objectives. However, the actual use of policy evaluation was based on a lack of understanding of the relationship between policy instruments and policy context. Policy instruments are implemented in policy contexts in constant movement. Policy evaluation was implemented by a discrete process in the form of ex-ante and ex-post evaluation with little links between the two. To improve the usefulness of policy evaluation it is important that it be based on policy instruments and implemented as a continuous process.

Discussion

The theme of this volume is the evaluation and packaging of policy instruments. The first challenge was to propose a typology of policy instruments that is parsimonious, fruitful, and minimal. The basic, three-fold Vedung typology based on the degree of authoritative force meets that challenge. The division along the line of degree of authoritative force permits a better grasp of the different forms of instruments packaging we find in real situations. It also facilitates evaluation of the action content of policy instruments in different policy contexts. A good illustration of that is Winston's (1993) analysis of economic deregulation of American industry for different economic sectors. He defines economic deregulation as the state's withdrawal of its legal powers to direct the economic conduct of nongovernmental bodies. This definition bares no differences with the one proposed by Vedung for regulation instruments. Winston makes interesting comments about the deregulation of the savings and loan industry, that had left the public with an at least $150 billion bill to honor savings and loan obligations.

He objects to attributing the blame for the savings and loans crisis on the deregulation of that industry:

> From a policy perspective, one would have to conclude that society was hurt by this policy and that it would be desirable to return to stricter asset regulation. But the least cost solution is not a return to greater asset regulation, which would deny savings and loans the benefits of expanded investment opportunities, but more effective regulatory supervision of savings and loans' financial condition and reduced exposure to moral hazard problems. (Winston 1993: 1273)

As we can see the disagreement is on the action content of the regulatory instrument, not on the regulatory instrument per se. In fact, Winston's article is more about the effectiveness of different action contents of the regulatory instrument in a variety of policy contexts than actual deregulation.

The Vedung typology based on authoritative force helps to take into account the complexities of policy instruments by making the distinction between the technique of governance and the application of the technique in different policy contexts. It improves our capacity to evaluate the effectiveness of government intervention.

References

Arentsen, Maarten J. 1997. "The Invisible Problem and How to Deal With It," ch. 9 in M. Bemelmans-Videc, R.C. Rist, and E. Vedung (eds.), *Carrots, Sticks, and Sermons: Policy Instruments and their Evaluation*. New Brunswick, NJ: Transaction Publishers.

Aucoin, Peter. 1990. "Administrative Reform in Public Management: Paradigms, Principles, Paradoxes and Pendulums," *Governance*. 3 (2): 323–343.

Auld, D. and H. Kitchen. 1988. *The Supply of Government Services*. Vancouver: The Fraser Institute.

Bardach, E. 1980. "Implementation Studies and the Study of Implements," Proceedings of the American Political Science Association, Washington, DC, American Political Science Association.

Bartlett, Bruce. 1992. "Government Regulation and Control of the Economy from Ancient Times to the Nineteenth Century," *Journal of Regulation and Social Costs* 2(3): 208–223.

Canada. House of Commons. 1991–92. *Minutes of Proceedings and Evidence of the Sub-Committee on Regulations and Competitiveness of the Standing Committee on Finance*, issue no. 23. Ottawa: Queen's Printer.

Chambers, David. 1988. "Learning from Markets," *Public Money and Management* 8(4).

Church, W. Thomas, and Milton Heumann. 1989. "The Underexamined Assumptions of the Invisible Hand: Monetary Incentives as Policy Instruments," *Journal of Policy Analysis and Management* 8(4).

DeMarco, Edward J. and Ray C. Rist. "Government-Sponsored Enterprises as a Credit Allocation Tool in the United States," ch. 8 in M. Bemelmans-Videc, R.C. Rist, and E. Vedung (eds.), *Carrots, Sticks, and Sermons: Policy Instruments and their Evaluation.* New Brunswick, NJ: Transaction Publishers.

Doern, G.B. and R.W. Phidd. 1983. *Canadian Public Policy: Ideas, Structure, Process.* Toronto: Methuen.

Dunshire, Andrew, Keith Hartley, and David Parker. 1991. "Organizational Status and Performance: Summary of the Findings," *Public Administration* 69 (spring).

Elmore, R.F. 1984. "Instruments and Strategy in Public Policy," *Policy Studies Review* 7(1): 174–186.

Garten, Helen. 1991. *Why Bank Regulation Failed, Designing a Bank Regulation Strategy for the 1990s.* Quorum Books.

Hancher, Leigh and Michael Moran. 1989. *Capitalism, Culture, and Economic Regulation.* Oxford: Clarendon Press.

Hargrove, Erwin. 1976. *The Missing Link: The Study of Implementation.* Washington, DC: Urban Institute Press.

Herzlinger, Regina and Nancy Kane. 1983. *A Managerial Analysis of Federal Income Redistribution Mechanism: The Government as Factory, Insurance Company, and Bank.* Cambridge, MA: Ballinger.

Hood, Christopher C. 1986. *The Tools of Government.* Chatham, NJ: Chatham House Publishers.

Hull, Brian and St-Pierre. 1990. *The Market and the Environment: Using Market-Based Approaches to Achieve Environmental Goals.* Conference Board of Canada.

Isaia, Henri and Jacques Spindler. 1989. "Le Management des politiques publiques locales et la décentralisation," *Revue française de finances publiques.*

Jackson, R.J., D. Jackson and N. Baxter-More. 1987. *Contemporary Canadian Politics.* Scarborough: Prentice-Hall.

Kettl, Donald F. 1988. "Government by Proxy (Mis?)managing Federal Programs," *Congressional Quarterly Inc.*, (ISBN 087187429-6).

Law Reform Commission of Canada. 1985. *Crimes Against the Environment.* Working Paper no. 44.

———. 1986. *Policy Implementation, Compliance and Administrative Law.* Working Paper no. 51.

Lerner, G. 1984. *Probing Leviathan: An Investigation of Government in the Economy.* Vancouver: Fraser Institute.

Linder, Stephen H. and B. Guy Peters. 1984. "From Social Theory to Policy Design," *Journal of Public Policy* 4(3): 237–259.

———. 1989. "Instruments of Government: Perceptions and Contexts," *Journal of Public Policy* 9(1): 189–202.

Lowi, T.J. 1972. "Four Systems of Policy, Politics, and Choice," *Public Administration Review* 32(4): 298–310.

May, Peter J. 1981. "Hints for Crafting Alternatives Policies," *Policy Analysis* 7(2): 225–235.

McCraw, Thomas K. 1984. "The Public and Private Spheres in Historical Perspective," in Harvey Brooks, Lance Liebman, and Corrine S. Schelling (eds.), *Public-Private Partnership: New Opportunities for Meeting Social Needs.* Cambridge, MA: Ballinger.

McGarity, Thomas O. 1991. *Reinventing Rationality: The Role of Regulatory Analysis in the Federal Bureaucracy.* Cambridge: Cambridge University Press.

Metcalfe, Les and Sue Richards. 1987. *Improving Public Management.* Newbury Park, CA: Sage Publications.

Moe, C. Ronald. 1987. "Exploring the Limits of Privatization," *Public Administration Review* (Nov./Dec.).

Netherlands Ministry of Justice. 1991. "Legislation in Perspective," The Hague (Oct.).

Norwegian Official Reports. 1992. "Improving the Structure of Legislation in Norway," Oslo.

Ostrander, Susan A., Stuart Langton, and Jon Van Til. 1987. *Shifting the Debate: Public/Private Sector Relations in the Modern Welfare State*. New Brunswick, NJ: Transaction Publishers.

Palumbo, D.J. and D.J. Calista. *Implementation and the Policy Process*. New York: Greenwood Press.

Popper, Frank. 1985. "Why I Don't Do Much Federal Consulting Anymore," *Journal of Management Consulting* 2(3): 4–9.

Prichard, R. 1983. *Crown Corporations in Canada: The Calculus of Instruments Choice*. Toronto: Buttersworth.

Rocher, G. and R. Vandycke. 1986. "Droit et Pouvoir: Pouvoirs du Droit," *Sociologie et Sociétés* 18(1): 3–10.

Rose, Richard. 1990. "Charging For Public Services: A Paradigm For Practical Analysis," *Public Administration* 68(3).

Ripley, R.B. 1966. *Public Policies and their Politics: Techniques of Government Control*. New York: W.W. Norton.

Salamon, Lester M., ed. 1989. "Beyond Privatization: The Tools of Government Action," Washington, DC: The Urban Institute.

Schultz, Richard. 1992. "Paradigm Lost: Explaining the Canadian Politics of Deregulation." Working Paper no. 60, Department of Political Science and CSRI.

Schultze, Charles. 1977. *The Public Use of Private Interest*. Washington, DC: Brookings Institution.

Seidman, Harold and Robert Gilmour. 1980. *Politics, Position, and Power, from the Positive to the Regulatory State*. New York: Oxford University Press.

Stanbury, W.T. 1986. *Business-Government Relations in Canada: Grappling With Leviathan*. Toronto: Methuen.

Thurow, Lester C. 1974. "Cash Versus In-Kind Transfers," *American Economic Review* 64 (May): 23–35.

Vedung, Evert, 1998. "Policy Instruments—Typologies and Theories," ch. 1 in M. Bemelmans–Videc, R.C. Rist, and E. Vedung (eds.), *Carrots, Sticks, and Sermons: Policy Instruments and their Evaluation*. New Brunswick, NJ: Transaction Publishers.

Winston, C. 1993. "Economic Deregulation: Days of Reckoning for Microeconomists," *Journal of Economic Literature* 31: 1263–1289

Woodside, K. 1986. "Policy Instruments and the Study of Public Policy," *Canadian Journal of Political Science* 19(4): 775–794.

3

The Carrot: Subsidies as a Tool of Government—Theory and Practice

Frans L. Leeuw

Subsidies: A Popular but Problematic Tool of Government?

Referring to the inventory of policy instruments (see ch. 1 and especially figures 1.5 and 1.7), subsidies and grants can be characterized as affirmative economic policy instruments (incentives). Taxes, charges, and levies have the character of negative economic policy instruments or disincentives.

In a number of industrialized countries, subsidies and grants are important tools of government (Salamon 1989; Vedung 1991). Organization for Economic Cooperation and Development (OECD) data show that the public expenditures for grants and subsidies[1] in countries like Germany, Belgium, The Netherlands, France, and Denmark vary between 20 and 35 percent of the GNP.

With regard to subsidies and focusing on The Netherlands in particular, data from the Dutch Ministry of Finance show that subsidy expenditures rose from 4.8 billion guilders in 1970 to 42 billion guilders in 1993. In large part this increase has been linked with the development of the political concept of the welfare state, in which context subsidies play an essential role.

Underlying Behavioral Assumptions

A subsidy is defined as the conditional transfer of funds by government to (or for the benefit of) another party for the purpose of influenc-

This chapter is largely based on research carried out the The Dutch National Audit Office (Algemere Rekenkamer).

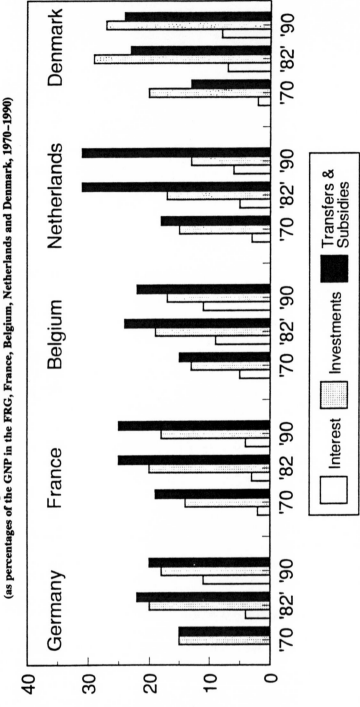

FIGURE 3.1

Public Expenditure in Terms of Interest, Investments, Transfers and Subsidies

(as percentages of the GNP in the FRG, France, Belgium, Netherlands and Denmark, 1970–1990)

Source: Ministerie van Financiën, Milfoenennota 1991, Den Haag, 1990

ing that party's behavior with a view to achieving some level of activity or provision.

A first feature of subsidies is that the government does not itself carry out the activities but instead seeks to achieve its goals by influencing the behavior of subsidy-recipients. According to Wolfson, subsidies try to affect behavior through income and substitution effects. "The income effect describes how people react to the alleviation of the budget constraint as affected by the resulting increase in income available for private use. The substitution effect describes how people react to changes in relative prices. The two effects tend to come in tandem."[2] Subsidies therefore intend to act as a financial incentive prompting the recipient to undertake activities which will achieve the goals of the subsidy provider, in this case the government. To this end the transfer is subject to certain conditions, formulated by the provider and pertaining to activities to be undertaken. It is therefore important that a subsidy leads to behavior which realizes the goals the government has formulated.[3]

Difficulties

Not only are subsidies are not only a popular policy instrument, but they are also characterized by a number of difficulties (Douma 1981; Heij and Vranken 1987; Gerritse 1990). As a policy instrument, subsidies are said to lack clarity and coherence, with no systematic provision being made for comparing costs and benefits, while the conditions attached to subsidies vary widely and are not clearly formulated. The financial administration of funds received and the procedures for monitoring compliance with the conditions attached have been criticized as inadequate; often no adequate picture of the efficiency and effectiveness of subsidies is available. Haider (1989: 114) notes that there are difficulties regarding the enforcement of grant conditions and requirements, as well as the often rather vague and elusive goals and objectives of grants. De Kemp (1987) has indicated that subsidization can be cost-ineffective: recipients might already have decided to behave in the desired way, in which case subsidization has been unnecessary.

Wolfson mentions a perverse effect of subsidies: increasing the tax wedge. "Regardless of the merits of individual subsidies, experience shows that the wedge created by taxation in the disposable income of labor and capital develops an endogenous growth of its own. As income available for private use is reduced, people claim to new subsidies to maintain their real income, widening the tax wedge again, and so on and so forth" (1990: 6).

Another perverse effect is benefit snatching: subsidies that are intended to provide benefits to consumers turn out to be a benefit for producers. This effect occurs when producers indicate that the costs of making goods and services eligible for subsidization will increase and subsequently prompt the government to increase the subsidy level. The consequence is that producers do not run the risk of decreasing demands. Had there been no subsidy available, the increase in production costs might not have taken place at all.

Finally, Wiseman (1977) and Jasinowski (1973) note a darker rationale underlying this tool of government: "to trade subsidies for votes" or even "to keep the constituents happy."

Lack of Empirical Knowledge

It should be noted that the ascribed negative aspects of subsidies are often based on investigations focusing on *specific* (types of) subsidies in *specific* policy fields like producer and industrial subsidies (Gerritse 1990; Ford and Suyker 1990), environmental subsidies (Vermeulen 1991; 1992) and subsidies in the field of housing (Priemus 1989).

In The Netherlands, a comparative study of problems and pitfalls with regard to *all* subsidies the government produces has long been lacking. Nevertheless, it is almost common wisdom to consider subsidization a typical case of policy failure. However, there are also examples of subsidies that have been successful. Restricting the story to industrial subsidies, Ford and Suyker (1990: 58) refer to successes like the subsidies for new industries in France (*train à grand vitesse* [TGV]) and The Netherlands (Fokker-airplanes). However, to which extent governments have adequate *management information* available on (the effects of) subsidies has been unknown in The Netherlands for a long time. Another problem is that although this tool of government is under severe criticism, even the very number of subsidies the Dutch government issued has for a long time been unclear. This was partly caused by definitional problems, partly by a lack of effort in inventorying facts and figures.[4]

By stressing pitfalls, thinking about and developing management instruments to curb the ascribed problems has been hampered. Why would anyone invest in developing "best practice guidelines" in order to improve the management of this tool of government when problems and pitfalls are so evident? Also, when authors, despite these critiques, formulate questions with regard to the improvement of the management of subsidies, as Peacock (1990: 28) did, it is rather unclear what can be expected from the improvements suggested. He suggested carrying out (more) ex-post evaluations through which it is possible to obtain adequate information about costs and benefits of subsidies. However, to what extent subsidies are already covered by these kinds of evaluations remains unclear. The other suggestion Peacock (1990: 30) gave focused on ways to reduce the uncertainty that subsidies are able to realize the goals set. "[This] may be the requirement that a time limit as well as an expenditure limit has to be placed on the subsidy provision." Again, Peacock does not indicate to what extent subsidies (in different nations) are already characterized by such a provision. It has also been suggested to pay more attention to the feasibility of the enforcement of subsidy conditions (Haider 1989) and to increase knowledge about the transaction costs involved in producing subsidies.

For at least three reasons this *lack of empirical knowledge* with regard to the management, goals, costs, and effects of subsidies is problematic. First, lack of data makes it almost impossible to answer the question to which extent (and which types of) subsidies are confronted with particular difficulties. Secondly, lack of knowledge makes it difficult to ascertain what the effects will be of the suggested improvements. In order to recommend improvements, one needs to be knowledgeable about existing provisions. Thirdly, lack of empirical knowledge can have immediate consequences within day-to-day politics.

In a time when countries like the United Kingdom, Germany, Sweden, or The Netherlands are experiencing substantial budgetary problems and retrenchments are the talk of the day, reducing or abandoning subsidies can be a solution. However, when there is no adequate knowledge available on the beneficial effects of subsidies, it is also unclear which negative (unintended) effects will occur when the use of this policy instrument is reduced or even abandoned. Counterfactual analysis may uncover new insight, but this approach presupposes knowledge about the goals subsidies have.[5]

Research by the Dutch National Audit Office:
Questions to be Answered

During the late 1980s the Dutch Algemene Rekenkamer (National Audit Office) carried out a government-wide investigation dealing with several of the aforementioned issues (Algemene Rekenkamer 1989; 1991; Kordes, Leeuw, and Van Dam 1991; Leeuw 1992).

The audit focused on the following questions:

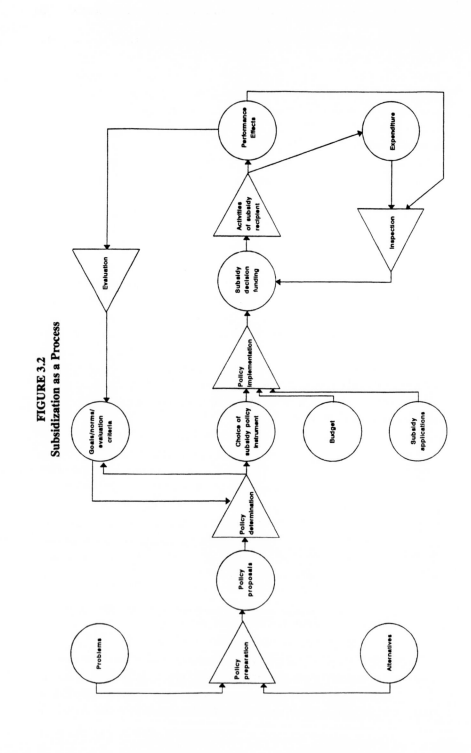

FIGURE 3.2
Subsidization as a Process

1. How many subsidies were issued by the Dutch government and which policy fields were covered by these subsidies? Who gave what to whom?
2. What information did the Dutch government possess with regard to the following management aspects of this instrument: goal-directedness, implementation/transaction costs, and ex-post evaluation of subsidies?[6]
3. Were there differences between types of subsidies on the one hand and coverage by ex-post evaluations on the other hand?

Theoretical Framework

In assessing the management of subsidies we made use of an approach developed by Bressers and Klok (1987; Klok 1991). These authors make a distinction between the *process to be regulated* (that is, the processes or activities which subsidy recipients are intended to institute within society) and the *policy process*, in this case that of the subsidy-provider, that is, the administration/ministry/agency issuing subsidies. For reasons of clarification, one might therefore also speak of, on the one hand, processes within society and on the other hand administrative processes. As an analytical aid, the policy (or administrative) process can in turn be divided into a number of components: preparation, decision, implementation, control, and evaluation.

With their respective inputs and outputs the processes can be set out in diagrammatic form as follows.

The triangles in the diagram represent the components of the policy process, and the circles their inputs and outputs, including the effects of subsidies within society. The policy (or administrative) process should be set up in such a way as to maximize the extent to which it promotes the desired action by recipients while minimizing the cost to the government.

Systems thoery helped analyze how the subsidy-provider gave concrete shape to this process. In this theory an organization is conceived as a system in which processes directed at achieving certain goals (a particular output) take place. Central to the approach is the notion that the goal-directed processes should not or cannot take place in uncontrolled fashion, but that a number of *other* processes are needed to *control* them, that is, to ensure that they operate effectively and efficiently. In systems-theory terms this implies that the goal-directed processes must incorporate a number of points at which measurement and control are possible. The measurement points make it possible to check that inputs and outputs meet the required criteria, and if they are found not to do so it must be possible to make the necessary adjustments.

Management Aspects

Against this background the adequate management of subsidies requires that the policy process incorporate mechanisms for data collection and processing and for control which keep the subsidy-provider informed as to the processes taking place within the subsidized organization and enable control to be exercised as necessary. Information must be gathered and used and control exercised in systematic fashion. With this in mind we have distinguished three aspects of management on which the subsidy-provider should focus; they are linked with the (actual and potential) problem areas identified earlier. The purpose of this aspect-by-aspect approach is the identification of strong and weak points in the management of subsidies. The following *management aspects* were distinguished.

Goal-Directedness of Subsidies. Here we are concerned with the manner in which the introduction of a subsidy is prepared. A goal-directed policy implies that, before a subsidy is introduced, attention is focused on the intended scope and effect of the subsidy, so that control mechanisms can be put in place in good time. In particular it is necessary to perform ex-ante evaluations. These studies aim at producing knowledge about one or more of the following subjects:

- the relationship of the subsidy and the policy goal(s): has the relationship been specified?
- the behavioral mechanisms underlying the subsidy: why do policymakers believe that subsidization will be able to solve or reduce problems? Put differently: has the policy theory underlying the relationship between instrument (choice) and policy goal(s) been articulated?
- the estimation of the implementation/transaction costs of subsidies;
- foreseeable problems dealing with the implementation of subsidies within society;
- the possibilities of fraud;
- the necessity of limiting the duration of the subsidy.

Implementation of Subsidies. Implementation covers the manner in which subsidy applications are processed, advance payments are made, and subsidy amounts are determined within the machinery of central government. Adequate management in this context implies that information is collected on the implementation and transaction costs associated with subsidy provision, and that the implementation process includes control mechanisms in the form of time limits for applications, decisions, and the determination of the amounts to be paid. When referring to transaction costs, we are concerned with inside bureaucracy costs. Although administrative and transaction costs for individuals and corporate actors within the society can and probably will be substantial,[7] no data related to our set of subsidies is as yet available.

Ex-Post Evaluation of the Effectiveness of Subsidies. Ex-post evaluation relates to the manner in which information is collected on the effectiveness of the subsidy and the efficiency of the activities undertaken. Adequate evaluation implies that information is systematically collected on the scope, goal-achievement, effects, and costs of a subsidy and that adjustments can be made on the basis of this information.

For each of these three aspects the National Audit Office looked at the instruments which are (or should be) available to central government, if it is to remain informed as to the progress being made in the process of subsidy provision and, where necessary, to make adjustments.

An Institution-Free Approach

The approach outlined is considered "institution-free." No attention has been paid to the impact that social, legal, political, and geographical characteristics related to different policy fields and subsidies *can* and probably *will* have on the management of subsidies. Subsidizing youth welfare hospitals in a rural area is quite different from subsidizing environmental activists in inner cities, while handling grants on behalf of crime prevention programs in slums is different from managing subsidies to the research and development activities of multinationals. However, the National Audit Office stressed that there are criteria that have to be met by *all* subsidies, without taking into account differences between policy fields or organizations. It was argued that, as its goal was to carry out a comparative study in order to increase the attention paid to the management of this tool of government, it would be wise to focus on a *limited* number of *management aspects* relevant for *all* subsidies in a relatively general way, instead of going into detail with regard to *specific* institutional and field characteristics of *some* subsidies. After the publication of this government-wide study, the Audit Office started several research projects focusing on *specific* subsidies in *specific* situations, such as youth guidance programs, crime prevention, and childcare activities.

FIGURE 3.3
General Overview of Subsidies
Total HFL 41,521,076 (1992)

Ministry

1 - Office of the Prime Minister
2 - Foreign Affairs
3 - Justice
4 - Home Affairs
5 - Science and Education
6 - Finance
7 - Defense
8 - Planning, Housing &
      the Environment
9 - Tranport, Public Works
      & Water Management
10 - Economic Affairs
11 - Agriculture, Nature
      Management & Fisheries
12 - Social Affairs & Employment
13 - Welfare, Cultural Affairs
      & Health

Other subsidies
(not related to a specific ministry)

14 - Development Aid
15 - Miniorities
16 - Subsidies on behalf of the
      Dutch Organization for
      Applied Scientific Research

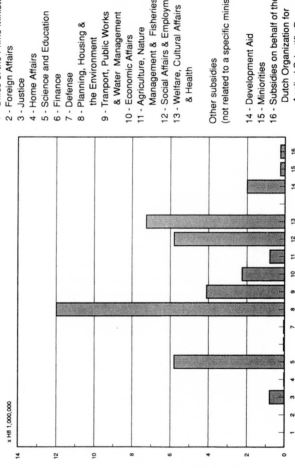

Design of the Research

All thirteen ministries of the Dutch central government, located in or near The Hague, were involved in the investigation. Currently some 140,000 civil servants in total are working within these ministries.

Omitting piloting activities, data were collected in two stages. The first round of data-collection took place in 1987 and referred to fiscal year 1986. The Audit Office started with taking an inventory of the number of subsidies in operation during fiscal year 1986 by scrutinizing financial information systems of the ministries. As there was no central registration of subsidies and as there were also definitional problems (what "is" a subsidy?) (Bruce 1990), it was impossible to obtain reliable data from the financial units of the ministries directly. Therefore, interviews of policy and staff units within central government that might use subsidies as a policy instrument were conducted. Information was also obtained from so-called "subsidiologists," that is, profit organizations specializing in obtaining grants and subsidies from the government. They usually operate on a no-cure–no-pay basis. The Audit Office cross-checked several of their lists by going back to the financial units of the ministries in order to find out what was known about unknown subsidies. Ultimately, the National Audit Office produced a list of all subsidies available during fiscal year 1986. The number was 722, while public expenditure circled around 30 billion Dutch guilders (approx. U.S. $16 billion). More recent information pertaining to 1993 shows that the number has increased to 730.

The second round of data-collection took place in 1990 with the goal of assessing developments that had taken place since 1986–1987. Data-collection and analysis were restricted to the 31 largest subsidies. Moreover, the second round was limited to only one management aspect, that is, ex-post evaluation.

After the publication of the study, Parliament urged the Dutch ministries and in particular the Ministries of Finance and Justice to launch a project to go into more institutional detail with regard to the twenty-five or thirty largest subsidies. Among other categories, attention was paid to the management of the subsidy, the level of goal achievement, the possible unintended side effects of subsidization and the possibilities of fraud and abuse of subsidies. Attention was also paid to the international comparison of several subsidies (Hamer 1992).

FIGURE 3.4
Percentage of Ex Ante Evaluations that Took Place

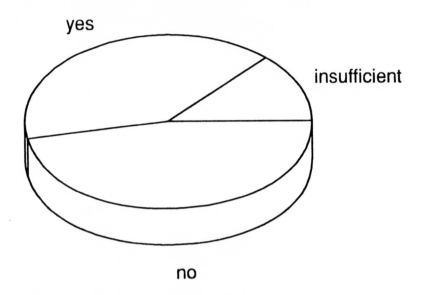

FIGURE 3.5
Percentage of Subsidies about which Evaluation Criteria were Formulated

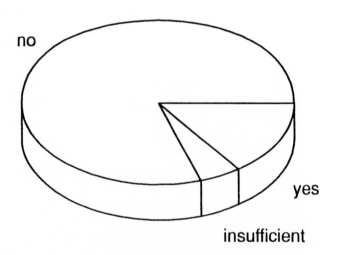

Research Question No. 1: Number of Subsidies Issued by The Netherlands Government: Who Gives What to Whom?

The question of who gave what to whom seems easy to answer but, as was already indicated, in practice appeared to be rather complicated. The 722 grants and subsidies analyzed were divided among fourteen government departments and one budgetary fund (the Investment Account Fund [IAF]). The amount budgeted for these subsidies in 1986 was 28.9 billion guilders; cash expenditure totalled 30.1 billion guilders (approximately U.S. $18 billion). It appeared that the Ministry of Housing, Physical Planning, and the Environment; the Ministry of Welfare, Health, and Cultural Affairs; and the Ministry of Transport, Public Works, and Water Management are the biggest spenders in terms of expenditures, while the Ministry of Welfare, Health, and Cultural Affairs; the Ministry of Agriculture, Nature Management, and Fisheries; and the Ministry of Sciences and Education were front-runners in terms of number of subsidies issued.

A recent update based on data from the Ministry of Finance and regarding fiscal year 1992 shows a total expenditure of somewhat over 40 billion guilders. It also shows changes with regard to the relative position of the departments.

As information on the three previously mentioned management aspects is mainly available with regard to the 1992 data, the following findings largely pertain to the earlier National Audit Office results.

Research Question No. 2: Information Available on Goal-Directedness, Implementation Costs, and Ex-Post Evaluation of Subsidies

Information Available on the Goal-Directedness of Subsidies

Given the uncertainties attached to the effects of subsidies, it is important that the introduction of subsidies be prepared with careful attention to the goals they are to serve. This involves compiling information on the way in which the subsidy in question is intended to help achieve the goals set, on alternative options, on the costs of the subsidy and of possible alternatives, and on the form which implementation and monitoring are to take place. To this end, *ex-ante evaluations* are needed.

Goal-directedness also means that the purposes of the subsidy must be set out in operational terms. Only by formulating *criteria for evalu-*

ation in this way is it possible to assess after the fact whether the goals have been achieved.

Interest in ex-ante evaluation began to grow in The Netherlands at the start of the 1970s, partly under the influence of the work of the Committee for the Development of Policy Analysis (COBA), which in 1974 issued a report focusing specifically on criteria and measures for use in cost-benefit analysis. A 1976 COBA report into subsidies also looked in detail at ex-ante evaluation. Therefore it was decided to withdraw from the analysis all subsidies that were decided upon before 1975. We also excluded a number of subsidies founded on EC directives and regulations; this was because where the decision to introduce a subsidy is taken in an international framework the work of policy preparation, including ex-ante evaluation, is not primarily a Dutch government responsibility. Finally, in the case of subsidies involving only small sums of money it may be decided not to carry out an ex-ante evaluation because the costs would outweigh the benefits. For this reason the following analysis excludes subsidies of less than one million guilders. Due to these restrictions the total number of subsidies analyzed is 281.

Results from the analysis are presented in figures 3.4 and 3.5.

Figure 3.4 indicates that with regard to 42 percent of the 281 subsidies examined, it could be shown that an ex-ante evaluation had been carried out covering one or more of the items mentioned. With respect to 10 percent of the subsidies, it appeared that the ex-ante evaluations had not been properly documented. Figure 3.5 indicates that with respect to more than 80 percent of the 281 subsidies investigated, no evaluation criteria had been formulated. In 5 percent of the subsidies the ministries indicated that criteria were formulated, but they were not capable of documenting them.

Information Available on Implementation and Implementation Costs of Subsidies

Various earlier studies found that inadequate attention is devoted to the question of implementation when subsidies are brought in: subsidies are introduced without any steps being taken to forecast and resolve problems of implementation and the costs of implementation are not included in cost-benefit analyses (Heij and Vranken 1988).

Efficient implementation can be promoted by setting time limits for the submission of applications, preliminary commitment, consultation,

FIGURE 3.6

Extent of Evaluation—Ex Ante and Ex Post—Number of Subsidies and Sums Involved

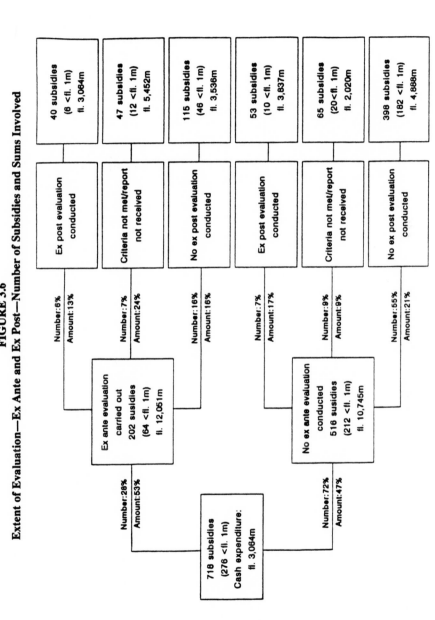

FIGURE 3.7

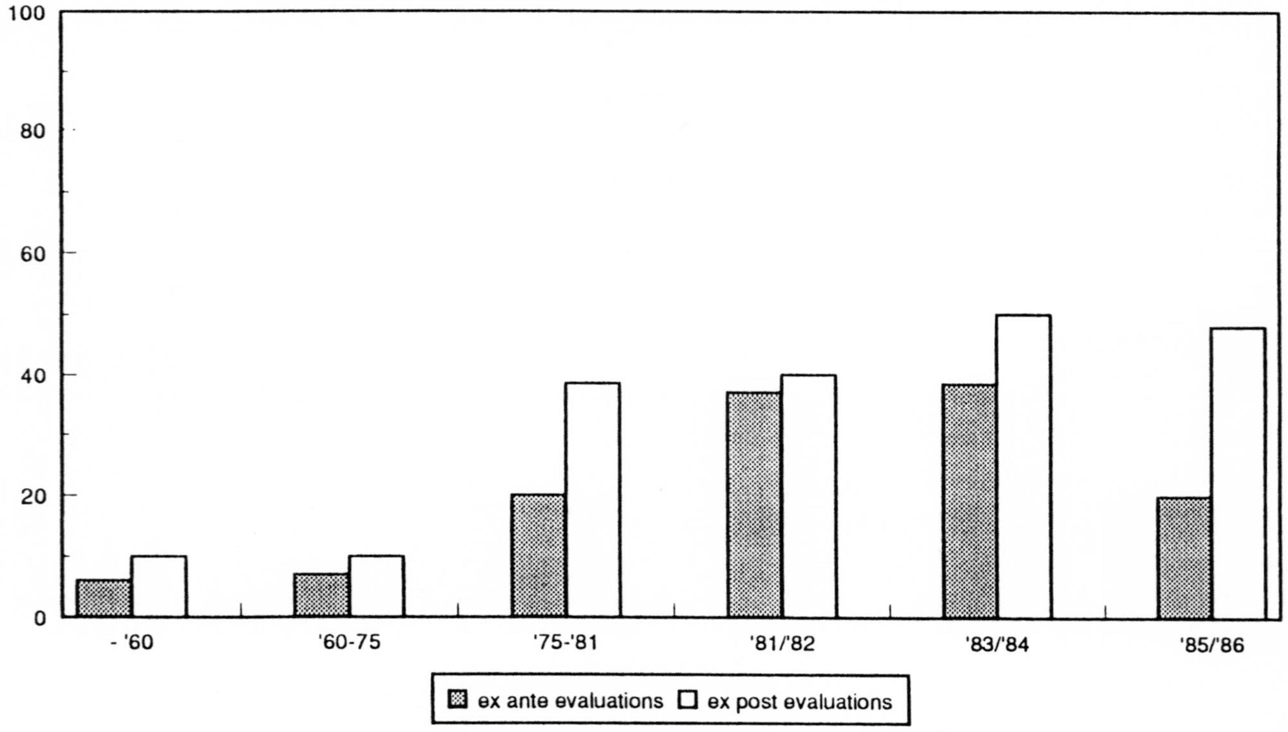

Percentage of Evaluations and Year of Establishment of the Subsidy

and the final decision on the amount to be paid. Inefficiency can then be diagnosed if these limits are regularly exceeded or there are long delays in the processing of applications and final decision making on subsidy amounts.

The National Audit Office's investigation focused principally on the question of the extent to which departments can give a reasonable estimate of the costs of implementation. Two limited checks were made in this connection: an indication was requested of the costs of implementation (on an annual basis), together with a rough breakdown. Respondents were also asked to indicate how many officials (in terms of full-time equivalents) were involved in implementing the subsidy (defined as transaction costs).

In 89 percent of the 722 subsidies considered, it was possible to give an estimate of the number of officials charged with implementing the subsidy every year. In 29 percent of cases it was possible to obtain some picture of the amount of implementation costs. However, the respondents' data were not based on any kind of a time-registration system. Therefore, most of the respondents decided not to report on the "actual" figures. As a consequence, no valid information on transaction costs was available to government of The Netherlands.

The investigation also found that for 44 percent of the subsidies examined time limits were set for applications; the proportion of cases in which departments had set themselves time limits for dealing with applications was much lower (16 percent). In the case of 36 percent of the subsidies which involved an advance payment, a time limit was set for the final decision on the amount of the subsidy.

Information Available on the Ex-Post Evaluation of Subsidies

The importance of (regular) evaluation follows from the nature of subsidy as a policy instrument. By definition subsidies are resource transfers which bypass the market, with the result that there can be no market signals. The links between payment, decision, and benefit are broken: subsidy costs are borne by the taxpayer, decisions are taken by politicians or civil servants and the benefit goes to the subsidy recipient or user of the subsidized facility. This underlines the importance of other signals which enable the effects of subsidies to be pinpointed and corrective action to be taken as necessary. Such signals can be obtained from the regular and systematic ex-post evaluation of subsidies.

As part of the investigation The Netherlands Audit Office looked at the extent to which subsidies had been subject to evaluation culminating in written reports, and further assessment of the usefulness of the reports produced. Three criteria were formulated which reports were expected to meet:

1. the report should either specify the purpose or goal of the study or set out its problem/questions or structure;
2. it should relate to empirical research; and,
3. it should cover either the effectiveness or the efficiency of the subsidy.

To emphasize the importance of regular evaluation the investigation covered only reports published since 1982. Only subsidies amounting to 1 million guilders (approx. U.S. $550,000.00) or more were considered; in the case of smaller subsidies the costs of ex-post evaluation may outweigh the benefits, and other forms of information may then offer a more efficient way of obtaining a picture of the effectiveness of the instrument or the efficiency of implementation. The total number of subsidies was reduced from 722 to 410.

Of the 410 subsidies for which an amount of 1 million guilders or more was budgeted in 1986 it was found that 268 had *not* been evaluated since 1982. In the case of 67 subsidies, written evaluation reports were mentioned which did *not* meet our criteria; the reports on the remaining 75 subsidies did meet the criteria.

To assess government departments' *overall* evaluation efforts we looked at the extent to which there was an association between ex-ante evaluations and ex-post evaluations. Figure 3.6 shows the extent of evaluation, both ex-ante and ex-post, in terms of both numbers of subsidies and of the sums involved (cash expenditure, FY 1986). To give as complete a picture as possible figure 3.6 covers the *complete range of subsidies*, with the exception of the four types payable under the Investment Account Act; these last four were primarily excluded because the large sums involved—some 7.4 billion guilders—would greatly distort the overall picture.

As figure 3.6 shows, 28 percent of the subsidies examined were subjected to ex-ante evaluation. The sum involved in the 202 subsidies for which ex-ante evaluation was carried out represented 53 percent of the total (cash expenditure, FY 1986).

Ex-post evaluations meeting the criteria were carried out for 13 percent of the subsidies examined. The sum involved in the 93 subsidies evaluated ex-post represented 30 percent of the total (cash expenditure, FY 1986).

A number of Dutch social science and governmental publications have concluded that too little evaluation is carried out within the Dutch civil service (Hoogerwerf 1990; De Kemp et al. 1989; Ministerie van Financiën 1991; Commissie Vraagpunten 1991). This is a state of affairs which is blamed, among other things, on an insufficiently developed evaluation culture and—as figure 3.6 shows—levels of evaluation research on subsidies do indeed leave something to be desired. It appeared that in total *only 40 out of 718 subsidies (6 percent) were covered by both ex-ante and ex-post evaluations meeting the criteria of the National Audit Office*. The sum involved in these 40 subsidies represented 13 percent of the total cash expenditure as of 1986.

The aforementioned findings are to a certain extent static. Figure 3.7 presents some information of a more dynamic nature.

The figure indicates that since 1974 the percentage of subsidies that have been ex-ante evaluated increased. The figure also shows that until 1984–1985 there is an increase in the number of ex-post evaluations of subsidies. From 1985 on there is a decline. However, the reason for the decline in 1985–86 might be data-technical in nature: the first round of data-collection on behalf of the government-wide audit data on subsidies were collected in 1987 and they referred to FY 1986. Hence it can be argued that rather young subsidies had a smaller chance of being evaluated ex-post than had older subsidies.

To shed more light on the increase or decrease in number of ex-post evaluations of subsidies, the National Audit Office in 1990 updated a part of its data regarding the 1988 investigation. For 31 of the largest subsidies (cash expenditure, FY 1989: 21.8 billion guilders), data on evaluations performed between 1986 and 1990 were collected. It appeared that 15 of the 31 subsidies (cash expenditure, FY 1989: 11 billion guilders) had since then been evaluated according to National Audit Office criteria. Comparing these findings with the ones from the first round of data collection led the Audit Office to conclude that although there is an increase in number of ex-post evaluations over time, still more than half of the 31 largest subsidies were nevertheless not evaluated properly.

Referring to FY 1993, the Dutch Ministry of Finance claimed that approximately 70 percent of all 730 subsidies now have been evaluated or are in the process of being evaluated (Ministerie van Financiën 1993). The claim is based on information obtained from the ministries.[8] However, a closer inspection of the data with regard to five ministries and 346 subsidies (Office of the Prime Minister; Foreign Affairs [including Development Aid], Justice, Science, and Education; and Welfare, Cultural Affairs, and Health) leads to the following conclusions.

First, the aforementioned methodological criteria relevant to characterize an activity as an evaluation appear to have been abandoned. Secondly, 54 of the 346 subsidies were carried out by an external organization and eighty-three evaluations by the ministry itself, 192 subsidies have not been evaluated as of 1993, while the remaining 17 cases could not be categorized.[9] Thirdly, to a large extent the internal evaluations focused on inside bureaucracy questions concerning the administrative organization of the ways in which subsidies are handled. Hence, they do not provide information about the behavioral and societal effects subsidies may have within society. According to Sharpf (1983), this type of information is essential in judging subsidies as a tool of government.

We concluded that instead of the proclaimed 70 percent only approximately 40 percent of all central government subsidies have indeed been evaluated, in the proper sense of the word. We included evaluations directed at administrative procedures and similar inside-bureaucracy variables.[10]

Research Question No. 3: Types of Subsidies and Coverage by Ex-Post Evaluations

In order to answer this question, the National Audit Office distinguished between three types of subsidies. The typology is based on two dimensions: the extent to which subsidies are structural or incidental and the focus of the subsidy (towards encouraging activities as such or towards the continuation (upkeep) of organizations/corporate actors that can or cannot perform certain activities). The first type, *program subsidies;* have a structural character and are primarily oriented towards continuation of organizations. The second type is labeled *project subsidies;* are of a more incidental nature and are clearly linked to the performance of activities as such. Finally, *operating subsidies* are structural in nature and are linked with the continuation/"upkeep" of organizations.

It was hypothesized that, dependent upon the type of subsidy a government issues, there is more or less information available with respect to the evaluation of these subsidies. For example: government officials *might* (rightly or wrongly) be of the opinion that given the usually restricted duration of project subsidies when compared with program subsidies, there is a lesser need for ex-ante and ex-post evaluations to take place with respect to project subsidies.

Indeed, there appeared to be a relationship between types of subsidies and ex-post evaluation activities. With respect to 50 percent of the program subsidies (data were related to the FY 1986), an ex-ante evaluation had been reported, while for project subsidies this percentage was 29 and for operating subsidies it was 32. It was also shown that for 24 percent of the project subsidies an ex-post evaluation was reported, while for the two other types the percentages were 21 and 14.

Discussion and New Research Questions

In The Netherlands information with regard to subsidies as a tool of government has for a long time been available in a very restricted quantity. Encouraged by the critical National Audit Office report and by Parliament, the government indeed utilized the audit findings and was prompted to change its "behavior" on subsidies drastically. In the course of 1991 the "integrated policy on subsidies" was launched with the aim to periodically assess the goal-directedness, relevance, efficiency, and effectiveness of all large subsidies. Reconsideration as well as abandonment of subsidies is to be expected and indeed already is taking place. From 1992–93 a register of subsidies is available, on request, from the Ministry of Finance. There is also progress in the *quantity* of information available with regard to the aforementioned management aspects. However, as indicated, the *quality* of the information with regard to the "evaluation" aspect raises serious doubts.

In our opinion the approach and data outlined in this chapter are relevant for policymakers as well as scientists. This is primarily so because the data allow the formulation of explanatory questions. Usually, auditors are not very much engaged in presenting explanations for their findings, but rather focus primarily on judging and valuing (Leeuw 1992). We therefore suggest the following explanatory questions.

Firstly, why do certain fields and organizations receive significantly more central government subsidies than others? Secondly, what has been the role of the earlier expansion of the welfare state in this respect and which predictions are possible with regard to the future of this policy instrument, now that this concept is under serious attack? Thirdly, what are the (unintended) negative consequences for society when governments abandon subsidies? Here a counterfactual approach might be helpful (Winston 1993). Fourthly, why do countries like the United Kingdom, Germany, and Sweden strive for rather strong cuts in subsidies, but the current U.S. administration appears to be moving in the opposite direction? Even taking into account the actual differences in levels of government spending on behalf of this tool between the countries, this question is worth posing. A fifth topic is the investigation of (the costs and consequences of) *chains of subsidies*: problems related to the unintended consequences of certain subsidization programs which are reduced through other subsidies is also worth considering. An example is the (partial) subsidization of the tobacco industry in Western countries and—in order to reduce the adverse health effects of smoking—the simultaneous issue of new subsidies for youth-targeted anti-smoking campaigns.[11] And the final question to raise is how do we explain that taxpayers, individuals as well as corporate actors, have accepted that subsidization went on and on without baseline information on goals, transaction costs and evaluations to be readily available? We argue that it has been caused by the neocorporatist structure of the Dutch economy and its multiparty system. Essential for this structure is consensus-building between actors in such a way that there appear more *visible winners* than *detectable and activist losers*. Increasing the tax wedge may, in the perception of large parts of the population, be caused by a number of activities, like foreign aid, trying to reduce environmental problems, or participating in United Nations activities. In their perception, it will *not* or only *marginally* be related to government spending on subsidies, leading to a situation of many non-visible and non-activist losers. On the other hand, the many recipients of the more than 700 Dutch subsidies are *visible* and *thankful*. According to Wolfson (1990), they are probably also active in trying to reduce the tax wedge by obtaining subsidies from the central government.[12] It will be clear that this mechanism resembles the mechanism which underlies the free-rider problem in the production of collective goods (Olson 1965).

As the editors have indicated in their introduction: "institutions do matter." Now that there is a database on Dutch subsidies, time is here to investigate the institutional conditions under which subsidies are produced, have the intended consequences, and are cost-effective. There is a long way to go.

Notes

1. Including income transfers. Often they are categorized together with subsidies and grants. This is also the case with regard to the data we use here and that stem from the Annual Budget.
2. Wolfson (1990: 2) mentions the classic exception: the inferior good. When margarine is subsidized, the income effect is that people will buy butter instead of more margarine.
3. This is evident with regard to merit goods. There the government believes it is necessary to subsidize behaviors or behavioral options, because otherwise people will not be engaged in these behavioral options.

4. For a discussion on the definition of the term subsidy we refer to Ford and Suyker 1990 and Bruce 1990.
5. For a recent application of this approach, see Winston 1993. His interesting study dealt with the consequences of the economic deregulation which took place during the 1980s.
6. These three management aspects directly relate to already mentioned problems and pitfalls. The study of the National Audit Office also included an analysis of information ministries had available with regard to three *other* management aspects. One concerned the way in which subsidies are legally regulated, a second concerned the inspection of subsidy-conditions (including the verification of financial statements) while the third aspect focused on cash-flow and cash-control mechanisms applied.
7. Allers 1992 is involved in research at the University of Groningen (Department of Economics) focusing on administrative and transaction costs for citizens and corporate actors of subsidies, income transfers and taxes. Data with regard to citizens indicate that some 2.6 billion Dutch guilders (approx. U.S. $1.4 billion) annually are involved, which is roughly equal to 1.6 percent of the total public expenditure of these tools of government.
8. The information is brought together in a register of subsidies. Apart from information about evaluations, also financial information is reported, information about the legal status of the subsidy, the way in which financial control has taken place, what the target groups of the subsidy are and to what extent the subsidy is considered eligible for fraud and misuse.
9. Inspecting the subsidy register revealed a number of other interesting points, such as subsidies that were evaluated externally although no report was available and annual reports and accounts of subsidized organizations which were labelled as "evaluations."
10. Frans L. Leeuw, "Efectiviteit subsidies zwaarder toetsen (A Plea for Testing the Effectiveness of Subsidies More Thoroughly)," in *Staatscourant* 108 (1993): 5.
11. The author thanks Evert Vedung for this suggestion.
12. Cf. S. Mestelman 1989.

References

Algemene Rekenkamer. 1988. *Jeugdhulpverlening*. The Hague: SDU.
———. 1989a. *Verslag 1988* (1988–1989 session), 21080, nos. 1–2. The Hague: SDU.
———. 1989b. *Bestrijding kleine criminaliteit*. The Hague: SDU.
———. 1990. *Achtergrondstudie Onderzoek naar subsidies*. The Hague: SDU.
———. 1991a. *Tijdelijke stimuleringsmaatregel kinderopvang*. The Hague: SDU.
———. 1991b. *Verslag 1990* (1990–1991 session), 21080, nos. 1–2. The Hague: SDU.
———. 1991c. *Voorlichtingscampagnes van het Rijk*. The Hague: SDU.
Allers, M.A. 1992. *Kosten van overdrachten voor particulieren en huishoudens*. Research memorandum no. 483, Department of Economics. Groningen: University of Groningen.
Bressers, J.T.A. and P.J. Klok. 1987. *Een voorlopige instrumententheorie van het overheidsbeleid*. Enschede: Twente University.
Bruce, N. 1990. *Measuring Industrial Subsidies: Some Conceptual Issues*. Working Paper no. 75, Department of Economics and Statistics, OECD. Paris.
Chelimsky, E. 1990. "Expanding GAO's Capabilities on Program Evaluation," *GAO Journal* 8: 43–52.
COBA. 1976. "Het instrument subsidie, een leidraad voor het subsidieonderzoek," *Beleidsanalyse*, no. 1.

Douma, S.W. 1981. *Ondernemingsfinanciering en overheidssteun*. Leiden: Stenfert Kroese.

Ford, R. and W. Suyker. 1990. "Industrial Subsidies in the OECD Economies," *OECD Economic Studies* no.15 (Autumn): 37–82.

Gerritse, R., ed. 1990. *Producer Subsidies*. New York: Pinter Publishers.

Hamer, H. 1992. Lecture on the Ministry of Finance policy with regard to evaluating and curbing subsidies. Symposium organized by The Netherlands Institute for Chartered Accountants (NIVRA). The Hague.

Haider, D. 1989. "Grants as a Tool of Public Policy", in L.M. Salamon (ed.), *Beyond Privatization: The Tools of Government Action*, pp. 93–123. Washington, DC: The Urban Institute Press.

Heij, P.R. and P.H.J. Vranken, eds. 1987. *Subsidie in revisie*. Instituut Onderzoek Overheidsuitgaven. The Hague: VUGA.

Hoogerwerf, A. 1990. "Policy Evaluation and Government in the Netherlands: Meta-Evaluation Research as One of the Solutions," in J. Mayne (ed.), *Advancing Public Policy Evaluation: Learning from International Experiences* (1992), pp. 215–229. Amsterdam: North-Holland.

Jasinowski, C.J. 1973. "The Great Fiscal Unknown: Subsidies," *The American Journal of Economics and Sociology* 32.

Kemp, A. de, W. van der Mei, J. van Dam, and F.L. Leeuw. 1989. "Evaluatie van subsidies: uitdrukking van een tekortschietende of een ontwikkelde evaluatiecultuur?" *Beleidsanalyse* 18: 12–19.

Kordes, F.G., F.L. Leeuw, and J.H.A. van Dam. 1991. "The Management of Government Subsidies," in A. Friedberg et al. (eds.), *State Audit and Accountability*, pp. 280–299. Jerusalem: Government Printer.

Leeuw, F.L. 1992. "Government-wide Audits in The Netherlands," in J. Mayne et al. (eds.), *Advancing Public Policy Evaluation: Learning from International Experiences*, pp. 131–141. Amsterdam: North-Holland.

Mestelman, S. 1989. "Taxes, Subsidies, Standards and Social Choices," *Public Finance* 41: 268–283.

Mueller, D.C. 1989. *Public Choice II*. Cambridge: Cambridge University Press.

Netherlands Commissie Vraagpunten. 1991. *Rapport bijzondere commissie vraagpunten*. Tweede Kamer (1990–1991 session), 21 427, no. 3. The Hague: SDU.

Netherlands Ministerie van Financiën. 1991. *Miljoenennota* (1990–1991 session), 21 800, no. 1. The Hague: SDU.

Netherlands Parliament. Lower House. Inquiry into Rijn-Schelde-Verolme Shipbuilders, Committee Report (1984–85 session), 17 817, no. 16.

Netherlands Parliament. Lower House. Inquiry into Housing Grants, Committee Report (1987–88 session), 19 623, no. 30.

Peacock, Alan T. 1990. "Identifying and Applying Norms for Subsidies to Industry," in Ronald Gerritse (ed.), *Producer Subsidies*, pp. 20–32. New York: Pinter Publishers.

Remery, C., F.L. Leeuw, and J. de Haan. 1993. "Zwaartepuntvorming in de maatschappijwetenschappen en overheidsbeleid," *Mens en Maatschappij* 68: 59–70.

Rist, Ray C. 1990. "Management Accountability: The Signals Sent by Auditing and Evaluation," *Journal of Public Policy* 9: 355–369.

Salamon, L.M., ed. 1989. *Beyond Privatization: The Tools of Government Action*. Washington, DC: The Urban Institute Press.

Vedung, E. 1990. "Policy Instruments," paper, Department of Government. Uppsala, NJ: Uppsala University.

Vermeulen, W.J.V. 1991. "Ending PCB Use: Dutch Experiences in Applying Financial Incentives," *Zeitschrift fur Umweltpolitik und Umweltrecht* 1: 53–70.

———. 1992. *De vervuiler betaal*. Ph.D. thesis, University of Utrecht.

Winston, C. 1993. "Economic Deregulation: Days of Reckoning for Micro-economists," *Journal of Economic Literature* 31: 1263–1289.

Wiseman, J. 1977. "The Economics of Subsidies: Some Taxonomic and Analytical Problems," *Quarterly Journal of the Piraeus School of Industrial Studies* 2: 455–461

Wittman, D. 1989. "Why Democracies Produce Efficient Results," *Journal of Political Economy* 97: 1395–1425.

Wolfson, Dirk J. 1990. "Towards a Theory of Subsidization," in Ronald Gerritse (ed.), *Producer Subsidies*, pp. 1–20. New York: Pinter Publishers.

Zuckerman, H. 1991. "The Careers of Men and Women Scientists: A Review of Current Research," in H. Zuckerman, J.R. Cole, and J.F. Bruer (eds.), *The Outer Circle: Women in the Scientific Community*. New York: The Free Press.

4

The Sermon: Information Programs in the Public Policy Process— Choice, Effects, and Evaluation

Evert Vedung
Frans C.J. van der Doelen

Information as a public policy instrument covers government-directed attempts at influencing people through transfer of knowledge, communication of reasoned argument, and moral suasion in order to achieve a policy result. The information dispensed may concern the nature of the problem at hand, how people are actually handling the problem, measures that can be taken to change the prevailing situation, and reasons why these measures ought to be considered and adopted by the addressees. It may also be just plain facts. However, no more than pure transfer of knowledge, persuasive reasoning, or exhortations are offered to influence the public or some segment of the public to do what government deems desirable.

Information is used here as a catch-all term for outright public communication campaigns; diffusion of printed materials like brochures, pamphlets, booklets, folders, fliers, bulletins, handbills, and posters; advertising; labeling; demonstration programs; counselling; custom-made personal advice; training programs; education efforts; and other forms of amassing, packaging, and diffusion of knowledge and recommendations.

This chapter deals with the theoretical question of why information programs are chosen as a policy instrument, what their effects are, and in which ways this policy instrument is evaluated. The article also contains a comparison of the role of information programs in Dutch and Swedish energy conservation policies after the 1973 Oil Crisis.

Information: The Most Lenient Tool of Government

In ordinary language as well as in information theory, "informing" is identical with providing correct, objective facts about some state of affairs. Naturally, this basic meaning has been retained in public-sector jargon. Yet, in public policy, government can also "inform" the citizenry about what is good or bad, right or wrong. Moreover, government can "provide information about" what people are allowed to do, or how they should act and behave. The information category covers, in other words, not only true knowledge about the world, but also judgments about which phenomena and measures are good or bad, and recommendations how the targets should behave. In public policy literature, information has come to embrace much more than transmission of knowledge.

As with economic tools of statecraft, no government obligation is involved. Under no circumstances are the targets mandated to act in the way outlined in the information. Whether or not to follow the recommendations are entirely up to the addressees because, by definition, information includes no stronger means of influence than plain recommendations and concomitant reasoning. This absence of obligation makes information different from regulation which, by definition, contains mandatory rules of conduct (see ch. 1, "A Basic Scheme"; for a different view, see ch. 5).

Yet, information is different also from economic policy instruments in that no handing out or taking away of material resources is involved. The information diffused may very well include arguments to the effect that targets will actually benefit materially from taking the measures recommended. However, government neither materially rewards people who take the action, nor materially deprives people who neglect the message. Only data, facts, knowledge, arguments, and moral appeals are offered.

All in all, information is the softest and most lenient instrument in the government tool-kit.

Types and Packages

Information-dispensing is a multifaceted tool of government. The ways in which information can be used as a governance instrument are innumerable. Five possibilities will be briefly mentioned here.

Types

A useful distinction is between *mass-mediated* and *interpersonal* government information. Under mass-mediated information-dispensers, we list not only information diffused via television, radio, film, and newspapers, but also information disseminated via other printed matter such as books. Advertisements in newspapers, distribution of booklets, television trailers, and instruction films are cases of mass-mediated information. Interpersonal government information include not only personal advice and custom-made audits but also ordinary classroom education and on-site demonstrations in built-up facilities.

Public information efforts may go on *continuously* or be designed as *campaigns* with time limits. According to Everett Rogers a "communication campaign" is a preplanned set of communication activities designed by change agents to achieve certain alterations in receiver behavior in a specified time period (quoted from Rogers and Storey 1987: 819). Modifying Roger's definition, a government information campaign would be a preplanned set of communication activities designed by government officials to reach and motivate a relatively large number of targets to effect some cognitive, attitudinal, or behavioral objectives in a specified time period. A continuous information program on the other hand is intended as something more permanent, since there is no specific set time-limit.

Still another important, though somewhat muddy, distinction is between *general, group-targeted* and *custom-made* information (Hood 1983: 24ff.). General information is a standardized message beamed at the world-at-large or to whomever it may concern. A brochure directed at the general public concerning the importance of electricity conservation would be an example of general information. Group-targeted information is designed to hit subsets of the population rather than anybody. A brochure fashioned to reach the industrial sector concerning the importance of electricity conservation would be a case in point. Custom-made information is individually tailored to each recipient. An energy audit in a specific industrial facility would be a case of custom-made information. Admittedly, this trifold scheme is not very clear at the edges.

On the basis of the direction of the communication we may differentiate between *one-way* and *multi-way* communication. One-way information goes in one direction from senders to receivers, without feedback.

Two-way or multi-way information engenders some give-and-take between at least two participants in the communicative effort. A communication sequence may consist of a search stage where the sender and a few potential addressees together formulate appropriate messages, a dissemination stage where the potential senders spread the messages across the board, but where some addressees still are active and channel the information to others, and an evaluation and feedback stage where information on achieved results mainly goes back from the addressees to the senders. Mass-mediated information is mainly one-way, whereas interpersonal information almost always is multi-way.

In many contexts it is also important to differentiate between *government-initiated* and *field-initiated* information. Knowledge of the first kind is spread by the sender with no active efforts on the part of the receivers to retrieve it, while knowledge of the second type requires some effort on the part of the receiver to get it and tune into it.

Cases of government-initiated information include fliers, folders, and booklets, which are transmitted by mail to multiple households. Another case is an energy audit performed after the municipal energy advisor has made a telephone call to the property owner and asked him for permission to come and perform the audit. The purpose of government-initiated information is to reach targets without know-how, or with know-how but no urge to act. Cases of field-initiated information include insights spread when receivers of their own initiative visit exhibitions, demonstration facilities, or when they requisition some written material.

Packages

Information can be joined to other policy instruments to form program packages. Our discussion will be limited to two possibilities. Information can be employed as a *metapolicy instrument* to disseminate knowledge of the availability and content of other policy instruments. A subsidy program may illustrate our point. If prospective applicants do not know that they may get subsidies if they apply, the program cannot function. To this end, government must inform prospective applicants about the existence and substance of the subsidy program. In this case, information is a metapolicy instrument.

Governments may spread information by their *own organizations* or use *intermediaries* to transmit the message to the public. Intermediating institutions can be *paid* to collect, package, and disseminate the information. For instance, the government can contract-out information campaigns to private advertisement firms, trade associations, or even municipalities. In this case, economic policy instruments are used to implement information efforts. Often, however, governments can also *require* go-betweens to broadcast some message. It can take the form of mandated labeling or obligation to display. In this case, government authorities apply regulation to promote dissemination of information.

When Should Information-Dispensing Tools be Used?

A crucial problem in information-instruments theory is when to apply them. When is it appropriate for governments to govern their citizenry by means of information-dispensers? When should other policy instruments be used instead? We shall discuss here one distinct, negative theory of information use by governments and several affirmative ones (cf. Vedung 1996).

Negative Theory of Universal Compliance

Information instruments should not be utilized when *universal compliance* is considered necessary. Nobody can tolerate that people are murdered, thefts are committed, or contracts are broken. Therefore, the government must choose regulatory measures in these situations. Information is cautioned against for two reasons. First, governments want to make clear that homicides, thefts, and breaches of contract are condemnable and cannot be tolerated. Regulation is the only instrument that carries such connotations. Information, on the other hand, contains just exhortations and admonitions which the recipients are not forced to follow. Secondly, since information is predicated upon voluntary behavior of the targets, compliance will never be 100 percent. If, on the other hand, it would be sufficient that 5 or 10 or 20 percent of the addressees comply, an information campaign might be considered.

Theory of Coinciding Interests

The *theory of coinciding interests* proposes that information should be applied when the desired actions are in the private interests of the targets as well as in the public interest of the state. Conversely, information should be constrained when the coveted behavior is not in the private interest of the addressee even though it is in the public interest of the state.

When we maintain that a particular action is in the interest of the addressee it means that the action will probably have consequences which lead directly to distinguishable advantages. An obvious case is economic benefits, but it can also be advantages in the form of better health, greater security to life and limb, increased needs-satisfaction, greater happiness, and greater utility. That an action is in the public interest, on the other hand, suggests that if taken by the addressees, it will produce a net benefit to society as a whole.

The interests or benefits we desire may occur, even if those concerned know nothing about them. To illustrate, let us assume that comprehensive insulation of a considerable set of single-family dwellings would reduce oil use, which would curtail emissions of sulphur into the atmosphere, which in turn would diminish acid rain and contribute to alleviating dependency on unsafe petroleum deliveries from the Middle East and improve the balance of trade which in turn would be in the best interest of the country. By the same token, this would reduce heating expenditures for the property owner so that the extra cost of the investment would be made up for after a couple of years. The specific measure of lower costs would then be in line with the private interest of the property owner, even if unaware of the larger interests of cleaner air or a more favorable balance of trade for the country. The private interest of the information targets and the public interest would still coincide.

Of course, it might well be the case that property owners know nothing at all about this. The price of insulation materials may have plummeted and the cost of energy may have increased without the prospective addressees being quite conscious of what has happened. The knowledge they once had about their self-interest has turned obsolete. Furthermore, it might well be that consumers do not regard insulation as a feasible alternative. It might also happen that the home-owners do not have the capability of calculating the life-cycle cost of the investment. Even though their initial expenditures for an investment are substantial, they may not realize that the total cost distributed throughout the whole life of the property, would be less if it were insulated than if it were left uninsulated.

In this case, we would say that comprehensive insulation is in the property owners' interest, although the latter do not know. It is in this sense of material gain that the word "interest" is used. On the other hand, we are definitely not arguing that the interests are objective in the qualified sense that value objectivists use the term.

The strongest case for information-dispensing action can be brought to bear in situations where the target individual is unaware that the action lies both in his own and in the community's interest. Another potentially interesting situation is the case where the potential targets know that the action lies in the interest of the community, but do not know that the individuals' own interest would be promoted as well. Were they to be informed about this, it would seem reasonable to assume that their propensity to act would increase.

A third situation would in principle seem amenable to government information-dispensers as well. In this case, the individual is aware that the action lies in his own interest, but does not realize that it also lies in that of the community. Were he to be informed of the latter, his motivation for acting might increase.

In a fourth governance situation, the individuals have perfect knowledge that the measure would serve the public interest as well as their own. If they do not act even then, it must be for some reason other than lack of knowledge. Thus, the potential need of government information, in the sense of transfer of knowledge, disappears entirely. Persuasion in the sense of transmission of norms and values might naturally come to the fore, in order to focus the interest on the particular functional area at hand and to bring up the measure on the agenda.

What then about situations in which the measure is not in the private interest of the potential addressees, although they are squarely in the public interest? We venture to assert that information would be a less suitable instrument in these circumstances. Almost all experience teaches us that simply appealing to people's feelings for the public good is doomed to fail. The general environment of government information provision must be very favorable, indeed, before people can be enticed to refrain from personal advantages in order to promote the common good. In general, stronger policy instruments than information efforts are required in these circumstances.

Paternalism

The paternalistic theory of information governance asserts that information is particularly appropriate in situations where the government intervenes in order to effect the recipients to act in their own not very well-understood interest. We have never seen in the literature such a theory but formulate it ourselves in a provisional fashion.

The paternalistic theory does not maintain that paternalistic interventions are justified in general or under some circumstances. Its modest assertion may be formulated in the following fashion: *given that paternalistic interventions are justified*, exhortation is more appropriate than regulations or even economic tools of government since it constitutes the mildest form of intervention.

The paternalistic theory of exhortation is predicated on the precondition that the measure is good for the recipient, but not necessarily for the society. A spontaneous reaction would be that government should not intervene in such situations. Yet, there are cases where this has happened and happens. A benign community attempts to urge the recipient to act in accordance with their self-interest. This presupposes either that the recipients have no insight into their self-interest, cannot judge it in any reasonable manner or know it and make a reasonable judgment of it but cannot persuade themselves to take action to attain it. These situations are perfect cases of *paternalism.*

"By paternalism I shall understand roughly the interference with a person's liberty of action justified by reasons referring exclusively to the welfare, good, happiness, needs, interests or values of the person being coerced," writes Gerald Dworkin (1979: 78). Like most other authors, Dworkin joins the concept of paternalism to coercive government measures. Actually, the discourse on paternalism is carried on as if there are no other policy instruments around besides regulation. Here, a much broader view is adopted. Paternalism covers all public intervention for the purpose of influencing the addressees' own self-interest. Even public interventions through economic means and exhortation are cases of paternalism, provided they are motivated by a concern for the addressees' own good.

Empirical cases of pure, paternalistic interventions are not easily found. Dworkin mentions laws mandating motorcyclists to wear helmets, laws prohibiting swimming in public swimming places when there are no guardians on duty, laws regulating certain sexual behavior, for instance, love relationships between homosexuals, laws against suicide, and laws mandating people to deposit parts of their present income into future pensions.

The philosophy of paternalistic intervention is both developed and convoluted. A straightforward and clean line of argument dating back to John Stuart Mill says that paternalism is always unjustified except for one situation: individuals should not be allowed to sell themselves as slaves. A milder line of argument is that paternalism is justified provided the individual in the future in all likelihood will give his consent to the measure that the government wants him to take at the present. It is probably this idea that Eckhoff (1983: 119) has had in mind in maintaining that it might be justified to the state to inform people of what is in their long-term self-interest. What they might do may produce damaging or dangerous consequences to themselves. As an example he mentions propaganda for good mountaineering practices, sailing behavior, traffic culture, and warnings against tobacco, alcohol, narcotics, or sexually transmitted diseases.

In this context, however, it is not necessary to justify paternalism because the paternalistic theory of exhortative policy instruments takes for granted that this issue is already solved. But since paternalism is always problematic in free societies, the use of exhortative policy instruments in paternalistic situations is more reasonable than use of other, more intrusive inventions.

Crisis Theory

The theories of universal compliance and coinciding interests suffer from indecisiveness. More specific are two theories customarily proffered by economists. Informative policy instruments are used either during short but disturbing crises, or when effective oversight over regulatory compliance or economic policy instruments administration is not feasible.

According to the crisis theory, exhortation is resorted to in acutely evolving crises, which are deemed to be short. The reason for this is that the alternatives, that is, economic means and regulation, cannot be implemented sufficiently fast due to, among other things, the fact that they presuppose rather comprehensive administrative monitoring arrangements. Baumol and Oates (1979) provide some examples from the environmental field. A sudden and unexpected atmospheric inversion over a city, which leads to life-threatening pollution levels, requires fast changes in people's activity patterns and leaves no time for the inauguration of an elaborated monitoring machinery. Much depends on the will of thousands of motorists to leave their cars at home or on cooperation of myriads of small businesses each of them contributing only a minimal part of the emissions. The authorities can control the activities of the large polluters. But it is difficult or impossible to monitor numerous small economic processes. Therefore, they have to appeal to people's reason, moral values, and voluntary commitment.

Baumol and Oates also maintain that public information efforts can produce real results during short spells of crisis. One of their examples concerns water conservation in periods of drought. During one such period in the middle of the 1960s the City of New York asked the citizens to conserve water. These appeals led to savings of approximating 4 to 6 percent of normal water consumption (Baumol and Oates 1979: 297).

Theory of Difficult Oversight

Exhortation is also used under normal circumstances when regulations and economic policy instruments are too difficult to monitor. The effectiveness of economic and regulatory policy instruments is to some extent contingent upon the authorities' ability to discover and oversee the activities to be controlled. If the emissions of an industry into a river cannot be adequately measured, the authorities cannot decide how large the environmental fees the industry ought to pay should be or even if there is a violation of a law.

There are cases when systematic oversight is exceedingly difficult to implement. Baumol and Oates (1979) use pollution of wilderness areas by visitors as a case. Since hikers often camp alone and spread out over large areas, it is practically impossible to effectively monitor what they do. In these situations there are only two alternatives. Pollution can be prohibited and the persons who are discovered discarding trash can be fined to warn other polluters. Even if this would work, people would probably regard it as unreasonable. The other possibility would be to leave the area unregulated but via exhortative messages appeal to the moral and general goodwill of the visitors. The latter option emerges as the most reasonable one.

As an example of a successful information program of this type, the American "Smokey the Bear" campaign against forest fires ought to be mentioned. Purporting to educate Americans to be careful with campfires in national parks, the information efforts were launched in 1942. The first poster with the bear as the symbol of the campaign was produced by Walt Disney. During the first thirty years, man-made forest fires diminished from 201,000 to 105,000 acres (Baumol and Oates 1979: 295). Before 1942, 30 million acres were destroyed by forest fires, in 1989 the number had decreased to less than 5 million (Rice 1989: 216).

Legitimating Theory

According to the legitimating theory, as we have chosen to call this theory, information programs are launched in the light of other more constraining policy instruments. The legitimating theory comes in one pessimistic and one optimistic form.

The pessimistic variant suggests that information is used for the political purpose of paving the road for stronger interventions. Decision makers realize that public intervention is needed to deal with a social predicament. They also understand that the predicament can only be alleviated or solved through strong measures like regulations or economic means, but that public opinion is not ripe for such drastic programs. In these situations, information is resorted to in order to soften public opinion and adjust it to public intervention in the area. Since information efforts are cheap, easy to enact, and most of all based on voluntary participation, they are supposed to be easier to accept for the general public. When stronger measures are inaugurated, the decision makers may legitimize their actions by arguing that softer measures have already been tried to no or little avail.

According to the pessimistic legitimating theory, information is not utilized to directly solve or alleviate the societal problem at hand but to accord legitimacy to stronger measures thought to master the problem. This type of legitimating theory is probably most applicable to paternalistic interventions to save individuals or collectivities against their own actions.

The series of steps taken to introduce the Swedish Safety Belt Act may be regarded as an application of the pessimistic legitimating theory. Public propaganda to urge people to use safety belts in automobiles includes paternalistic traits. While lowering social costs for rehabilitation in connection with traffic injuries has been an important concern, there is also an element of concern that individuals should be safeguarded against their own actions. The Safety Belt Act was preceded by a period of informing; when information did not help, Parliament regulated the matter.

The optimistic legitimizing theory on the other hand suggests that decision makers sincerely hope that the perceived problem will be solved through ample use of informative policy instruments and that stronger measures can be avoided. The optimistic theory suggests that, ideally, public intervention ought to be avoided to solve the problem, but since intervention in spite of everything is deemed necessary, the most lenient government tool is resorted to with the hope that information will be sufficient. In these situations, threats of regulation are often used as an argument to support the messages in the information program.

Clearly, the optimistic theory has been a motivating force behind some Swedish energy conservation programs. In the "Reduce the Risk of Rationing Campaign," the optimistic legitimating theory was included already in the name. Information was utilized in the hope of avoiding oil rationing in combination with prohibitions against some uses of oil. Also in the 1970 electricity savings campaign the avoidance theory played an important role. One theme in the information campaign was "help us to avoid electricity rationing." Again, regulation and information are packaged into a collected whole.

Token Theory of Information

According to the token theory, information is utilized for symbolic rather than substantive motives. The motivating force is not to solve a substantive societal problem but to divert attention from it or avoid criticism for passivity and negligence. A campaign is started as a show-off to the public that something important is occurring. Decision makers want to win prestige or increase their trust within the general public. Information campaigns may constitute "token attempts at change" (Salmon 1989: 28).

Demands for informative policy instruments may be raised for tactical reasons to divert attention from stronger means of government. In their discussion of "voluntaristic response" or "campaigns of moral suasion" Baumol and Oates write:

> Economists have...been wary of the use of voluntarism as a diversionary tactic. When an effective environmental program (that threatens some vested interest) is proposed, often those threatened find it expedient to urge the superiority of voluntary compliance, in order to block the enactment of the program...The fear of this sort of diversion under the cover of voluntarism has not been entirely groundless. (1979: 282f.)

Baumol and Oates show in their book that companies with an interest in continued pollution have actively supported information campaigns to weaken the public support of demands for stronger interventions to safeguard the environment. They offer active support to voluntary information efforts as a step in their fight against the introduction of emission charges or regulations concerning, for instance, throwaway cans or bottles (Baumol and Oates 1979: 293).

Effects and Evaluation of Government Information Programs

Weiss and Tschirhart (1994) reviewed 100 campaigns which cover a variety of policy fields like health issues (smoking, drugs, alcoholism, nutrition); safety (crime prevention, traffic safety, fire prevention); and production, consumption, and conservation of energy. The review shows that the political benefits of campaigns are considerable: public campaigns meet the political needs of governments; the democratic consequences are paradoxical; and the effectiveness of campaigns is in fact troublesome in many cases. The general conclusion of the authors is rather positive against the backdrop of this empirical evidence:

> Policy instruments with the capacity for effective intervention, which are politically feasible to use in a wide variety of circumstances, and with positive consequences for democracy and citizenship, are scarce indeed. Public information campaigns do not deliver on all three counts every time; but the remarkable thing is that they are capable of delivering on all three counts. (Weiss and Tschirhart 1994: 104)

In order to get a more complete view and a more balanced judgement it is necessary to make a more comprehensive effort to classify effects and inventory the way evaluation research takes into account these features of information programs. Such an effort will be undertaken in the next section.

Effects of Government Information Programs

The effects issue is complicated as with most policy instruments. First, there are effects and then there are effects. From a public policy perspective, it is always illuminating to differentiate main intended effects from null effects, perverse effects, and side effects. From a program instigator viewpoint, the main intended effect can be defined as the central substantive impact that the program supporters wanted to achieve intentionally by introducing the program. Null effects mean that the program produces no consequences at all in the target area. In the perverse effects case, consequences are produced in the target area but contrary to the ones intended. Side effects, finally, occur outside the target area. They may be positive or negative, anticipated or unanticipated.

Researchers rarely discuss side effects of government information programs. One of the few issues raised in this area is the problem of information gaps. "An *information gap* is the widening difference in knowledge or other communication effects between the information-rich and the information-poor in an audience, as a result of an information campaign" (Rogers and Storey 1987: 840). This differential rate of knowledge growth might be considered an interesting side effect of a communication campaign.

The term "knowledge-gap" was coined by Tichenor, Donohue, and Olien in a 1970 article. The authors wrote:

> As the infusion of mass media information into a social system increases, segments of the population with higher socioeconomic status tend to acquire this information at a faster rate than the lower socioeconomic segments, so that the gap in knowledge between these segments tends to increase rather than decrease.

Perverse effects of official information efforts are sometimes discussed in the literature under the label "boomerang effects." A boomerang effect is usually defined as "a shift in the attitude in the direction opposite to that intended" (Blake and Haroldsen 1975: 71).

In a discussion of Robert Merton's ideas of boomerang effects, Sieber (1981: 34f.) argues that boomerang effects seem to be some sort of a regressive intervention, or what we have called perverse effects. Sieber continues:

> But despite the provocative title used to designate this effect of propaganda, virtually all of the examples that are offered are not regressive, but only null. That is, they refer to propaganda efforts that, instead of creating a reverse effect, simply fail to achieve their ends. The one rather clear example of a reverse effect is termed, interestingly enough, a "distinct boomerang"...but this case was not repeated in Merton's later and more theoretical treatment of the boomerang effect....

An interesting case of the boomerang effect is clearly illustrated in the history of forest fire protection campaigns of the Dutch government (Stielstra 1993), a kind of modern equivalent of the well-known "Smokey the Bear" campaigns in the United States and Canada. After 1985, the Dutch government stopped with radio and television spots that warned against forest fires in the summer. The television spots showed someone carelessly dropping a cigarette in a wood, after which a huge fire and scared running deer were shown. The reasons for stopping the campaign were multiple. They were shown too often, as there was not enough money to produce new spots. But there was also another reason. It was noticed that immediately after broadcasting the spots, sudden fires occurred. Forest managers suggested to the policymakers that the spots drew unwarranted attention and triggered pyromaniacal behavior. Ex-post facto investigations further showed that the underlying programming assumptions of the information campaign apparently were false. Experiments under extremely hot weather conditions showed that it was very hard to start a huge forest fire with a discarded cigarette, an action warned against in the information campaigns. The conclusion was that fires with unknown causes were deliberate actions of malicious people and that information campaigns were not useful for this target group.

The results were notable. Researchers of the Ministry of Agriculture are reluctant to suggest a causal relationship between the canning of the information campaign and a decrease in the number of forest fires, but the figures are almost self-evident. In the seven years before and during the information program, there were 175 fires per year, and an average loss of 256 hectares of forest. In the seven years after the campaign's end, there was an annual average of 98 fires and a loss of 177 hectares of forest. The category "deliberate fires" decreased from an annual average of 51 to an average of 18.

Evaluation of Information Programs

Unlike incentive and regulation programs, the use of information programs as an instrument of public policy do not necessarily contain an automatic feedback mechanism. Information programs on radio and television do not automatically generate knowledge about the number of listeners or viewers and the way they generally respond. The same holds true for information programs using written communications, like advertisements in newspapers or free leaflets disseminated to the public. Still, these forms of information campaigns are used most often because they are relatively cheap and easy to launch. Their general visibility makes them extremely useful as an instrument of democratic policy, as we have outlined in the previous paragraphs.

The importance of good and firm evaluation concerning the use of information programs is obvious. A review by the Dutch National Audit Office of about seventy information programs of the central Dutch government gives interesting results. As far as there were good evaluations available, it appeared that the information programs had relatively little effectiveness. The various information programs resulted—according to a review of evaluation surveys of the target groups of the campaigns—in a change of knowledge ranging from 6 to 18 percent, a change of attitude ranging from 0 to 12 percent and a change of behavior in a range from 0 to 13 percent. It also appeared that the budgeting of the information programs was not transparent, that the target groups were too large and amorphous, that some information programs weakened the effect of others, and that the effects in general were very hard to evaluate (Algemene and Rekenkamer 1991).

A striking feature in this review is that while most evaluations of information programs concern knowledge effects, little evaluation pertains to attitude changes, and almost no research at all is directed at behavioral changes. Research methods in which peoples' behavior is observed in more or less experimental settings are very rare. The policy instrument with very hard to detect effects seems to have a very weak evaluation culture. How is this paradox to be explained?

The reaction of the Dutch ministries concerning the report by the National Audit Office gives some insights into the difficulties of evaluation in the context of communicative policy strategies. The Minister of Justice, for example, first emphasized that firm evaluation of this relatively inexpensive policy instrument would be more costly than the use of the instrument itself. Second, he noted that information campaigns are often used in crisis situations where the government has to act very quickly. Information programs are the most suitable policy instrument in these situations because they are flexible and burdened with little bureaucratic and legal red tape. In such situations it is also very difficult to design a good evaluation with a control group. The correspondence between the National Audit Office and the Dutch policymakers shows that the relative inexpensiveness and flexibility of information programs contribute to a weak evaluation culture.

The Role of Information Programs in the Energy Conservation Policies of The Netherlands and Sweden

Energy conservation is one of the most exemplary policy areas—perhaps matched by health care—in which information programs play a considerable, even dominant role in the policy process. The study of energy conservation policies provides good opportunities to gain systematic knowledge of the functioning of information programs over a longer period of time and in relation to other policy instruments. We shall describe here the development of information programs after the oil crisis of 1973 in The Netherlands and Sweden, and from these two cases try to formulate some more general conclusions concerning the use of information programs as a policy instrument.

Information Programs in Dutch Energy Conservation Policy

The energy situation of The Netherlands has three key features: a large reservoir of natural gas, a strong opposition to nuclear power, and a relatively energy-intensive economy. These three interconnected elements determine the internal national dynamics of Dutch energy policy.

Energy conservation policy has been an integral part of energy policy, but has also had several ups and downs in the last two decades. It emerged after the first oil crisis of 1973, when The Netherlands was hit by a supply boycott of Arabian oil- producing countries. After the boycott ended and national security was no longer jeopardized, national attention faded. The second oil crisis of 1979 triggered energy conservation again. This time energy conservation was the answer to raising energy costs, especially for the Dutch energy-intensive industries. When prices lowered, attention faded and the energy conservation policy budget was cut. The third revival appeared in 1989 when environmental issues, like the greenhouse effect and acid rain, dominated the Dutch elections. Again, energy conservation policy was intensified, but this time in order to save the natural environment.

Although the underlying rationale of the energy conservation policy (national security, international economic competition, environmental protection) changed over the years, these changes do not account for the chosen and implemented policy instruments. A review of the Dutch energy conservation policy by the European Commission showed that the implementation of information and grants programs was strongly developed compared with other members of the European Community (EEC 1984). Policy instruments like price regulation and compelling directives, on the other hand, did not seem to be emphasized. Dutch policymakers appeared to choose to reward and stimulate conservation behavior rather than to directly punish or constrain the use of energy. Meanwhile the large reserves of natural gas have been used by the Dutch government to strengthen the competitive position of Dutch greenhouse cultivators and the chemical and metallurgical industries by providing gas at low prices. The European Commission has protested several times against this kind of price regulation and argued that it is a distortion of economic competition (van der Doelen and de Jong 1990). An analysis of the white papers in the 1970s and 1980s show that there were essentially six different policy instruments chosen to advance energy policy objectives: publications, an "advice bus" visiting organizations, grants for energy audits, premiums for certain types of investment, loans for certain types of investment, and financial support (grants and loans) for experimental demonstration projects (van der Doelen 1989).

In order to compare the different effects of these policy instruments two research strategies were used: (1) a review of the twenty existing evaluations of the separate instruments, and (2) a study of 210 energy-intensive industrial companies, consisting of both users and non-users of the policy instruments involved. The review of twenty governmental evaluations showed that, in general, the information instruments (publications, advice bus, grant for audits) led to a 10 to 30 percent greater level of effort to practice energy conservation. The investment incentives (premium, loans, and grants) led to additional energy conservation investments by 10 to 50 percent of the involved organizations.

The survey among the 210 energy-intensive industrial companies compared the effects of the above-mentioned six instruments on four types of energy conservation: good housekeeping, retrofitting investments, new capital investments, and investments for cogeneration. A regression analysis showed that, besides the very dominant effect of the rising energy costs, the information and grant programs had only a limited and partial effect on the different kinds of energy conservation behavior. The governmental publications, for example, stimulated good housekeeping and the premium stimulated investments in cogeneration. Both the review of twenty governmental evaluations of separate instruments and the more directly comparative regression analyses of six policy instruments led to the same general conclusion: the effects of energy prices on energy conservation behavior tended to be predominant, while the effects of (investment) grants were moderate, and those of (oral or written) information campaigns were only modest.

This research suggests that information programs have a mainly symbolic function. This idea is strengthened when one takes into account the justification for using these policy instruments over the years. In the 1970s, Dutch policymakers mainly implemented mass media information programs. Evaluation of these mass media information programs during the years showed rather disappointing results. The mass media information programs changed attitudes, but did not change energy conservation behavior (Klop 1979). In the 1980s the Dutch government implemented more direct and selective information programs (advice buses, grants for audits, special campaigns for target groups), in which economic advantages of energy conservation were stressed especially. The empirical results also showed no impressive effectiveness of these types of information campaigns. At the end of the 1980s the budget was cut and the minister of economic affairs wanted to stop information programs. In 1988 it was argued that after such a sustained set of information campaigns, most Dutch people had sufficient knowledge about the problems and the solutions. New information programs could not add very much. But the elections of 1989 were dominated by environmental issues and all the political parties stressed their "green" identity. The result was that information programs on energy conservation were again intensified, but now in conjunction with environmental "green" argumentation, especially concerning acid rain.

The Swedish Energy Conservation Programs and Nuclear Power

The current Swedish energy conservation program started with some scattered measures in 1974 and a fully comprehensive program in 1975. In a chapter in the 1977 volume by Leon N. Lindberg called *The Energy Syndrome*, Måns Lönnroth intimated that the 1975 decision marked the beginning of a new, innovative energy policy. In hindsight, it is arguable whether the 1975 decision really constituted such a cornerstone of a new, conservation-prone energy policy. Lönnroth underrated the political motives for pushing energy conservation and overemphasized the substantive energy motives.

Sweden's energy conservation policies in the 1970s and 1980s are not unique in the Western world. Most Western countries introduced energy conservation programs in the wake of the 1973 oil crisis. The oil crisis is usually taken as the main impetus for conservation. In the Swedish case, however, the peculiar *political* background is also important: the Social Democrats long history as the governing party, the challenge of this hegemony by the Center Party along the environmental dimension, and more particularly the impact of the nuclear energy issue all framed Swedish energy policy. The way the Center Party transformed nuclear power into an issue in Swedish politics in the spring of 1973, *before* the oil crisis, and the way this issue turned into a threat to the "state-carrying" Social Democratic Party is the main explanatory factor. In order to save the hard core of the nuclear program, placate internal party opposition, and retain the party's hegemonical strength in the electorate, the Social Democratic leadership had to demonstrate that it was in favor of resource conservation and other "green" values. Argued Robert Sahr (1985: 5): "The Social Democratic emphasis on conservation was at least partly an attempt to deflect concern over nuclear power, an issue that continued to be divisive both inside and outside the party."

Before 1975, neither an overall energy policy nor the concept "energy policy" itself did exist in the Swedish context. Government intervention was supply-oriented, particularly aiming at efficient production and distribution of hydroelectric power. Through the 1975 decision, state intervention was directed at energy in general, the total level of energy supply and use, and the distribution of energy use among different use-sectors. The foremost innovations in the new energy policy was that Parliament set targets that were lower than the forecasts; that measures were taken to direct supply; and, above all, that demand management—conservation—was included.

The planned slowdown of the growth of the pace of the energy supply had been designed to hit the residential/commercial sector harder than transportation and considerably harder than industry. The Swedish people have been called upon to save energy in homes and offices in order that transportation and, above all, industry would get what they needed. This tendency was gradually strengthened during the period.

In comparison with economic means and regulation, information activities over the past twenty years have been assigned a substantial role as an independent policy tool in the Swedish energy conservation program. The information efforts have been both pervasive and diversified (Vedung 1995, Furubo 1983 and 1984, Furubo and Sandahl 1984).

Another striking fact about policy instruments in the Swedish energy conservation program is that besides information, other "soft" policy measures like grants and subsidies have been preferred to "hard" policy measures, such as mandatory price regulations. Instead of introducing a harsh command-and-control type of regulatory system, the Swedish national government chose to encourage and exhort energy consumers to voluntarily make their energy use more efficient by offering them free brochures, booklets, folders, and other types of printed information, as well as audits, personal advice, and education on the best ways to save energy and the economic benefits of doing so. Over the past years, consumers have also been offered generous grants and loans for certain prescribed measures to save energy. The Swedes have not been obligated by their political leadership to save energy. This strategy, governed by the *Principle of Client Voluntariness,* is strikingly similar, if not identical, to the "Give" part of the so-called "give-and-take strategy" (see ch. 5). Starting in 1974, and strengthened by the major parliamentary decisions in 1975, 1978, 1979, 1981, 1985, and 1991, the energy conservation program in all sectors has contained surprisingly few mandatory directives, standards, and regulations. Clients and energy users have been free to decide by themselves whether they want to conserve energy or not (Vedung 1996).

There are, to be sure, exceptions to the general rule of voluntariness. Some regulations have been enacted. Generally, regulatory techniques are directed to buildings under construction and activities about to start. The principle has been to regulate the upcoming and let voluntariness reign in the existing.

In industry, to provide an example, a package of information and economic incentives has overshadowed everything else in the area of existing structures and processes. With respect to creation and siting of energy-demanding new industrial facilities, a system of compulsory licensing was introduced in 1975 through amendments and changes in the Building Act § 136a. But since the annual addition constitutes only a tiny part of the total stock of industrial buildings and processes, it is no exaggeration to maintain that client voluntariness and the "give strategy" is the fundamental policy instrument philosophy behind the Swedish energy conservation program in industry and in other sectors as well.

The Swedish energy conservation program with its emphasis on information and economic incentives as tools of government has had some success. The conservation goals set by Parliament since 1974–75 have been accomplished with ample margins. Overall energy supply was lower in 1993 than in 1970 in spite of, for instance, a forecasted 50 percent increase from 1973 to 1988. Total energy supply in 1993 was 439 tera-watt hours (TWh) as compared to 457 in 1970. The conservation goals were achieved to an even higher degree with regard to the supply of oil. The level for 1993 was far below the level of 1970, 185 versus 350 TWh, respectively. Sweden has drastically diminished its dependency on foreign oil from 70 to about 43 percent of the total energy supply (Energifakta 1994).

Whether and how public information efforts have contributed to this achievement is not substantiated beyond all doubt. Most studies seem to indicate that information has had some effect, albeit rather small and limited in time. Certainly, it has precipitated a reduction that would have come later because of price hikes. In general, however, information campaigns seem to have had little impact on energy use. Economic incentives have been much more effective (Vedung 1996).

The organization of public information efforts may have contributed to the tiny successes that can be found. The Swedish government has tried several models. It has used established networks of private third parties between consumers and government agencies to collect, package, and disseminate information to end-users. The third parties include institutions like professional organizations, trade associations, unions, employers' confederations, and the network of organizations around electricity and other energy production and distribution. Trades and professions as well as the mass media have been important channels. Another typical feature is the use of local governments and the Association of Local Authorities, their interest organization. In addition, a notable portion of the information has been research-based, produced within the peculiar Swedish system of so-called sectorial or applied research. The corporatist, trades-and-professions, mass media, local government, and research approaches to government information have all contributed to the success of the communication programs (Vedung 1996, Klingberg and Similä 1984).

Information has been somewhat successful in influencing consumers who have economic incentives, to take conservation measures but who do not know exactly how to go about doing so. It has been more productive with consumers who can influence directly their energy environment (homeowners, owner-occupants) than with those who cannot (tenants). Specific information on how-to skills have been more instrumental than general motivation knowledge. Information activities with perpetual evaluation of outputs and outcomes and incessant feedback of the results not only to program managers but also to the addressees are more successful than information efforts without a proper evaluation function.

Dutch and Swedish Energy Information Programs: Some Comparative Conclusions

Both Swedish and Dutch energy conservation policy may very well be regarded as massive information and persuasion efforts coupled with generous economic incentives. Swedish and Dutch cabinets and parliamentary majorities have denounced sticks and relied upon a package of sermons and carrots to bring people in line with national goals for energy conservation. How effective is such a "give" strategy?

Time-series of the OECD countries suggest that available energy-savings techniques make a conservation of 40 percent possible and that energy prices are overwhelmingly determining the degree of energy conservation. There is, for instance, a strong correlation between gasoline prices and the purchase of energy-efficient cars. Schipper and Meyers (1992) estimate that subsidies have an effect of 20 percent, while there is no indication in their study that information campaigns effect energy conservation.

Typically enough, though, the price on government produced energy is not officially used as an instrument of energy conservation policy. On the other hand, information programs are often chosen and implemented as part of a national energy conservation policy. They have generally appeared not to be very effective. These two instrumentation features strongly suggest a token function or a legitimation/symbolic-use function of the information programs in energy conservation policy, as is illustrated in our comparison of Sweden and The Netherlands.

Recent developments in The Netherlands and the development in Sweden since an overall energy policy was introduced in 1974–75 confirm this token use of information also from another point of view: a weakly instrumented energy conservation policy is mainly symbolic and, in fact, a side step for introducing or continuing with nuclear power. This especially accounts for the recent official Dutch emphasis on acid rain as a main side target of energy conservation policy instead of, for example, the greenhouse effect.

General Conclusions

This chapter deals with the question of why information programs are chosen as a policy instrument, what their effects are, and in which ways this policy instrument is evaluated.

In democratic policy-making, information is the most lenient tool of government. There are several reasons for choosing information as a policy instrument. In this paper we have enumerated several: when universal compliance is not necessary, when private interests are in line with the public interest, in paternalistic situations, in sudden crisis situations, when compliance with other instruments cannot be monitored, when counterinformation is not present, to legitimate the later use of more intrusive instruments, and to give an appearance of concern.

Information may have, like all policy instruments, different effects. Surprising are the perverse effects of information programs. Often information programs assume that lack of knowledge is the cause of undesired behavior. On the other hand, it may be that self interest is the cause of the behavior. In general, information programs seem to have effect when they strengthen well-reasoned self-interest. Information programs are generally not very costly and the effects on behavior are often hard to detect. This leads to an evaluation paradox: the policy instrument that perhaps needs the most intensive evaluation, due to the inherent invisibility of its impacts, is less evaluated because of its relative cheapness and flexibility.

After this general, theoretic exercise the Dutch and Swedish energy conservation policies have both been compared on an empirical level.

In both countries information programs are very important instruments in the central governments' tool kits in this policy area. Energy conservation policy is a field in which information programs play a crucial role. It is a policy area in which public and private goals seem to coincide: using less energy for the user also means, in general, less energy costs. It seems quite rational for government to presume that lack of information is the reason why people do not show the desired energy conservation behavior. In both countries the contributions of information programs to the ambitious energy conservation policy targets is significant but inherently modest, due to the program's voluntary character. It is striking that neither country has influenced or intends to influence energy prices as a means of stimulating energy conservation.

This missing element in an effective tool kit provides additional insight into the reasons why governments use information programs. In The Netherlands and Sweden, energy conservation is of crucial importance because of the popular opposition to nuclear power in the countries. The information programs are highly visible and give the impression that government has undertaken massive efforts to stimulate energy conservation. After a long time, when this policy does not solve the energy problem, the resistance against nuclear power may fade away and old reactors can continue to operate and new plants can be built to provide a supply-side solution to the energy issue. In this context, it appears that information programs may have a strong symbolic and legitimating political function.

References

Algemene Rekenkamer. 1991. *Voorlichtingscampagnes van het Rijk* (Central Government Information Campaigns). The Hague: The Netherlands General Accounting Office.

Baumol, William J. and Wallace E. Oates. 1979. *Economics, Environmental Policy, and the Quality of Life*. Englewood Cliffs, NJ: Prentice-Hall.

Blake, Reed H. and Edwin O. Haroldsen. 1975. *A Taxonomy of Concepts in Communication*. New York: Hastings House.

Doelen, Frans C.J. van der, and J.M. de Jong. 1990. "Energy Policy," in Menno Wolters and Peter Coffey (eds.), *The Netherlands and EC Membership Evaluated*, pp. 62–70. New York: St. Martin's Press.

Doelen, Frans C.J. van der. 1989. *Beleidsinstrumenten en energiebesparing: De effectiviteit van voorlichting en subsidies gericht op energiebesparing in de industrie van 1977 tot 1987* (Policy Instruments and Energy Conservation: The Implementation and Effectiveness of Information Programs and Subsidies Directed at Dutch Industrial Energy Conservation from 1977 to 1987). Enschede: Twente University.

Dworkin, Gerald. 1979. "Paternalism," in Peter Laslett and James Fishkin (eds.), *Philosophy, Politics, Society*, 5th series, pp. 78–96. New Haven, CT: Yale University Press.

Eckhoff, Torstein. 1983. *Statens styringsmuligheter, særlig i ressurs—og miljøspørsmål.* Oslo: Tanum-Norli.

European Economic Community. 1984. *Comparative Research Concerning Energy Conservation Programs of the EC-member States,* Com (24) 34 def. (Feb.), Brussels.

Energifakta. 1994. Stockholm: AB Svensk Energiförsörjning, September Report.

Furubo, Jan-Eric. 1983. *Information som styrmedel* (Information as a Policy Instrument). Statens Offentliga Utredningar, no. 34. Stockholm: Liber.

———. 1984. "Information on Energy Conservation," in T. Klingberg (ed.), *Effects of Energy Conservation Programs,* pp. 51–63. Bulletin M84: 2. Gävle: Swedish Institute for Building Research.

Furubo, Jan-Eric and Rolf Sandahl. 1984. *Energihushållnings-programmets effekter* (The Effects of the Energy Conservation Programs). Stockholm: National Energy Administration.

Hood, Christopher C. 1983. *The Tools of Government.* London: Macmillan.

Jasper, James M. 1990. *Nuclear Politics: Energy and the State in the United States, Sweden, and France.* Princeton, NJ: Princeton University Press.

Klingberg, Tage and Matti Similä. 1984. "Do House-Owners Use the Energy Advisers?" in Tage Klingberg (ed.), *Effects of Energy Conservation Programs,* pp. 65–73. Bulletin M84: 2. Gävle: Swedish Institute for Building Research.

Klop, C.J. 1979. "De Campagne 'Verstandig met energie'—hoe effectief kan voorlichting zijn? (The Campaign 'Sensible about Energy'—How Effective Can Information Programs Be?)," in *TNO—project,* no. 12, pp. 445–458.

Lönnroth, Måns. 1977. "Swedish Energy Policy: Technology in the Political Process," in Leon N. Lindberg (ed.), *The Energy Syndrome: Comparing National Responses to the Energy Crisis,* pp. 255–283. Lexington, MA: Lexington Books.

Rice, Ronald E. and Charles K. Atkin, eds. 1989. *Public Communication Campaigns.* Newbury Park, CA.: Sage.

Rogers, Everett M. and J. Douglas Storey. 1987. "Communication Campaigns," in Charles R. Berger and Steven H. Chaffee (eds.), *Handbook of Communication Science,* pp. 817–846. Newbury Park, CA.: Sage.

Sahr, Robert C. 1985. *The Politics of Energy Policy Change in Sweden.* Ann Arbor, MI: University of Michigan Press.

Salmon, Charles, ed. 1989. *Information Campaigns: Managing the Process of Social Change.* Newbury Park, CA: Sage.

Schipper, Lee. 1983. *Energy-Efficient Housing in Sweden.* Berkeley, CA: Lawrence Berkeley Laboratory, mimeo. (The full report of this project, *Coming in from the Cold* by Lee Schipper, Stephen Meyers, and Henry Kelly, was published in 1985 by Seven Locks Press, Cabin John, MD.)

Schipper, Lee and Stephen Meyers. 1992. *Energy Efficiency and Human Activity: Past Trends, Future Prospects.* Cambridge: Cambridge University Press.

Sieber, Sam D. 1981. *Fatal Remedies: The Ironies of Social Intervention.* New York: Plenum Press.

Stielstra, Theo. 1993. "Bos brandt beter als de overheid geld uitgeeft aan voorlichting (Forests Burn Better when Government Spends Money on Information Campaigns)," *De Volkskrant* 26 (July).

Tichenor, Philip J., George A. Donohue, and Clarice N. Olien. 1970. "Mass Media Flow and Differential Growth in Knowledge," *Public Opinion Quarterly* 34: 159–170.

Vedung, Evert. 1988. "The Swedish Five-Party Syndrome and the Environmentalists," in K. Lawson and Peter M. Merkl (eds.), *When Parties Fail: Emerging Alternative Organizations,* pp. 76–109. Princeton, NJ: Princeton University Press.

————. 1996. *Statliga informationskampanjer: Svenska energisparprogram* (Government Information Campaigns: Swedish Energy Conservation Programs). Unpublished ms., Uppsala University, Department of Government.

Weiss, Janet A. and Mary Tschirhart. 1994. "Public Information Campaigns as Policy Instruments," *Journal of Policy Analysis and Management* 13(1): 82–119.

Wittrock, Björn and Stefan Lindström. 1984. *De stora programmens tid: Forskning och energi i svensk politik.* Stockholm: Akademiförlaget.

5

The "Give-and-Take" Packaging of Policy Instruments: Optimizing Legitimacy and Effectiveness

Frans C.J. van der Doelen

A man can build himself a throne of bayonets,
but he can not sit on it.
—William Ralph Inge (1860–1954),
dean of St. Paul's (London)

Introduction

Politics is sometimes described as the deliberate shaping of future society. However, the questions of what government wishes to achieve with its policy ("ends") and how it wishes to accomplish this ("means") are not always easy to answer. This is partly because the goals of government policies are sometimes vague, changeable, and even mutually contradictory. It is also because the application of instruments in policy can sometimes better be explained by reference to ingrained civil service traditions or fashionable political rhetoric than by reference to deliberate efforts to shape the future. Notwithstanding these reservations, analyses of political action and public policy in terms of goals and instruments is often very illuminating and quite feasible.

It is good to know something about the potential effects of different policy instruments before one chooses among them. The famous quote in the beginning of this article, for example, points out in a nutshell that the effectiveness of state interventions cannot be separated from their legitimacy. The question whether government should attain its goals by punishment or reward is not hard to answer: government should act one way and not hesitate to implement the other way as well. In an adequate political strategy, the iron fist and the silk glove should be combined in balance (Balch 1980). The central thesis of this article is that government should in a balanced way simultaneously give and take: the giving contributes to the legitimacy, the taking to the effectiveness. And government can "give and take" by combining restrictive and stimulative policy instruments.

Policy Instruments, Effectiveness, and Legitimacy

The degree to which certain types of policy instruments contribute to the policy goal can be differently estimated. Nagel (1975) composed his personal "top ten" of policy instruments for compliance with environmental law in the following order. Policy instruments with relatively high compliance potential are discharge taxes or fees, contingent injunctions, and finally, tax rewards and subsidies. Policy tools with medium compliance potential are objective civil penalties, publicizing wrongdoers, and selective government buying power. Instruments with low compliance potential are fines, jail sentences, and persuasion.

Nagel offers here a very interesting ranking of policy instruments. But the categorization lacks theoretical underpinning and the concept "compliance" is rather vague. This may cause confusion. For example, the ranking tempts the Dutch sociologist Schuyt (1985: 120) to formulate the general thesis that, in general, behavior can be better changed by rewarding than by punishing. The implicit assumption of this thesis is that when government is nice to the citizens, the citizens will be nice for government. This general conclusion, though, is debatable. It seems that the concept "compliance" puts the legitimacy of a policy too easily in line with its effectiveness. Though it is true that the more compliance-enhancing instruments typically evoke little resistance during policy implementation, this does not mean automatically that these policy instruments are therefore also effective and that they lead to instrument-induced behavioral changes in the citizens or their organizations. Lack of resistance is not the same as realization of the aimed changes of behavior. Though there might be a positive correlation between legitimacy on the one hand and effectiveness of a policy on the other hand (see Introduction), there are also good arguments underpinning a negative relation. In democratic policy-making, there is often a trade-off between the effectiveness and legitimacy of policy instruments.

In order to elaborate this thesis, the central concepts in this chapter have to be described.

A *policy instrument* can be described as everything a policy actor may use to obtain certain goals. Of course this is a general description and multiple classifications are possible on this subject. In this book, the division of policy instruments into the communicative, economic, and judicial control models is the dominant viewpoint. These models are sometimes respectively classified in such a way as to suggest an increasing degree of coercion. The ordering from weak to strong authoritative force or constraint runs from communication through economic incentives—by means of subsidies and charges—to, ultimately, judicial directives (Geelhoed 1983). In this section we will elaborate and refine this idea of increasing constraint, which also throws a more complicated light on the logic of packaging policy instruments, compared to a straightforward one-dimensional ranking.

Legitimacy is sometimes discerned from compliance and acceptance. In this chapter, legitimacy is used as an overall term for the degree to which a certain policy is accepted by the citizens and their organization. The legitimacy of a policy instrument is expressed by the degree to which the policy instrument is assessed to be feasible by the policymakers and evokes actual acceptance among citizens and their organizations.

The *effectiveness* of a policy should be discerned from its goal attainment. Effectiveness of a policy is the degree to which the chosen policy instruments themselves contribute to attainment of the policy goals. The goal attainment of a policy might very well be due to other external factors than the chosen and implemented policy instruments. Thus, its effectiveness could be low while the end results could be notable.

Increasing Degrees of Coercion: Education, Engineering, and Enforcement

Communication is often seen as a weak model of coercion. Economic incentives, like subsidies and levies, are regarded as being in the mid-range between weak and strong coercion. In the case of economic incentives there is still freedom of choice. The individual is, in principle, still free to choose a particular form of behavior. However, the attractiveness of the options is materially altered. The degree of coercion is already greater, therefore, than in the case of the provision of nonbinding information. According to this line of reasoning, the point at which freedom turns into coercion is situated somewhere between the two poles of this economic control model, namely between control through subsidies on the one hand and control through levies on the other. By their very nature, subsidies encourage and levies discourage certain forms of behavior. At the other end of the scale of increasing degrees of coercion are judicial directives. Certain courses of conduct are made compulsory by prescription. In the case of judicial directives the individual does not, in principle, have the freedom to choose a particular course of conduct, but is instead obliged to do or refrain from certain acts (orders and prohibitions respectively). On the basis of this classification, analysts have developed strategies on how to pursue a feasible and effective policy. The three control models are sometimes linked together in a particular sequence. Often reference is made to the three E's strategy: education, engineering, and enforcement (Paisley 1981). The idea is that over time a policy problem is tackled in three different ways: first by the provision of information (education), subsequently by the application of selective incentives (engineering) and lastly by the establishment of rules and regulations (enforcement). Here too, we find an increasing degree of coercion implicit in this reasoning. The underlying notion is that in solving social problems the authorities employ instruments of increasing strength in successive stages. Gradually, the resistance of certain groups of individuals is broken, after which the authorities are, in due course, entitled to regulate the matters definitively by employing their most powerful instruments (rules and regulations).

Repressive and Stimulative Policy Instruments

It is necessary to refine these views on the increasing degrees of coercion of the various categories of policy instruments. This is evident, for example, from the fact that some regulations impose fewer constraints on conduct than some levies (Bressers 1988). This classification on the basis of increasing degrees of coercion—from communication through incentives to regulations—can also be challenged on theoretical grounds.

The distinction between stimulative and repressive forms of the three control models is based on the extent to which the individual is or is not free to use a particular policy instrument, that is, the extent to which the use of the instrument by the individual is *optional*. And, as far as this is concerned, a dividing line runs right through each of the three

FIGURE 5.1
Stimulative and Repressive Forms of the Communicative,
Economic, and Judicial Control Models

	Stimulative	Repressive
Communicative control model	Information	Propaganda
Economic control model	Subsidy	Levy
Judicial control model	Contract/Covenant	Order/Prohibition

control models, with the result that a stimulative and a repressive form can be distinguished in each of the models. This distinction is shown in figure 5.1, where the cells are named after relatively specific policy instruments.

The examples in figure 5.1 can be explained as follows. In the communicative control model, the repressive and stimulative forms are reflected in the distinction between information and propaganda. The object of providing information is to increase the knowledge of the individual, thereby enabling him or her to form an independent judgement. Propaganda, on the other hand, is intended to influence the will of the individual and attempts to undermine his or her capacity for independent judgement, which is in essence a very coercive way of changing a person's behavior (Vogelaar 1955).

Repressive and stimulative modes can also be identified in the case of the economic control model. An example of a repressive incentive is a levy. Although the individual is free to decide whether or not to follow a particular course of conduct, he is in fact financially discouraged. An example of a stimulative incentive is a subsidy. In principle, a subsidy may or may not be applied for when a particular course of conduct is to be followed. An individual may apply for a subsidy, but he is free not to do so (see ch. 3).

In the case of the judicial control model, the dimension of stimulation and repression can be characterized by the distinction between contracts and covenants on the one hand and orders and prohibitions on the other. Orders and prohibitions are norms of conduct which are imposed unilaterally by the authorities on the individual and which the individual is obliged to observe. In the case of contracts however, there is reciprocity. It is a legal commitment which is voluntarily entered into and entails mutual rights and duties. The distinction coincides with that between Von Hayek's twofold division of legal systems in *Nomos* and *Thesis* (Barry 1979: 76–103) and Hood's (1983) characterization in positive and negative directives.

The argument outlined above can be summarized by saying that it is not fruitful solely to classify the communicative, economic, and judicial control models on a scale of increasing degrees of coercion. Not only does such a classification fail to recognize the coercive nature of a form of communication such as propaganda, but it also takes no account of the optional nature of a legal instrument such as a contract or covenant.

The Give-and-Take Strategy

The distinction between repressive and stimulative forms of control models is not merely of academic importance. From the assumption of an increasing degree of coercion in the communicative, economic, and legal control models was derived the rule of conduct of the three E's strategy. However, a more refined and varied rule of conduct can be based on the introduction of the stimulative and repressive dimension, namely the give-and-take strategy. As will be argued in the three following sections, the use of stimulative and repressive policy instruments has certain effects. Stimulative policy instruments (information, subsidies, and contracts) legitimate a policy, whereas repressive policy instruments (propaganda, levies, and orders and prohibitions) effectuate it. By combining stimulative and repressive forms of control models, in other words by giving and taking, the authorities enhance the feasibility and effectiveness of a policy. In the next three sections this give-and-take strategy is elaborated with respect to each of the three control models.

Judicial Control: Orders/Prohibitions and Contracts/Covenant

To quote Koopmans (1970), the character of the law has changed over the years from codification to modification. Whereas the law originally concentrated on recording existing customs and relationships in society, it has increasingly been used in the twentieth century as an instrument for modifying social developments. Private law, whose dominant legal form is the contract, is often associated with codifying law and corresponds to the stimulative legal control model. Public law, whose dominant legal form is orders and prohibitions, is frequently seen as modifying law and corresponds to the repressive, judicial control model.

Orders and Prohibitions

In the 1980s, in The Netherlands, there was a stagnation in the historical progression from codification to modification. This was initially reflected in the moves towards deregulation. Many individuals and organizations were of the opinion that the proliferation of laws was resulting in a surfeit of extremely detailed and often mutually inconsistent government regulations (Geelhoed 1983). The sheer volume of orders and prohibitions promulgated by the authorities generated considerable opposition. By way of reaction, the authorities took a step backwards from the repressive legal control model.

The enforcement of the many orders and prohibitions has proved in practice to be the Achilles' heel of the repressive legal control model. It appears, for example, that many of the businesses which require a permit under the Nuisance Act (Hinderwet) do not, in practice, have any such permit. Moreover, even where they do have the official permit, the regulations under the permit are often inadequate. In reality, the potential effectiveness of the unilaterally peremptory orders and prohibitions is limited. For various reasons, legal sanctions are seldom applied in the case of regulations, and a number of regulations are ignored on a large scale. The application of peremptory orders and prohibitions which are theoretically very effective proves difficult in practice because of the resistance such regulations zencounter from individuals and businesses.

Contracts and Covenant

In the 1990s the pendulum of the law in The Netherlands appears to be swinging back from modification to codification: the process of deregulation is evidently giving way to a process of self-regulation. The present administrative trend is for unilaterally coercive government regulations to be replaced by bilateral, voluntary agreements concluded between the authorities and interest groups. Voluntary agreements between equal partners in the form of codes of conduct, gentlemen's agreements, contracts, and covenants are becoming very common. The stimulative legal control model is in the ascendant.

De Ru (1987: 81) submits that unilaterally coercive regulations are often regarded as less legitimate and effective than multilateral agreements: "It is striking that management agreements in agriculture are regarded as more coercive than orders. The parties bind themselves more explicitly." This view is becoming more and more popular among Dutch policymakers in general and as a consequence such policy agreements are mushrooming in, for example, the environmental sector in the 1990s. The Dutch authorities hope to achieve more in this way. Klok (1989) examined the effectiveness of all product-oriented environmental covenants signed by 1 August 1988. His cautious conclusion is that the effectiveness of the covenants in question does not appear to be very great, although the situation is better than in cases where there are no such covenants. According to Klok (1989: 180), the limited effectiveness is partly due to the fact that the instrument is used in situations in which the objective would be largely attained even without an instrument. Although Klok makes a reservation by pointing out that covenants have been in existence for only a short time and there has been no comparison with other instruments, their effectiveness appears only limited.

The popularity of covenants as a policy instrument should therefore be explained by other characteristics. Covenants as a policy instrument have various other advantages and disadvantages. The disadvantages are mainly a result of the shadowy legal status of covenants. The advantages are mainly related to the improvement in the structure of consultations with industry and the greater degree of acceptance. In other words, industry is treated as an equal partner, recognizes the social problem, and is thus made partly psychologically responsible for solving the problem. The conclusion is clear: covenants above all promote the legitimacy of a policy.

Judicial Give-and-Take

Broadly speaking, this leads to the following picture of the legitimacy and effectiveness of the legal control model. The potential effectiveness of repressive variants of the legal control model such as orders and prohibitions is often not achieved. Their application encounters resistance from the individuals and groups concerned. On the other hand, stimulative forms of the legal control model in the nature of various types of agreements have great legitimacy but little impact. They are ineffective in inducing individuals and organizations to make an effort to change their behavior. The combination of stimulative and repressive regulations of—"may" and "must"—seem to benefit both the legitimacy and the effectiveness of policy. Covenants make organizations partly responsible for solving the social problem concerned and legitimatize government policy on the subject. Not infrequently, the threat of coercive regulations is used as a stick to encourage the parties to conclude covenants. The organized social groups often do not come voluntarily to the authorities to regulate their own forms of behavior. By keeping the threat of unilaterally coercive regulations in reserve, the authorities can often achieve their policy goals.

The give-and-take strategy within the legal control model is of course an ideal type. In reality, there are many kinds of legal policy instruments, and between the stimulative agreements on the one hand and the repressive orders and prohibitions on the other there is a mixture of legal instruments such as authorizations, exemptions, concessions, and permits. But, working with these extremes clarifies matters and makes it possible to analyze public policy-making more fruitfully.

Empirical research in the area of Dutch consumer policy revealed that self-regulation agreements on consumer affairs come into being only very gradually and at a very slow pace. The majority of the projects supervised by a ministerial steering group on self-regulation did not result in new self-regulation agreements. Even advocates of self-regulation can scarcely avoid the conclusion that almost the only way of tackling the problem posed by the lack of progress with self-regulation in consumer policy is by holding in reserve the threat of legislation. Many forms of present legislative work originated historically from previous attempts at self-regulation. Such originally self-regulatory policy fields as house building, social security, and education have gradually been incorporated into the new legislation. The present Dutch trend towards self-regulation is probably the gateway to new repressive regulations (van der Doelen and Bakker 1991).

Economic Control: Levies and Subsidies

As a result of the lessons learned in the economic crisis in the 1930s and the construction of the postwar welfare state, the ideas of John Maynard Keynes gained wide acceptance. In brief, Keynes argued that public spending was a suitable instrument for stimulating economic growth. The economic crisis in the 1970s undermined confidence in the effectiveness of this instrument of economic policy. The monetarist

Friedman articulated the new view by contending that the public sector was not the solution, but the cause of the problem. In fact, the consequent debate about the "foundation of the economy" concentrates on the effectiveness and legitimacy of financial instruments such as levies and subsidies.

Levies. According to Frey (1983), a sizeable body of research shows that levies and forms of tax disincentives—which according to our theoretical scheme are the repressive mode of the economic control model— are very effective instruments of government policy. Dutch research also reveals that these kinds of negative incentives bring about major changes of behavior on the part of both individuals and businesses. In the case of Dutch water-quality policy in the 1970s, for example, levies proved to be the most powerful stimulus in changing the attitude of businesses to water pollution (Bressers 1988). And the rising energy prices of the 1980s proved to be the main motor behind energy conservation moves in The Netherlands (van der Doelen 1989). Like Bressers (1988), one can pose the rhetorical question why policymakers do not use repressive, economic incentives more frequently. Frey supplies the obvious answer for each target group. The use and potential effectiveness of levies are limited by the resistance which they generate. Individuals find levies unjust as they tax the poor as heavily as the rich. And there is resistance from officials as they have a ingrained preference for laws prescribing the course of conduct considered necessary. Interest and pressure groups are opposed to levies because they know only too well how effective they are.

Subsidies. The resistance to repressive economic instruments can be reduced, according to Frey (1983), by the simultaneous use of a stimulative subsidy that encourages the desired behavior. Subsidies extinguish conflicts and enhance the feasibility of policy acceptance. Subsidies work as a kind of tranquillizer, ensuring that a policy to which there is great resistance can still be implemented. The advantages of subsidies are therefore mainly in the political sphere. Frey's view is that subsidies are relatively ineffective and do not in themselves bring about the desired instrument-induced change in behavior. Subsidies merely redistribute resources, without stabilizing economic development or permanently allocating certain public goods.

Relatively little systematic research has evidently been conducted on the way in which the provision of subsidies actually facilitates policymaking (see ch. 3). There are indications that subsidies ease the administration of policy, reduce resistance, and thus strengthen the legitimacy of policy. Vermeulen (1988) concludes that the provision of subsidies in the context of the Dutch regional policy on management of the disposal of toxic metals was not effective in a direct sense. He did, however, find evidence that the allocated subsidy served as a way for governmental officials to come into contact with polluting industries and as "loose change" in the bargaining process. It fulfilled an indirect function in support of policy. The process of subsidization thus legitimated the application of other (repressive) policy instruments.

Economic Give-and-Take

Broadly speaking, the above description leads to the following picture of the effectiveness and legitimacy of instruments of the economic control model. Increasing the costs of certain courses of conduct by imposing levies is an effective means of altering the behavior of individuals and their organizations. However, levies arouse too much resistance and are therefore used only sparingly. Increasing the benefits of certain courses of conduct by providing subsidies appears to lessen the resistance to a given policy. By taking with one hand, through the levy, and giving back with the other, through the subsidy, the authorities can increase the feasibility and effectiveness of a policy.

In practice it is virtually impossible to define subsidies and levies if the existing tax structure is not taken into account at the same time (Ricketts 1985). Between the more purely stimulative instrument of the "subsidy on request" on the one hand and the "levy" on the other, there therefore lies a great variety of economically oriented policy instruments such as credits, support, grants, guarantees, tax deductions, asset-sharing, refunds, price measures, tariffs, and taxes. Stimulative and repressive economic instruments are used in combination in various parts of Dutch environmental policy in order to ensure feasibility and effectiveness. Firms are "punished" by means of levies if they pollute the environment and "rewarded" by means of subsidies if they act in the desired manner in order to spare the environment. On the basic premise that "the polluter pays," the proceeds from all kinds of environmental levies are used to pay subsidies intended to promote the adoption of clean technology.

In 1985, the two-edged sword of levies and subsidies was cleverly applied in the policy designed to introduce "clean" cars with catalytic converters. Fiscal measures were used to promote the sale of clean cars. The rates of the special tax on cars were altered in such a way that buyers of clean cars obtained a discount of between 850 and 1,700 Dutch guilders. The rebate on the tax rates for clean cars was financed by an overall increase in the tax rates for new cars. Klok (1991) notes that this combined system of subsidies and levies was effective. The supply of models fitted with catalytic converters from the various importers increased. The consumers took full advantage of this windfall, and increasing numbers bought cars fitted with catalytic converters. In the first three years, sales of clean cars rose faster than had been anticipated when the policy was formulated in 1985. A market share of 10 percent, 30 percent, and 45 percent had been expected in 1986, 1987 and 1988 respectively. In reality, the market share in these years was 13 percent, 46 percent, and 70 percent.

Communicative Control: Propaganda and Information

Dutch postwar thinking on the provision of government information can be divided into three stages. Immediately after the war, the aim of government information was to inform the public on the very existence of public policy in certain areas. At the end of the 1960s, the advent of the welfare state resulted in the addition of a second dimension: the authorities assisted consumers of the social welfare facilities by providing helpful information about the services. And in the early 1980s the provision of information assumed another new aspect: the authorities used information as a means of persuasion with a view to changing people's behavior and thus achieving the objectives of a democratically accepted policy.

Propaganda

According to Vogelaar (1955: 61), who may have had the experience with the German propaganda machine in mind, the variant of the manipulative communicative control model—namely propaganda—is in principle an extremely effective instrument for altering people's behavior:

> As times become more difficult and the community feels increasingly threatened or a concerted effort is required on the part of all its members, the need for manipulative information grows. The deeper one wishes to dig in order to mobilize even the lowest echelons of society, the greater the necessity to simplify logical arguments (slogans) and emphasize emotional arguments.

In a constitutional democracy, there is quite a lot of resistance to intensive forms of persuasive communication such as indoctrination and brainwashing. The application and effectiveness of more moderate forms of persuasive government information (advertising, marketing, and public relations) also prove in practice to be limited by the resistance which these forms of communication arouse among the general public. Among Dutch government information officials, there is a debate between those who stress the need for strictly neutral modes of government information and those who want to use more persuasive information. The view taken by the advocates of neutral government information is that if individuals are not merely provided with neutral information but are also cajoled and persuaded, this threatens their ability to form an independent opinion and thus also undermines the basis of democratic decision-making. In view of these forms of resistance towards persuasive information programs, it is perhaps hardly surprising that nowadays those who provide information for the Dutch government prefer to be known as "information officers" rather than as "propagandists."

Information Programs

Since the use of propaganda arouses public resistance, the alleged effectiveness of this medium (as outlined, for example, by Vogelaar above) is seldom actually realized. However, the literature on the effectiveness of information provided to increase knowledge—the stimulative variant of the communicative control model—also presents a rather gloomy picture. Hyman and Sheatsley (1947) argue that mass media information campaigns often fail because there is always a significant amount of people who are not reached and it is mainly people who are already interested in the subject who obtain the most information. Furthermore, people tend to gather information which confirms their existing attitude, they interpret the same information differently, and information by no means always changes people's attitudes. Advocates of the so-called knowledge-gap theories (Tichenor, Donohue, and Olien 1970; Gaziano: 1983) even argue that information campaigns tend to strengthen rather than weaken the existing unequal division of information. A Dutch study by van der Haak (1972) on the introduction of the National Assistance Act (Bijstandswet) in the period 1962–1968 confirms this proposition. The government information provided as a service to get the public acquainted with this act, widened rather than narrowed the existing knowledge gap between members of the public.

The effectiveness of information campaigns designed to increase knowledge is usually small. In view of these characteristics, it is hardly surprising that analysts attribute to motives other than those of effectiveness the choice by public authorities of the information instrument. Despite its limited effectiveness, such information does have various other attractive qualities. Dahme and Grunow (1980: 139) observe that information campaigns are an ideal instrument for pursuing a symbolic policy. They enable the authorities to bring their activities in a positive way to the attention of the public without inducing any actual changes. Information is relatively cheap and has a high profile. It seems that the use of information campaigns, which are so often ineffective, can be explained by the desire to obtain political support.

Communicative Give-and-Take

The more informative and instructive ("knowledge-augmenting") campaigns are generally ineffective, but because of their high profile they promote the idea that the authorities take the given objective seriously. They increase the legitimacy of a policy. At the same time, the more motivating and promotional ("preference-manipulating") campaigns fail to realize their high potential effectiveness because such forms of information-transfer arouse opposition among the public. The combination of the two essential elements ("knowledge-augmenting" versus "preference-manipulation") in a single communication campaign should theoretically enhance the legitimacy and effectiveness of a policy. The communication should contain both an informative and instructive aspect on the one hand and a motivating and promotional aspect on the other hand.

Naturally, it is scarcely possible to define the instructive and manipulative part of a communicative message with any accuracy. Between the extremes of purely stimulative information on the one hand and purely repressive propaganda on the other, there are countless different communicative forms such as education, advice, marketing, public relations, and advertising. However, as the next case will illustrate, an analysis carried out by reference to these two poles of the communicative control model can throw an interesting light on the present functioning of the Dutch government's communication strategy.

In recent years, the number of Dutch television and radio ads has increased and their tone has become more "persuasive." The characteristics of manipulative communication listed by Vogelaar ("simplification of logical arguments (slogans) and emphasis on emotional arguments"), have therefore been much more evident in the increasingly intrusive television ads referring to available government information leaflets. Examples are the anti-vandalism ads which show young vandals wearing nappies (voice-over: "Vandalism is *so* childish!"), the anti-shoplifting ads which depict shoplifters as rats (voice-over: "Shoplifting. You should just see yourself.") and the anti-sexual violence ads which show obtrusive men being put in their place by assertive women (voice-over: "Sex is natural. But should never be taken for granted.").

Although this approach to government information ads is in principle effective, there are increasing objections to it. The debate on the 1992 budget of the Ministry of General Affairs, under which the Government Information Department and hence the ads for government information leaflets come, was dominated almost entirely by the discussion of television and radio ads, posters, and brochures in which the government tries to influence the behavior of the public. The discussion mainly concentrated on whether it was not all a bit too much for the public, and whether the campaigns did not impinge too much on one another, as Prime Minister Lubbers suggested at the start of the debate. Members of Parliament of all political parties expressed the view that government information should be cooler, more factual, and more practical. The general feeling that "patronizing" television ads had overstepped the mark was represented very graphically by Mr. Mateman, a member of the Christian Democrat party, who said:

> If you go home for a meal and leave the TV on, you first hear that you shouldn't smoke too much. During the meal the authorities warn you that your food shouldn't contain too much fat. And at the end of the meal you're instructed to close the curtains. Before you go to bed, you're told that sex is okay provided there's no violence.

Opportunities and Limitations of an Instrument Doctrine

The central thesis of this chapter has been that the communitive, economic, and judicial control models each have a stimulative and repressive mode. The stimulating, rewarding modes of these three control models (information programs, subsidies, and covenants) enlarge the alternatives of behavior. They promote the political support and legitimacy of a policy. The repressive, punishing modes (propaganda, levies, and prohibitions) limit the alternatives of behavior. They contribute to the change of behavior in the desired way and therefore to the realization of the goals of a policy. In order to have an accepted and effective policy, governments strive to combine both stimulating and repressive policy instruments. Policymakers should simultaneously "give and take" by choosing different mixes of policy instruments.

For a full understanding of the elaborated "give-and-take strategy," it is important to be aware of the opportunities and limitations of the approach. In our view, the use of this taxonomy of policy instruments offers great opportunities for policymakers. It allows for a quick and systematic comparison of types of instruments and their effects. Thus policymakers can map out the basis of a feasible and effective policy by using a particular package of stimulative and repressive policy instruments. In optimizing the stimulative and repressive elements by packaging the instruments, the policymaker will have to opt for the lesser of two evils. On the one hand, a repressive instrument arouses so much public resistance that it will be difficult to implement, and therefore will be not effective. On the other hand, a stimulating instrument, which is accepted by the public and has a large legitimacy, will not really lead to instrument-induced changes of the desired behavior. The balanced package of stimulation and repression instruments is often one of the factors most susceptible of manipulation by policymakers in order to influence the feasibility of a policy. It is therefore a package which can barely be missed in practice.

The application of the give-and-take strategy also has some limitations. It is important to realize that the proposition is a model-like approach to reality. First of all, the stimulative or repressive character of a specific policy instrument is by no means easy to determine in reality, because there is a grey area between the two extreme poles of stimulation and repression of the three control models. Second, in the case of explaining the legitimacy of a policy instrument, factors other than the type of policy instrument (repressive or otherwise) play an important role (see the Introduction). Third, the strategy is essentially "institution free." In recent literature the importance of the institutional setting for the functioning of policy instruments is stressed more and more. Arentsen (see ch. 9) stresses the need for "linking public policy and organizational theory." Leeuw (1992) stresses the cohabitation of "institutional analysis and effect measurement." Frey (1990) concludes that "institutions matter" and Ostrom (1991) observes that "institutional details are important."

This explicit recognition of the opportunities and limitations of an instrument doctrine is of great importance in preventing political misuse of scientific research. The history of economic theory offers useful lessons. To estimate the status of a instrument doctrine, the conclusions of Hennipman (1977: 7273) concerning the status of economic theory is very memorable:

> In addition to academic insight, qualities such as experience, common sense, good judgement, feeling for relationships and other virtues possessed by a good politician will be essential for an effective policy, and it will have to be accepted that notwithstanding all the good intentions and efforts the theoretical optimum—even measured by reference to the welfare function of the government—will be remain a Fata Morgana."

References

Balch, G.I. 1980. "The Stick, the Carrot and Other Strategies: A Theoretical Analysis of Governmental Intervention," in J. Brigham and P.W. Brown (eds.), *Policy Implementation: Penalties or Incentives*, pp. 4368. Beverly Hills: Sage.

Barry, M.P.B. 1979. *Hayek's Social and Economic Philosophy*. London/Basingstoke: MacMillan.

Bressers, J.Th.A. 1988. "A Comparison of the Effectiveness of Incentives and Directives: The Case of Dutch Water Quality Policy," in *Policy Studies Review* 7(3): 500–519.

Dahme, H.J., and D. Grunow. 1983. "Die Implementation persuasiver Programme," in R. Mayntz (ed.), *Implementation Politischer Programme II: Ansätze zur Theoriebildung*, pp. 117–141. Opladen: Westdeutscher Verlag.

Doelen, F.C.J. van der. 1989. *Beleidsinstrumenten en energiebesparing: de toepassing en effectiviteit van voorlichting en subsidies gericht op energiebesparing in de industrie van 1977 tot 1987*. Enschede: University Twente (diss.).

Doelen, F.C.J. van der and G.P.A. Bakker. 1991. "De terugtredende overheid: het consumentenbeleid," in *Openbaar Bestuur*, no. 8, pp. 2327.

Frey, B.S. 1983. *Democratic Economic Policy-Making: A Theoretical Introduction*. Oxford: Martin Robertson.

———. 1990. "Institutions Matter: The Comparative Analysis of Institutions," in *European Economic Review 34*, pp. 443–449.

Gaziano, C.G. 1983. "The Knowledge Gap: An Analytical Review of Media Effects," in *Communication Research* 10(4): 447–486.

Geelhoed, L.A. 1983. *De interveniërende staat: aanzet voor een instrumentenleer*. '_-Gravenhage: Staatsuitgeverij.

Haak, C.P.M. van der. 1972. *Bekend maken en bekend raken: evaluatie van de eerste vijf jaar overheidsvoorlichting van de Algemene bijstandswet (1962–1967)*. 's-Gravenhage: Staatsuitgeverij.

Hennipman, P. 1977. "Doeleinden en criteria der economische politiek," in J. van den Doel and A. Heertje (eds.), *Welvaartstheorie en Economische Politiek*, Alphen aan den Rijn, pp.17–113 Brussel: Samson.

Hood, C.C. 1983. *The Tools of Government*. London/Basingstoke: MacMillan.

Hyman, H.H., D. Sheatsley. 1947. "Some Reasons Why Information Campaigns Fail," in *Public Opinion Quarterly* 11: 412–425.

Klok, P-J. 1989. *Convenanten als instrument van het milieubeleid*. Enschede: Twente University.

———. 1991. *Een instrumententheorie voor milieubeleid. De toepassing en effectiviteit van beleidsinstrumenten*, (diss.). Enschede: Twente University.

Koopmans, T. 1970. "De rol van de wetgever," in *Honderd jaar rechtsleven*, pp. 221–235. Zwolle: Tjeenk Willink.

Leeuw, F.L. 1992. *Produktie en effectiviteit van overheidsbeleid: Institutionele analyse en effectmeting*. 's-Gravenhage: Vuga.

Mayntz, R., ed. 1983. *Implementation politischer Programme II: Ansätze zur Theoriebildung*. Opladen: Westdeutscher Verlag.

Nagel, S.S. 1975. "Incentives for Compliance with Environmental Law," in S.S. Nagel (ed.), *Improving the Legal Process*, pp. 341–356. New York: D.C. Heath and Company.

Ostrom, E. 1991. "Rational Choice Theory and Institutional Analysis: Toward Complimentarity," in *American Political Science Review* 85: 237–243.

Paisley, W.J. 1981. "Public Communication Campaigns: The American Experience," in R.E. Rice and W.J. Paisley (eds.), *Public Communication Campaigns*, pp. 15–40. Beverly Hills: Sage.

Ricketts, M. 1985. "The Subsidy As a Purely Normative Concept," in *Journal of Public Policy* 5(3): 401–411.

Ru, H.J. de. 1987. *Staat, markt en recht: de gevolgen van privatisering voor het publiekrecht*. Zwolle: Tjeenk Willink.

Schuyt, C. 1985. "Sturing en recht," in M.A.P. Bovens and W.J. Witteveen (eds.), *Het Schip van Staat: Beschouwingen over recht, staat en sturing*, pp. 113–124. Zwolle: Tjeenk Willink.

Tichenor, P.J., G.A. Donohue, and C.H. Olien. 1970. "Mass Media Flow and Differential Growth in Knowledge," in *Public Opinion Quarterly* 34(2): 159–170.

Vermeulen, W.J.V. 1988. "De effectiviteit van een subsidie bij multi-instrumentele beleidsvoering: regionaal zware metalenbeleid als voorbeeld," in *Beleidswetenschap* 2(4): 345–359.

Vogelaar, G.A.M. 1955. *Systematiek en spelregels van de overheidsvoorlichting* (diss.). 's-Gravenhage: Staatuitgeverij.

Part II

Choice and Context

6

Choosing the Right Policy Instrument at the Right Time: The Contextual Challenges of Selection and Implementation

Ray C. Rist

In the abstract, the situation should not be that difficult. The policymaker faces the emergence of a policy problem that requires a policy response, a search for a solution. This is what policy-making is all about—being proactive, diagnosing the condition, and finding ways to solve problems before they get out of hand. After all, there are an array of tested and long-standing policy instruments available from which the policymaker can choose to address the problem. Should the response involve subsidies, loans, regulations, direct service, penalties, information, the use of force, or tax credits, to name but eight among many possibilities?

The policymaker picks one, or a cluster of several, to appropriately respond to the problem at hand. With the choice made, the baton is then passed to those responsible for implementation of the selected policy. Implementation takes place according to the blueprint for the selected instrument. The problem is contained, maybe even solved, and the policymaker moves on. Substantive policy goals are translated into concrete actions with demonstrable results.

In reality, it seldom if ever happens this way.

Every link in this long causal chain is in continual danger of breaking. Policy-making is neither so rational or so linear.

The views expressed herein by Ray C. Rist of The World Bank Group are his own, and no endorsement by the World Bank Group is intended or should be inferred.

What is faced, instead, is the chaos of political agendas, confusion over objectives, contradictions in political messages, partial understandings of the societal conditions, self-aggrandizement among the political actors, cross-currents of desired economic and political outcomes, organized groups of stakeholders, and more or less capable and committed public-sector bureaucratic systems. This is the world the policymaker faces when a problem arises. Making a decision and moving in any direction is never to be taken for granted. (Becoming risk-averse in such a political arena is entirely predictable and even rational.) But presuming some decision will be made, that is, a policy instrument needs to be chosen to address the condition, how and why is the selection made?

This chapter will focus on the political and organizational contexts in which decisions are made regarding the choice of one or more instruments to address a condition presuming to require a policy response. Two central themes will frame the chapter. First, there is the matter of how the policy problem is understood and what resolution is desired. The definition of the situation as well as the presumed remediation or resolution shape the political and institutional options available to the policymaker. A causal analysis is essential to the selection of a policy instrument. Stated differently, what is the context in which the policymaker strives to pick the right instrument in the hope of achieving the desired effect.

The second theme in this chapter is that of the context for implementation. Once a policy instrument is selected, there is the matter of it being operationalized. Choosing the right instrument but poorly implementing it is a prescription for a failed policy initiative. The likelihood of successful implementation (or not) of a selected instrument plays back into the original selection process. Here the potential trade-offs become apparent. Does one choose a weaker or less appropriate instrument where there is some confidence that it can be implemented and at least some change can be anticipated? Or does one take the risk of choosing a more robust instrument where the implementation difficulties are considerably greater and the likelihood of success more tenuous, but with a greater possibility of impact on the problem if successfully implemented?

Governments have to make choices all the time. In a reified fashion, the policymaker faces the choices embedded in a two-by-two table:

While the immediate reaction is to say that the box in the upper left corner (table 6.1) is where one ought to be, the message of this chapter

TABLE 6.1
Selecting a Policy Tool—The Policymaker's Choice

Robustness of Instrument	Likelihood of Implementation	
	High	Low
High		
Low		

is that such a decision can only be made in light of an understanding of the context of the problem, the array of available instruments, the trade-offs of effectiveness and efficiency, the capabilities of the implementing institution, the political and fiscal costs of selecting a particular instrument, and the different constituent pressures faced by the policymaker. In short, things are not always as they appear.

The Framing of the Policy Response

A strength of this book is that it makes clear the range of policy instruments available to the policymaker and how such instruments can address different policy agendas. Further, the contextual analysis of the selection and implementation of different instruments allows for an analysis of the multiple assumptions embedded in that instrument vis-à-vis (1) how the policy problem is defined and addressed; (2) the targets of the policy and how the instrument will effect the targets; and (3) the presumed costs and benefits from implementing the instrument. (McDonnell and Grubb 1991). Each instrument carries in its construction and application more or less unique answers to these three sets of assumptions. Elmore (1987: 175) echoes this view when he writes:

> ...certain types of problems predictably bring into play certain responses from policy makers; these responses, which we call instruments, entail certain operating characteristics, as well as certain distinctive design and implementation problems, which can be anticipated by analysis in a rudimentary and useful way; and certain instruments "fit" with certain problems and objectives better than other instruments.

In working through the analysis of when and why policymakers choose one instrument instead of several others, it is important to be mindful of the fact that the larger and more complex the policy issue, the less likely that the policymaker controls the context in which the selection has to be made. In this sense, the policymaker, particularly at the national or federal level, is operating within a set of constraints that are often external to their own sphere of influence. Our point of reference here are democratic societies, not those that are authoritarian. Policymakers, for example, cannot directly shape the forces of the global economy, or the explosion in information, or the climatic changes evident in global warming.

It is a matter of contention as to whether policymakers have more direct influence over the context as the scope of the issue or policy problem narrows. But whether local policymakers have more discretion and range of action than do national leaders is not the issue here. (It will only be a matter of degree in any event.) Policymakers operate in an environment in which they often have little to no influence in shaping the context that limits their policy options.

Indeed, the analysis by Howlett (1991) of "policy styles" in three countries suggests that policymakers in these three countries are politically and culturally constrained by state-society relations existing in each nation. The policy process is thus one of adaptation and incrementalism—finding ways to respond to problems within existing constraints and political assumptions. The proposition of different governments having preferences for certain types of instruments, based on their individual state-society relations, is borne out in the present collection of case studies as well.

Instrument choice is context bound. Thus the chapters here as well as the analyses by others of when and why different countries tend to opt for different instruments do not lend themselves to the basis for any separate theory of political life. Rather, the study of policy instruments in general and of the rationale for the selection of any individual instrument over and against another must, in Howlett's phrase, "exist as a part of a more general theory of national public policy making." (Howlett 1991: 15)

The Selection of the Policy Instrument(s)

It is not the intent here to move toward a general theory of national public policy making, but rather to go in the opposite direction towards a discussion of how the selection of a particular policy instrument, the diagnosis of the problem at hand, and the desired policy objective come together. This relation is often far more messy in reality than depicted here. Policymakers face a situation where the problem is not well un-

derstood, where the choice of instruments is constrained and the consequences not all that predictable, and where the policy objectives are
multiple, perhaps vague, and even at cross purposes (Rist 1995). Note
also that the term "instrument" is not equated with the term "policy."
They are different. Policies have multiple components, one of which is
the instrument(s) selected to achieve desired ends. Policy formulation
involves instrument choice. As Elmore (1987: 175) notes:

> ...we recognize the fact that policies are typically composed of a variety of instru-
> ments, and frequently the logic by which these elements are stuck together has
> more to do with coalition politics than with their operating characteristics, or their
> basic understanding of expected effects. Sometimes, however, policies form a
> more coherent package, combining what might seem at first like incompatible
> elements in a way that carries a distinctive message and considerable impact.

To rephrase Elmore and to reiterate the point made by Vedung in
chapter 1, any given policy may include multiple instruments. In fact, it
is more likely than not that there will be a cluster of instruments packaged together as part of the policy response to the problem or condition. If the policy has multiple objectives, there is a high probability
that there will be multiple instruments. Perhaps the most complete discussion on this issue of packaging policy instruments is found in chapter 5 by van der Doelen.

This general proposition appears to hold, regardless of whether the
problem and its policy response is defined in individual or institutional
terms. Seldom, for example, is a single "stick" instrument sufficient to
address a problem at an individual level, be that poor educational performance, criminal behavior, driving while intoxicated, failing to pay
the rent or mortgage on one's house, or spousal abuse.

The reverse seems no less the case. Seldom will a single "carrot"
also be sufficient to motivate or ensure the desired behavior of an individual, a group, or an organization. And if it is difficult to change behaviors of individuals with a single instrument, how much less can one
anticipate that a complex organization or bureaucracy will change its
behavior, based on a single instrument. Packaging instruments as part
of the policy response simply reflects the contextual reality of how one
brings about change, whether in individuals or in institutions.

The political context for the selection of a policy instrument is that
of policy formulation. It is in the formulation phase that a set of in-
structions are transmitted from the policymakers to the implementers
that spell out the intent of the policy, its objectives, desired effects, and

the means of achieving them. (Cf. Nakamura and Smallwood [1980].) Consider this description of the context for policy formulation from McDonnell and Grubb:

> Policies are designed in a political environment shaped by policymaker's ideology and interests, constituent pressures, and a variety of fiscal and institutional constraints. Those facts lead policymakers to view some problems as more worthy of their attention than others, influence how they define the problems to be addressed, and cause them to prefer some policy instruments over others. For example, ideology or interest may prompt officials to define a policy problem as the need to provide additional services to groups inadequately served by existing programs. A different set of interests and ideology might lead other policy makers to view the problem of as one of increasing U.S. competitiveness, and to consider distributional issues less important. In both cases, however, policymaker's preferences are tempered by the need to reach compromises that ensure legislative enactment and by a variety of other constraints such as the availability of resources and the competing demands of other policy arenas. (1991:9)

This chapter began with an observation that the policy world is not neat and tidy, it is messy. But even so, this does not dismiss the need for the policymaker to try and understand the context in which events and conditions appear that require a response. Working in an environment that is neither highly rational nor linear does not mean that there is no necessity of appraisal and analysis. Quite the opposite. Effective policymaking in such an environment requires bringing to bear what information and insight one can if there is to be some possibility of successfully impacting the emergent problem (cf. Rist 1994).

It is here that we come to the issue of evaluation and its role in informing the selection of one or more policy instruments. The analysis that policymakers need in developing a policy response is evaluative—both retrospective and prospective. There is an essential requirement in this process to scan the political arena and ask:

- What is the current condition?;
- Is it generating a real or perceived problem?;
- Who it is that thinks they have the problem?;
- Why is the present status quo not working or acceptable?;
- What is the desired outcome or condition?;
- How big is the gap between what is and what is sought?;
- What is known of causes and potential solutions?;
- Has the problem appeared before and if so, what approach was taken to address it?;
- How well or not did prior efforts succeed?;

- What options (choice of policy instruments) are available?;
- What constraints (organizational, fiscal, etc.) exist on the selection of possible instruments?; and
- Is there the political will to act?

These are indicative of the evaluation questions to be asked in the formulation of a policy response and the selection of policy instruments.

A reading of both Elmore's and Howlett's work suggests that how these questions are approached and addressed generates a distinctive "policy style" for different countries. These questions establish the context for political action. Their answers help frame the actual political response.

One key aspect of the instrument selection process that merits further attention here involves the antecedent issue of how the problem is defined. (If there is any sequence to this activity of policy formulation, it would be that instrument selection follows problem definition, not vice versa.) The definition of the problem is presumed to drive the policy response. But there are enough instances in the literature of failed policy initiatives to suggest that the failure is not in the crafting of the instrument or in its implementation, but in the prior failure to correctly assess the nature of the problem itself. Indeed, McDonnell and Grubb suggest three possible explanations for why disjunctures exist between the problem definition and subsequent instrument implementation and effects. They posit:

> First, policy design is often hampered by analysts' and policymakers' inability to diagnose a problem correctly. A problem that appears to stem from inadequate incentives may actually be caused by a lack of capacity; or a seeming need for more stringent or uniform performance standards may actually mask deep-rooted institutional problems that only a wholesale change in organizational structures can remedy.
>
> Second, an inappropriate match between problem definition and the instrument selected may also reduce the likelihood that policies will produce their intended effects. Policymakers often rely on instruments with a short time frame when the problem is the need to build long-term individual and institutional capacity...The reason for not choosing a capacity-building instrument is often political: Capacity building tends to be less visible than other instruments, and its payoff is typically distant and uncertain.
>
> Finally, inconsistency in problem definition across policy actors and governmental levels is a particular problem in an arena as fragmented and decentralized as education and training. Inconsistency may result from disparate beliefs about what constitutes appropriate roles for different governmental levels, or from different incentive structures, constituent pressures, and operating responsibilities. (1991:10–11)

The point here is not inconsequential. Insufficient attention to and inadequate or inaccurate definition of the problem to be addressed does not bode well for eventual policy success. The cases in the present book are noteworthy by their exception, save for one of the cases from the United States. To wit, there is a clear understanding in the cases reported of the problem being faced by the policy community in Canada, Korea, Sweden, Belgium, The Netherlands, and the United Kingdom. Problem definition appears justified and well-supported. Further, the link to the selected policy instrument can be clearly understood. In the case of the GSEs in the United States, there is an ambiguity of purpose that comes from a lack of a clear mission. They have remained static for so long that they face the possibility of obsolescence. Their mission as a quasi-public, quasi-private institution is increasingly vague, redundant, and ambiguous. Thus the urge of the GSEs to redefine themselves and break out of their present cul-de-sac, that is, completely privatize, reduce government oversight, and compete in new fiscal markets.

Policy Targets and Policy Effects

In the literature to date on policy instruments, there is one area that is often overlooked and where little research exists. This is the area of how the targets of instruments in fact behave and react to these same instruments. The context of policy instrument selection necessarily needs to take into account the political character and ideology of those making the selection, as well as logistics, fiscal costs, administrative burden, anticipated benefits, time frame, institutional capacity of the implementing institution, and so forth. But there is also a need to carefully assess who are the intended targets of the instruments, what is known of their attitudes, behaviors, motivations, and previous reactions to policy initiatives directed at them.

Policymakers may think they know what message they intend to send and what behavioral or institutional responses they wish to shape with the selection and implementation of an instrument. Yet there are more than enough examples of where instruments have been unsuccessful in bringing about the desired outcomes. All of the reasons discussed earlier still hold as to why the initiative was less than successful, for instance, weak design, poor institutional capability, lack of political will, and so forth. But if the policymakers are unaware or misinformed as to the values, beliefs, behaviors, and incentive systems of the intended recipients of the instruments—the targets—the initiative is likely to have a poor rate of success.

My own experience suggests this happens more often than we may wish to acknowledge. A government ministry or agency will undertake an initiative, working long and hard to carefully craft the instrument, secure the funding, arrange facilities and staff, build the necessary political support, ensure coordination with other units to avoid bureaucratic turf battles and duplication, and launch the effort with great enthusiasm. But amidst this flurry of effort, no one talks to the intended recipients. They are the silent and unacknowledged partners in this scheme. To say this creates vulnerabilities and risks for the policy initiative is to state the obvious. Holding only presumptions about how individuals or organizations will behave gives the policymakers just that—presumptions. Consider this description from McDonnell and Grubb:

> The selection of policy targets reflects the way policymakers view the incentive structures of those whose behavior they are trying to influence. Each instrument contains assumptions about the capabilities and incentives of its targets that shape responses to policy and, ultimately, the effectiveness of the programs. Politicians who choose to use mandates and inducements assume that if the right incentives (either negative or positive) are offered, targets have the capacity to act in accordance with the policymakers' expectations. Use of these instruments also assumes that policymakers can obtain reliable and valid information about whether targets are performing in a way that is consistent with their expectations. (1991: 11)

Introducing the recipient or target of an instrument into the contextual analysis creates a triadic relationship among the policy problem, the policy instrument, and the policy target. It is this triad that shapes the contextual study of policy instruments. Furthermore, it suggests both the parameters and vulnerabilities of any policy initiative. The parameters are formed in that the triadic relation is the focus and domain of the analysis. Each leg of the triad is shaped by and interacts with the other two components. The understanding of the policy problem is shaped by how the policymaker views the target population and also present and prior experiences with policy instruments that addressed this problem. The focus on instruments is linked to both the definition of the problem and the presumptions about the targets of that instrument. Finally, the behaviors and values of the target population help define the policy problem as well as influence the decision on which instrument to employ to impact the target.

With respect to this last point, it is also important for the policy initiative to establish the parameters of success, given that it is unlikely that the deployment of an instrument (or instruments) will achieve 100 percent compliance by the intended target. The target group will have its own agenda, its own self interest, its own context within which to respond—or not. Thus a policymaker who presumes complete compliance is most likely to be disappointed. How much less than 100 percent change or compliance can be tolerated within the policy and still be considered acceptable? The answer to this question helps to establish the basis for thinking about a successful policy initiative. Is 80 percent compliance sufficient to be successful? Would 50 percent be tolerated? Working through these tolerance limits becomes essential if one is to know at the end if the effort was successful or not. The degree of latitude that is granted has political, organizational, and fiscal implications.

Framing the relation among these three aspects of a policy initiative as a triad also makes immediately clear the vulnerabilities inherent in any such initiative. The requirements for a successful policy thus face the critical requirement for alignment among the three components. The policy problem must be accurately defined in relation to the actual condition and situation of the target audience. The selection of the policy instrument must actually reflect the intention of the policy design and also be effective in reaching the target. If expected outcomes do not materialize, it may well be due to the weak interactional effect that the instrument had on the target. The target must also understand the policy message being sent by the instrument (stop a negative behavior, begin a desired behavior, change an operational activity in your organization, commit resources to a long-term initiative, etc.) in the way intended.

Aligning all three aspects of this triad to the point where a policy initiative has a fair chance of success is difficult and ought not be taken for granted. Indeed, it is in some areas so seldom that successful instances become the gist of case studies. It might also be noted that the alignment of these components is not sufficient for successful policy outcomes. Alignment is a necessary condition. There are all kinds of externalities that can cause failure in a policy initiative, even if these three are aligned. One of the most prevalent is that of the quality, consistence, and accuracy of the implementation of the initiative.

It is to this dimension that we now turn in the last section of this chapter.

Policy-Instrument Implementation: Organizational Considerations

Successful policy implementation involves the translation of policy intent into policy action. While the failure to craft a thoughtful policy involving the choice of appropriate instruments can reasonably predict that the policy will not have the intended effects, so also can the failure to appropriately implement the policy ensure that the intended effects do not occur. Intention without execution leads nowhere.

Here again we immediately come to the issue of alignment—this time between policy design and policy implementation. The implementation has to be undertaken in the context of the design and the intended effects to be achieved. If design and implementation are not aligned, the likelihood of success is greatly diminished. Again, the intent should be to align a strong design with strong implementation. What happens all too frequently instead is: (1) a strong design that is weakly implemented; (2) a weak design that is weakly implemented; or (3) a weak design that is strongly implemented. In none of these three latter situations is the outcome optimal. Yet we have enough experience with policy implementation across countries, across ministries, and across programs to know that these latter three options are the more likely. Indeed, the classic book by Pressman and Wildavsky (1984) entitled simply, *Implementation*, makes exactly this point. They write:

> Our normal expectations should be that new programs will fail to get off the ground and that, at best, they will take considerable time to get started. The cards in this world are stacked against things happening, as so much effort is required to make them work. The remarkable thing is that new programs work at all. (p. 109)

The literature on policy and program implementation is extensive. There are multiple case studies, theoretical analyses, and "how-to" manuals available for the interested reader. The intent here is to identify several factors that tie policy instruments to the contextual challenges of implementation. The rationale for this attention is that the choice of the implementing organization influences: (1) how the problem will be understood, defined, and translated into an operational program; (2) how the client population will be served; (3) the efficiency with which the policy tool is implemented; and (4) the institutional flexibility to respond to changing circumstances in the definition and condition of the problem over time. It should be stressed that "the selection of an implementing organization is a key design choice that policymakers can make" (McDonnell and Grubb 1991: 16).

The first of the contextual factors is that of institutional capacity. Successful implementation requires the capacity in one or more organizations to carry out the policy initiative in an appropriate and adequate fashion. Not all institutions necessarily have that capability, even if they are in the appropriate domains. Consider that not all hospitals are equipped or staffed to provide all medical services. Establishing a policy that requires a particular medical function in all hospitals may founder on the reality of the lack of institutional capacity to do so. Small hospitals, rural hospitals, charity hospitals, none may have the capacity to provide that which is required. The same point can be made with other sectors in the society—be these, for example, education, public welfare, job training, environmental protection, or public transportation. The point is a straightforward one, but is oftentimes overlooked in establishing new services or functions.

A related contextual factor is that of the goals of the implementing organization. Choosing a welfare or charity organization to begin a social control function when the philosophy of that organization is to empower clients to make choices for their own lives is to immediately create goal and value conflicts in the organization. Implementation is likely to suffer. Each organization has its own order and logic. It also has its own values, core beliefs, and institutional memory. The task for the policymaker is to try and select implementing agencies that share at least broad common values and goals with the intent of the policy.

Yet another contextual factor related to implementation is that of the choice of whether to work through an existing institution or to create a new one. Policymakers often find themselves confronting a problem for which no existing institution is entirely appropriate as the implementing agent. The issue may be capacity, it may be political philosophy, it may be the weakness of the management team, or any number of other possibilities. The reality is that no institution seems quite right.

The decision either to opt for an existing institution or to create a new one is politically risky, regardless of which direction one goes. To create a new organization implies: the need for funding for start-up costs; the availability of persons to organize and manage the new organization; the tolerance for a time lag in getting the new organization fully functional; the political repercussions of not selecting an existing organization (maybe with powerful constituent groups); the policy problem being addressed stays the same long enough for the new organization to address it; and finally, that there may be significant political, fiscal, and constituent problems if the new organization is not successful. There will be no place to hide for the policymaker if things go badly. The new organization is his or her creation and if the policy problem stays unresolved, the blame will be at their feet.

But ironically, an equally risky set of potential conditions face the policymaker if the choice is made to locate the policy implementation within an existing organization. The existing organization has its own political history. There will be those pleased with the prior performance of the organization and others who are not. There will be those who have confidence in the leadership of the organization and those who do not. There will be those who want to see the expansion and increased prominence of the organization and those who do not. There will also be concerns about whether the organization can readily expand. Some organizations are appropriately structured for their present responsibilities and functions. An increase in functions and responsibilities can result in the present structure becoming dysfunctional to the new tasks at hand. To reach a new stage of functional performance means a restructuring of the organization, with the multiple costs any reorganization incurs. And finally, there is the matter of selecting one existing institution over others. One organization and its constituents will be pleased; other organizations and their constituents will be displeased. There will be more losers than winners with the decision.

One other contextual factor to be noted here that impacts upon the implementation process is that of the policy and organization web within which the implementing organization is placed. Organizations, particularly those working to implement public policies, do not operate in a vacuum. They are linked in multiple ways and via multiple channels to other organizations. They also do not have unlimited range of action. Consequently, their ability to successfully implement any policy initiative must be viewed in the context of other organizations supporting or competing with them. The ability of an organization to successfully function within this web clearly influences the capacity of the organization to move in the direction intended by the policy. Some organizations (whether public or private) are more adroit in negotiating this complex set of relations than are others.

What creates a difficult situation for the policymaker in this regard is that history may or may not repeat itself. An organization accomplished in working within one set of relations and among a known set of complementary organizations may or may not do well with a new challenge that takes it out of its existing patterns. Some organizations will be more adaptable at this change than will others. Current success is not an absolute predictor of future success.

Finally, and parallel to the organizational web within which the implementing institution must operate is the policy web that also defines the range of policy action as well as the other competing or complementary policies that must be accounted for in implementation. The

creation of any new policy may create competition if not outright contradictions with existing policies and how they are being implemented.
There is an existing policy system into which a new policy is being
interjected, wanted or not. Linking existing policies and institutions to
new policies and new institutions is almost inevitably difficult. There
are likely to be political land mines everywhere.

Working to frame a policy initiative requires of the policymaker a
substantial understanding of present and past policies and how they
will support, negate, or neutralize the policy being considered. There is
a need to undertake a political/policy scan of the environment in which
the new policy is to be implemented. It is not desirable to be caught
unaware in an elaborate web.

A Final Note

The contextual understanding of when and how instruments are selected as well as when and how they are implemented suggests a highly
idiosyncratic if not unpredictable environment for the policymaker.
Political and organizational dynamics keep changing. The fluidity of
the policy environment is a given. Yet for the policymaker, decisions
continually have to be made, instruments selected, and initiatives begun. And all of this has to be done with incomplete information on
present conditions, let alone potential future consequences.

But the focus on the context does provide some help to the
policymaker. First, it allows for comparisons between that which can
be learned or gleaned from other instances and that which is unique to
the present situation. Comparisons allow for assessing commonalities
as well as differences. Any given subsidy, for example, is like all other
subsidies, like some other subsidies, or like no other subsidy—depending on the level at which one compares among them.

Second, the study of context takes the selection of a particular instrument out of the theoretical and places it in the political and practical—in the end, in the world where policymakers work and seek success.
To the question of which instrument to choose when, the answer is, it
depends. And what it depends upon is the study of context. Thus the
contextual understanding is essential to the political success of the initiative, and by extension, to the political success of the policymaker.

Third, it creates the opportunity for the policymaker to gain an overall understanding of the possibilities of success for the initiative. The
contextual study of policy instruments links policies, problems, tar-

gets, and implementation into a coherent whole. It is the lens through which to assess the alignment of these various components. The assessment of the alignment is an assessment of the likelihood or not of the success of the policy initiative. It is a probability or risk analysis.

Finally, the study of context makes clear that the selection of the implementing organization to carry forward the policy initiative is central to the success of the policy itself. Not all organizations are equally adept at implementing any particular policy instrument, or cluster of instruments. Thus the selection process to decide how the policy is to be implemented via which instruments and which organizations is central to the entire endeavor. The contextual arena in which the implementation is to take place merits careful study and evaluation. Not doing so essentially leaves the policymaker flying blind—much as would attempting to fly through a storm with no instruments.

References

Elmore, R. 1987. "Instruments and Strategy in Public Policy," *Policy Studies Review* 7(1).

Howlett, M. 1991. "Policy Instruments, Policy Styles, and Policy Implementation: National Approaches to Theories of Instrument Choice," *Policy Studies Journal* 19(2).

McDonnell, L. and W.N. Grubb. 1991. *Education and Training for Work: The Policy Instruments and the Institutions.* Santa Monica, CA.: The Rand Corporation.

Nakamura, R.T. and F. Smallwoood. 1980. *The Politics of Policy Implementation.* New York: St. Martin's Press.

Pressman, J. and A. Wildavsky. 1984. *Implementation.* 3d ed. Berkeley, CA.: University of California Press.

Rist, R.C. 1994. "Influencing the Policy Process with Qualitative Research," in N. Denzin and Y. Lincoln (eds.), *Handbook of Qualitative Research.* Thousand Oaks, CA.: Sage.

————. 1995. "Introduction," in R. Rist (ed.), *Policy Evaluation: Linking Theory to Practice.* Hants, England: Edward Elgar Publishers, Ltd.

7

Contracting-Out and Program Evaluation: A Case Study

Joe Hudson
Richard Nutter
Burt Galaway

This chapter presents two case studies of purchase-of-service contracting for a particular type of social service—treatment foster care (TFC)—in the American State of Minnesota, County of Hennepin, and the Canadian province of Alberta, Edmonton Region. The statutory bases for contracting in the two cases are described, along with federal-state-county and federal-provincial-region relations, before attention is given to planning for evaluation research on purchase-of-service contracting arrangements.

Contracting as an Economic Policy Instrument

Contracting is a type of economic policy instrument that amounts to a decision by government to buy from private agencies rather than make or deliver goods and services. In turn, government's decision to contract leads to a series of decisions about:

- What specific services are to be purchased and which, if any, are to be delivered by government.
- What agents are eligible to provide or deliver the services.
- How contract agents will be selected.
- What types of contracts will be let (cost plus contract, itemized accounting, and so forth).
- How contractors will be evaluated, and by whom.

- What standards/rules/regulations will be imposed as a condition of the contract.

Once the policy decision has been made that government will use private providers to deliver a service, a series of tasks are usually carried out:

- Preparing and distributing requests for proposals;
- Preparing and submitting responses to the request;
- Rating and selecting proposals;
- Drafting, negotiating, and processing contracts;
- Implementing the contract and delivering services;
- Monitoring and evaluating performance; and
- Renewing or terminating contracts.

While these amount to key activities carried out by the two sets of parties most directly involved in contracting—government and private agencies—other parties, such as service recipients and individual service providers may be involved, each having rights and responsibilities. The more parties involved, the more complicated a contract arrangement is likely to be and, as discussed later, the more likely it will affect program evaluation research carried out on the purchase-of-service arrangement.

Treatment Foster Care Services

Treatment foster family care programs first appeared in the United States, Canada, and England in the early 1970s with the number of programs growing dramatically during the 1980s. Annual North American Treatment Foster Family-Based Conferences began in 1986. Incorporated in 1989, the North American Treatment Foster Family-Based Treatment Association currently has membership from most American states and half the Canadian provinces.

Among key characteristics of TFC programs are:

1. The program is explicitly identified as a TFC program with an identifiable name and budget;
2. Payments are made to caregivers at rates above those provided for regular foster care;
3. Training and support services are provided to the treatment foster family caregivers;

4. A formally stated goal or objective of the program is to serve clients who would otherwise be admitted to, or retained in, a non-family institutional setting;
5. Care is provided in a residence owned or rented by the individual or family providing the treatment services;
6. The treatment foster family caregivers are viewed and dealt with as members of a treatment team.

Using these six program attributes, a recent survey obtained information on 321 TFC programs in the United States and Canada (Hudson, Nutter, and Galaway 1993). Survey results show that the programs are relatively new with almost nine out of ten established since 1980. Approximately four-fifths (79 percent) of the TFC programs were operated by private agencies. Of these, the vast majority (96 percent) were private not-for-profit organizations with only a small proportion (4 percent) operating as private for-profit TFC agencies. Typically, these private agencies contract with government to carry out such key activities as recruiting, training, and supervising foster family caregivers; accepting referrals and placing foster children with the caregivers; and providing support and supervision to the caregivers in their work with the foster children. The private agencies contract with foster caregivers to provide services to the foster children and, in this way, serve as intermediary organizations between government and the caregivers.

Study Method

To collect comparative information on government contracting for TFC services, an American and Canadian jurisdiction were chosen. The American jurisdiction is Hennepin County, Minnesota; the Canadian jurisdiction is the Edmonton Region of the Alberta Department of Family and Social Services. Both Hennepin County and the Edmonton Region have long histories with TFC; both were sites for two of the earliest and best known programs (Galaway, 1978; Larson, Allison, and Johnston 1978), and both use purchase-of-service contracts. Persons from both jurisdictions are seen as leaders in the field, holding executive positions in the North American Foster Family-Based Treatment Association.

To obtain information on TFC contracting practices in these two jurisdictions, twelve open-ended, structured interviews were carried out with both government and private agency officials in Alberta and Minnesota.

Child Welfare Policy

Public child welfare policy in the United States and Canada is carried out by two intersecting types of organizations: public social service departments (government) and private social service agencies that may be for-profit or not-for-profit. These private agencies provide various types of social services under boards of directors responsible for setting agency policy. Financial support is provided through endowments, fees, contributions, and, increasingly, government purchase-of-service contracts. Public social service agencies are operated by departments or agencies of government, staffed largely by civil service employees, whose powers and duties are determined by statute and administrative regulations.

In the last hundred years there has been a series of major shifts in responsibility for the delivery of social services in Canada and the United States. First, private agencies were largely responsible for delivering most services, then government entered the market, followed by a more recent shift back to relying on private agencies in a "re-privatization" initiative. While a number of economic instruments have been used by government, including grants/subsidies, vouchers, and franchises, since the 1960s purchase-of-service contracts have become the primary policy instrument used to transmit public funds to private social service agencies (Gibelman and Demone 1983).

Contracting for Social Services in the United States:
Federal and State Mandates

Current U.S. federal legislation for child welfare originated with the enactment of the Social Security Act of 1935. This act provided in general terms for federal funding of selected child welfare services. The legislative intent was to assist the "homeless, dependent and neglected child, and the child in danger of becoming delinquent." Between 1935 and 1961, the act was amended to increase funding levels and to change the rules for allocation of funds to the states. In 1961, for the first time, federal funding was allocated for foster care of dependent children under Title IV of the Social Security Act. This amendment allowed the states to bring needy, dependent children under the federally aided program where a court of competent jurisdiction found that foster care is in the best interests of the child. Responsibility was given to the state agency to place the child in a foster family home. In 1962, the Social

Security Act was amended to add a provision allocating funds to children placed in non-profit private child care institutions. Since 1962 these provisions have been part of the Adoption Assistance and Child Welfare Act. The 1980 amendment established a separate Foster Care and Adoption Assistance program under a new part E of Title IV of the Social Security Act. For the most part, the existing rules governing foster care were continued, as were limitations requiring that only non-profit agencies were eligible.

The use of purchase-of-service contracts is authorized and encouraged in the U.S. federal legislation and there has been a dramatic increase in the amount of Title IV-E money going to foster care (GAO 1993). Several authors have noted that purchase-of-service contracting has been the major form of state human services delivery since the late 1970s (Benton, Field, and Millar 1978; Mueller 1980; Kettner and Martin 1987). The federal Department of Health and Human Services, all fifty state social service agencies, and a sizeable proportion of municipal and county human service agencies use purchase-of-service contracting (Martin 1986; Agranoff and Pattakos 1985).

Contracting-Out for Social Services in Canada— Federal and Provincial Mandates

The key piece of federal social service legislation is the Canada Assistance Plan (CAP). Enacted in 1966, the plan authorizes the federal government to enter into agreements with the provinces and the territories to pay 50 percent of approved provincial and municipal expenditures on social assistance and social services, including child welfare. Prior to 1966, the federal government was already reimbursing provinces 50 percent of expenditures in a variety of different programs. A major aim of CAP was to achieve a more comprehensive and integrated welfare system in Canada by replacing the separate cost-sharing arrangements and extending cost sharing to services provided through child welfare agencies. Sharable expenditures are defined by rules and by maximum allowable exemptions. Payments under CAP are transfers from the federal government to provincial governments for programs that meet minimum requirements.

CAP contributions are made for welfare services when they are provided by "provincially approved agencies." These include "...any department of government, person or agency, including a private non-profit agency...." The eligibility of non-provincial agencies nominated by the provinces, such as a private agency, is reviewed by federal officials and, if found to be acceptable, listed in a schedule appended to the provincial CAP agreement. Once listed and approved, costs incurred by these agencies can be shared. As in the United States, for-profit child welfare agencies cannot be included in the federal definition of an approved agency. Each month the provinces submit claims for cost sharing that federal officials review and process for payment.

In Canada, as in the United States, there has been a trend toward provincial and municipal governments contracting with private agencies to deliver a variety of social services, so that approximately 40 percent of all provincial submissions for coverage under CAP have been private agencies (National Health and Welfare 1993). Federal-provincial administrative procedures are also similar to those used in the United States.

Hennepin County Contract Procedures

The largest of Minnesota's eighty-seven counties, Hennepin covers the City of Minneapolis and several surrounding communities, having approximately one-third of the state's 4.2 million residents. County government delivers all child welfare services.

Minnesota state government is largely responsible for setting statewide rules and transmitting Title IV-E money to the counties as quarterly reimbursement for the child welfare services delivered. Two criteria are used by state officials when making decisions about the reimbursement claims submitted by the counties: First, whether the child welfare agency that provided the services is licensed under state child placement regulations, second, whether the family is receiving assistance under the income support program, Aid To Families With Dependent Children (AFDC), or if the family might be eligible for such assistance. A check of the state listing of child placement agencies verifies the first criterion. County social service workers are responsible for determining whether a family meets the income criteria and state officials accept this decision without further investigation.

Begun as a pilot project in 1982, Hennepin became the first county in the state to contract for the purchase of TFC services from private agencies. A request for proposals was issued, and four private agencies were subsequently placed on a qualified vendors list. Two other agencies were added in later years, so that six private agencies currently have purchase-of-service contracts.

Payment procedures with contracting agencies are based on the number of placement days of service provided. The current per diem amount varies slightly between the agencies, approximating $48. Of this, each private agency then pays approximately $30 to foster family caregivers as fees, with the remaining $18 allocated for agency administration and social work staff.

Contract monitoring procedures involve both state and county officials. Statewide licensing and program standards have been set and the State Department of Human Services is responsible for conducting annual agency reviews. These statewide standards cover procedures for licensing foster parents, record keeping, case planning, and review. Hennepin County also carries out annual program reviews: usually a visit by a program office official who checks that procedures outlined in the contract have been followed and case-planning documents are complete.

Edmonton Region Contract Procedures

The population of the Edmonton Region is approximately 800,000—about one-third that of the Province of Alberta. Almost two-thirds of the regional population is in the City of Edmonton, with the remainder scattered over a mostly rural area containing a few small communities. The first TFC program in the Edmonton Region was established in 1974. This program was begun and continues to be operated directly by the government. Beginning in 1989, the government entered into a purchase-of-service contract with one private TFC agency, this was followed in 1990 by an additional contract with another agency, three more in 1991, and two more in 1992. As of April 1992, seven private agencies with 81 placement spaces had TFC contracts in the Edmonton Region. The number of TFC private agency placement spaces is projected to increase to 138 and the total contract budget from $1.7 million to $3.4 million in the next two years (McCallum 1992).

Two sets of procedures are followed in selecting purchase-of-service contractors in Edmonton. One set relates to selecting first-time contractors and follows usual contracting activities—issuing a request for proposals, reviewing proposals, selecting successful contractors, and entering into formal contracts. Potential contractors are assessed on criteria such as proposal quality, cost, and history of the agency. Annual contract renewals amount to the government announcing the amount of any payment increases, renewing existing contracts accordingly, and, as necessary, issuing a request for proposal for new contractors.

Edmonton-region officials prepare an annual contract management plan estimating the number of TFC spaces required and their cost. Officials in the corporate office of the Provincial Department of Family and Social Services review this plan and allocate funds. Once they know the amount of approved funds, regional officials then decide on the number of TFC spaces to allocate to each operating agency and the number to be tendered to new contractors.

Contract payment procedures in the Edmonton Region are based on a specified number of placements to be purchased during the year. The regional authority limits the size of each agency by specifying the maximum number of foster care placements that will be purchased, as well as the payment rate. Most of the private agencies operating in the region have a limit of eighteen placements at a specified daily rate. Agencies are paid on a quarterly basis for the eighteen placements at the rate, regardless of whether the total number of placements have actually occurred. At the end of the fiscal year, the private agencies are then responsible for reimbursing the government for the number of placement days short of the number specified in the contract. Private agencies are able to retain the administrative portion of the daily fee but must return that portion of the fee allocated to caregiver services that were not, in fact, provided. The reason for allowing private agency contractors to retain the administrative portion of the fee regardless of a contracted space being empty is based on the view that agency administrative and professional costs are largely fixed. Requiring that these funds be returned could place private agencies in the difficult position of having to lay off administrative and professional staff when placements drop much below the contracted number. In short, the payment procedures amount to a financial guarantee of a fixed dollar amount to the private agencies regardless of whether the contracted number of placement beds have been filled. However, no such guarantee is extended to the actual caregivers, the persons who take challenging youth into their homes and care for them. Caregivers are generally paid only for the days they provide care, even though they have little control over how many days of care they will be asked to provide.

Financial, programmatic, and client matters are covered in contract-monitoring procedures. Both financial managers and program supervisors participate in the initial contract negotiations. One official is then responsible for monitoring financial conditions of the contract while program matters are handled by other managers. They collect information about contracted agencies from views expressed by departmental child welfare supervisors and social workers, as well as from occasional reviews of agency operations. Departmental child welfare social workers are responsible for monitoring the care of individual children placed in TFC programs. In practice, there is no clear line that can be drawn between programmatic, client, and financial matters. Program changes will usually have financial and client implications, and vice versa. Consequently the different sets of officials have overlapping responsibilities requiring continuous checking back and forth.

Provincial Department of Family and Social Services officials play no direct role in regional contracting procedures, and only collect some monitoring information for budget-planning purposes. Provincial program standards for TFC programs are just now being developed. Therefore, the department currently has no licensing role to play with private TFC agencies.

The Rationale for Contracting-Out

Hennepin County initiated purchase-of-service contracts for TFC in 1974, the Edmonton Region in 1989. In concert with a North American trend, both have expanded their original number of contracted agencies and the total number of TFC placements. Both the county and region used standard procedures for selecting first-time contractors and routinely renew contracts annually. While both pay on a unit cost basis, the payment procedures differ. Hennepin County pays essentially for the services delivered, while the Edmonton Region pays a fixed amount for administrative and professional services to a stipulated number of placement spaces, regardless of whether the placements were filled. While paying on a strict fee-for-service basis, as done in Hennepin County, limits the financial liability of government to actual services rendered, it has obvious disadvantages for the private contractors. Smaller agencies and those beginning operations can experience financial difficulties when the number of placements is too low to cover the minimum amount needed to pay staff. The fixed-payment system established in the Edmonton Region guarantees the survival of small agencies while potentially increasing the unit cost of services. However, while the Edmonton Region payment system may increase the security of agency staff, it probably does little to increase the security of the actual caregivers who are treated as independent contractors by the agencies and have no guarantees.

Both Hennepin County and the Edmonton Region can be seen as having a package of policy instruments in place—program and foster caregiver licensing procedures as types of regulation as well as two forms of purchase-of-service arrangements. One contractual arrangement involves the county or region with the TFC agencies; the other involves the TFC agencies with the foster caregivers.

Neither Hennepin County nor the Edmonton Region has carried out any periodic program-evaluation research of their contracted TFC agencies. In Minnesota, both state and county government carry out annual program reviews, using state standards and county contract provisions as review criteria. In contrast, Alberta has no provincial standards, and program reviews are mainly concerned with financial matters. Hennepin County and the Edmonton Region both use a team approach for carrying out monitoring activities with social workers handling programmatic monitoring while fiscal monitoring is carried out by financial managers. While such a team approach reportedly predominates in purchase-of-service contracting (Gwin et al. 1980; Herman 1978; Kettner and Martin 1987), it can be complicated and lead to an impasse in making contractor compliance decisions.

In line with explanations given in the literature on contracting (Allen et al. 1989; Conant and Easton 1987; Kamerman and Kahn 1989) several reasons are given by Hennepin County and Edmonton Region officials for the decision to contract for TFC services:

1. To obtain the special program services of treatment foster family care. In 1982, Hennepin County had no experience in delivering this type of service and private agencies were operating in the area and interested in helping meet service demands. In Edmonton, the region had over fifteen years experience at operating its own TFC program. Yet, when it was decided to expand the number of TFC placements and reduce congregate care spaces, the region decided to contract for additional services, rather than expand its own program. Alberta government bias toward de-institutionalized services and favoring service contracting were dominant considerations in this decision.

2. To reduce the cost of services and improve effectiveness. Both Hennepin County and Edmonton Region had been making extensive use of residential treatment settings for challenging young persons and by the 1980s this was seen as, at best, expensive and, at worst, damaging to the young people served. TFC was seen as a more economical and effective service option for challenging young people.

3. To provide government social workers with more choice of service providers and types of services. With six purchase-of-service contracts in Hennepin County and seven in the Edmonton Region,

government social workers are free to purchase service from that agency seen as best able to meet the placement needs of particular children.

4. To reduce, or at least not increase the size of government. Since the early 1970s in Minnesota and the 1980s in Alberta, there has been a strong push to reduce and keep small the size of government. In Minnesota this was strongly reinforced in a report published by the Minneapolis Urban Coalition, an influential public policy research group, recommending that government get out of direct service delivery responsibilities, restricting itself to deciding by setting policy, but not doing the decided. Alberta has a long history of conservative governments that nevertheless sponsored a dramatic growth in public services on the basis of oil wealth in the 1970s and early 1980s. With decreased oil revenues in the mid-1980s, purchase-of-service contracting with private agencies has been seen as a way to reduce the size of government.

These reasons given by Hennepin County and Edmonton Region officials seem to reflect the same biases as found in other studies done to understand the rationale of government purchase-of-service decisions. For example, a study done by Booz-Allen and Hamilton, management consultants (1969) concluded that there were four major reasons state agencies chose purchase-of-service contracting: (1) to provide for consumer choice and satisfy unmet needs; (2) to provide services not suitable to government delivery; (3) to increase the type and amount of services provided; and (4) to convert existing programs to new federal funding sources. Another study done by Wedel (1974), looked at all fifty state social service agencies and concluded that important reasons for contracting were government-private agency relationships, increased consumer choice, flexibility of service delivery, the opportunity to provide new services to clients, availability of potential contractors, and a desire to reduce the size of the public bureaucracy. An Urban Institute study (1978) focused on the implementation of social service programs in eight states and the most frequently mentioned criterion used in making purchase-of-service contracting decisions was tradition, followed by community policies and pressures. Another study by Pacific Consultants (1979) assessed social service purchase-of-service contracting in nine states, concluding that existing capacity is the strongest reason for contracting. In Minnesota, for example, the county did not deliver TFC services and once the decision was made to provide such services, purchase-of-service contracting was chosen. In Edmonton, the government had experience delivering TFC services but appears to have decided to contract for additional needed services beyond the government's existing capacity to deliver them directly, because of a government philosophy that purchase-of-service contracting is a more efficient and effective mode of service delivery or, at least, does not appear to increase the size of government. A 1981 study reported by The American Public Welfare Association asked state social service officials to rate the relative influence of seven variables on their purchase-of-service contracting decisions.

The study concluded that only one variable—enhancement of client services—was clearly a high priority with two variables—cost savings and availability of contractors—having a mixed effect. It is important to note that, although there is some consistency of rationale favoring service delivery by private contractors, this is largely assumptive and has not been tested by systematic collection and analysis of relevant data.

Evaluation Implications for Using Purchase-of-Service Contracting in the Social Services

Planning for evaluation research means answering the following questions:

- *Who* wants *what information*?
- About *what program*?
- *When* and at *what level of confidence*?

These questions amount to clarifying who the clients are, their perspectives on the program, the questions they want addressed, and the timing and rigor of the evaluation information. Answering these questions, however, can be particularly difficult when planning for the evaluation of purchase-of-service contracting arrangements that always involve two or more sets of officials in different organizations.

As described earlier, contract arrangements for TFC in Hennepin County and Edmonton Region are complex, involving a variety of officials in different government departments carrying out a variety of intersecting activities—federal-state or provincial mandates and funding arrangements, county government in Minnesota, a local administrative unit of the provincial department as in Alberta—and the contracted agency responsible for delivery of the TFC services. Thus, in both the county and region, four organizations are involved, each having a different perspective. The presence of four stakeholder groups complicates planning for evaluation, particularly in respect to answering the

FIGURE 7.1
Organizations Involved in TFC Contracting

Federal Department	Legislative Mandate; Program eligibility standards; Cost sharing; and Monitoring
State or Provincial Departments	Legislative Mandate; Program design standards; Cost sharing; and Monitoring
County or Regional Departments	Contracting for services procedures; Monitoring for local service needs and service demands; and Program monitoring
Private Agencies	Specific program designs; Manage program operations; Plan delivery of services; Support service delivery
TFC Caregivers	Deliver the treatment services; and Provide care to challenging youth

question: What is the program to be evaluated in purchase-of-service contracting for TFC?

Figure 7.1 shows the five sets of officials in different organizations, acting to carry out specific activities with each having intended and unintended consequences for the others. The outputs of one become inputs or consequence for others. These inputs and consequences are mutually causal. For example, the nature of the federal mandate will likely have direct implications for program design, financial conditions and procedures, as well as the standards set and monitored by state or provincial officials. In addition, state or provincial activities will have consequences for county or regional purchase-of-service contracting as well as the amount and type of services actually delivered by contracted agencies (Bella 1979; Dyck 1976; Splane 1985). The converse also occurs with contracted agencies interacting and affecting county or regional and state or provincial levels of organizations.

The relationships established between the different sets of officials amount to a set of transactions in which numerous matters are continuously established, reviewed, renewed, and revised. While each set of officials operates within certain organizational and legal constraints, they also have varying degrees of freedom. How this official discretion is exercised will have further consequences so that each set of officials has effects on others, and in turn is affected by them. Any federal official in the United States or Canada with responsibilities for dealing with state or provincial counterparts can attest to the mutual causal nature of these working relationships. State and provincial officials can affect actions taken or not taken by federal officials every bit as much as the reverse. Similarly, officials in state or provincial government departments are likely to affect and be affected by their counterparts at the county and regional level. Like the others, purchase-of-service contractors will be affected by and have the potential to affect any of the three levels of government. Each level of authority—federal officials, state or provincial officials, county or regional officials, and officials from private agencies—may serve as evaluation clients. Each set of officials may have a different definition of the program, and where definitions are shared, they will likely have different perspectives on the program and therefore different questions to be answered by an evaluation. Officials will be most interested in answers to inform their own decision making and less interested in answering questions to inform decisions to be made by others. Thus, initial questions to resolve in planning an evaluation of a contracted service are: *Who is the primary client for the study? What is their perspective on the program?* and *What are their evaluation question(s)?* Planning for an evaluation can only proceed to describe the program after selecting the primary evaluation clients and learning their program perspective(s). Figure 7.2 presents the resources, activities, and immediate results of purchase-of-service contracting from the perspective of county or regional department officials. This figure is intended to be read from left to right and from top to bottom. The "immediate results" in one row provide the essential conditions for the county or region "activities" in the next row. Failure to achieve the immediate results in a row would presumably result in redoing the activities for that stage or returning to an earlier stage in the process. For example, if the request for proposal process did not result in proposals from private agencies, this process would have to be repeated because purchase of TFC contracting as outlined here could not proceed without proposals from private agencies.

Figure 7.2 presents only the perspective and activities of the county or region. Figure 7.3 shows these same steps in purchase of TFC contracting from the perspective of a private agency.

Figures 7.2 and 7.3 show different but parallel resources, activities, and immediate results for purchase of TFC contracting and serve as appropriate frameworks for examining each purchase of TFC contracting step. However, figures 7.2 and 7.3 do not make explicit the *logic* or

FIGURE 7.2
County or Region Perspective on Purchase of TFC Contracting

Resources	Activities	Immediate results
1. Program designers Contract managers	Prepare and distribute request-for-proposals (RFP process)	Proposals from private agencies
2. Contract managers	Review and select proposals	Service providers selected
3. Contract managers	Draft and negotiate contracts	Contracts with private agencies signed
4. Contract managers Money	Implement contract by providing agreed financing	Private agencies develop TFC placements
5. Youth needing TFC Social workers*	Youths are identified and placed in TFC with private agencies	Youths receive the treatment they require
6. Contract managers Social workers*	Monitor and evaluate private agency performance	Private agency strengths and deficiencies identified
7. Program designers Contract managers	Renew, modify, or terminate contracts	New or modified contracts signed or RFP process begins

* One or more supervisory levels may oversee and approve these activities.

rationale that explains why the activities will produce the immediate results in each row, or why the immediate results of one row will help the activities in the next row produce the immediate results in that row. While the rationale implied in figures 7.2 and 7.3 may appear too obvious to bother stating explicitly, the value of an explicit rationale becomes apparent when a process fails to work as expected. For example, if a contracted private agency failed to develop TFC placements, county or regional officials would want to know why. Explanations for the failure and success of agencies could be developed, studies of the selection and contract negotiation processes would test these explanations, and the processes could then be changed to increase the probability of selecting agencies and developing contracts that would lead to good TFC placements.

FIGURE 7.3
Private Agency Perspective on Purchase of TFC Contracting

Resources	Activities	Immediate results
1. Board of directors, program designers	Prepare response to request-for-proposals (RFP)	Proposal to supply TFC delivered to county or region
2. Board of directors or administration	Negotiate contract	Contract to provide TFC signed and money secured
3. Social workers*, and potential TFC caregivers	Recruit, screen, train, certify, and contract with TFC caregivers	The contracted number of TFC placements are available
4. Youth needing TFC, social workers*, and TFC caregivers	Youths are accepted for TFC placement and matched with caregivers	TFC placements filled with appropriate youths
5. Youth in TFC, social workers*, and TFC care givers	Plan, deliver, and support the care and treatment received by youth in TFC	Youths receive the care they require in TFC and caregivers are supported
6. Social workers* and TFC care givers	Monitor TFC care and report to county or region as required	County or region receives information the require
7. Directors and administration	Renegotiate contract	Support for TFC program secured for another term

* One or more supervisory levels may oversee and approve these activities.

It is important to note that figures 7.2 and 7.3 show purchase of TFC contracting from the perspectives of two organizational levels, regional or county and private agency. These figures do not address in detail the nature of TFC programs nor their effects on the lives of TFC caregivers or the youths served by TFC. Questions about detailed outcomes for caregivers and youths would require expansion of rows 5 and 6 in figure 7.2 and rows 3, 4, 5, and 6 in figure 7.3. Expanded views of the TFC programs would show recruitment, screening, training, and support of TFC caregivers in sufficient detail to identify the immediate, medium-term, and long-term outcomes that should be measured. Similarly, selecting youth, matching them with caregivers, treatment planning, and treatment delivery would be described in detail so they could be systematically documented along with the specific immediate, medium-term, and long-term outcomes for youths. Thus, different questions, about different stakeholders, and for different clients require detail about different parts of the service-contracting process and the service(s) contracted.

One might ask how this approach to evaluating purchase-of-service contracting could be applied to the rationale given by Hennepin County and Edmonton Region officials for their decisions to contract for TFC services. Hennepin County began contracting for TFC services in 1982 and had no prior experience in providing TFC services. An evaluation question they could have asked is whether contracting with private agencies for TFC services was more efficient or effective than providing TFC services directly. Answering this question would require comparative models that identified similarities and differences in the two approaches and directed the collection of relevant data.

The Hennepin County rationale is very different from the Edmonton Region rationale that was essentially ideological, government bias favoring service contracting as opposed to direct provision of service. If regional officials were responding to perceived government bias, then the evaluation questions were (a) whether their perceptions of government bias were correct and (b) whether the bias was purely ideological or based on an assumed set of relationships that could be tested by gathering data. Regional officials would be the clients of an evaluation to discover if government was biased in favor of contracting. However, discovering the basis of the bias would be of interest to persons interested in changing government policy. Since the duty of regional officials is to carry out government policy, not change it, they would not have a direct interest in knowing the bases of that policy.

The second reason given by Hennepin County and Edmonton Region officials for contracting TFC services is not strictly about contracting versus direct provision of services, but is about comparison between TFC and congregate institutional treatment. The relevant evaluation would compare these two methods of treating challenging youths. Models could be developed that would help to ensure that relevant data from both treatment methods were systematically recorded for comparison purposes.

The third reason for contracting TFC services was to provide government social workers with more choice of service providers and types of services. It is unclear why providing social workers with more choice among types of services or service providers is thought to be a good thing. The evaluators' first task would be to identify with the county and region officials just why these choices were presumed to be good. It is possible that these officials think that choice is always a good thing, an ideological or value position that is not open to empirical examination. However, these officials may think that choice among types of service will lead to social workers choosing more appropriate services for individual youths and that choice among service providers will lead to competition that will increase the quality of the services provided and the benefit received by the youths. If the latter is the case, at least four evaluation questions might be engaged: (1) Are different types of service better for different types of youths? (2) Do social workers match youths to the best service available for those youths? (3) Do private agencies provide better services if there is competition among them than that which is provided by government when it operates as a monopoly? (4) Are the benefits to youths positively related to the quality of the services they receive? Again, each of these general questions is amenable to the development of program models that would identify the data that should be systematically collected in an evaluation to answer that question. The models developed for each question would be different, although they could be addressing the same set of programs.

To reduce or at least not increase the size of government is the fourth reason given for contracting for TFC services rather than providing them directly. If size of government is measured by number of civil servants, then models could be constructed to provide a comparison between the number of civil servants per private agency TFC placement as compared to number of civil servants per government TFC placement. These models would define all of the civil servants involved in these alternate forms of service provision. The answer may seem obvious—more civil servants in the government programs—but this may not be the case. Some models for organizing service design, provision, and monitoring may require more persons to purchase services than to provide them directly. These models would have to define how much of whose time was devoted to the RFP process, the contracting process, service-provision process, and the monitoring process. Similarly, if size of government means expenditure per TFC placement rather than number of civil servants per placement, different models should be developed to direct the collection of appropriate data.

The approach to evaluating purchase-of-service contracting suggested here is not different from the approach that we suggest for evaluating other aspects of social service provision. However the details of each particular evaluation will evolve from a process that includes: (1) identifying the primary client for evaluation; (2) clearly defining, with the client, primary evaluation questions; (3) developing with the client a program description that is appropriate for answering their evaluation question(s); (4) collecting and analyzing the data identified as relevant in the program model; and (5) presenting timely and understandable results to the client that will help the client make wise decisions.

Summary and Conclusion

Purchase-of-service arrangements are always interorganizational. In this case study, federal, state or provincial, and county or regional levels of government were involved plus private agencies and private caregivers, five levels of organization to provide a service to challenging youths. Each of these levels brings different realms of authority, different perspectives, and different questions to the evaluation enterprise. An evaluation planned for specific stakeholder clients may focus exclusively on their questions, ignoring relationships among the multiple levels and perspectives present in this multilevel delivery system. General models of the entire system that identify potential interactions among the organizations can help to consider the contributions of organizations in relation to each other. For example, questions about (1) what the different organizations contribute, directly and indirectly to service delivery; (2) the impact that the structure and processes of the different organizations have on specific program operations; (3) the nature and type of coordination across the different organizational boundaries and how these support or detract from service delivery; etc. Different perspectives of the same process are presented in figures 7.2 and 7.3. When planning an evaluation of contracting for providing service, questions should not focus on only one level of organization. It is important to attempt to capture important elements from different perspectives and to identify how changes at one level may affect and be affected by other levels of organization. Critically important are the effects that organizational changes may have upon the ultimate results, the welfare to the clients served.

References

Agranoff, R. and A.N. Pattakos. 1985. *Local Government Human Services, Baseline Data Report* 47(4). Washington, DC: International City Management Association.
Allen, Joan W., K.S. Chi, K.M. Devlin, M. Fall, H.P. Hatry, andW. Masterman. 1989.

The Private Sector in State Service Delivery: Examples of Innovative Practices. Washington, DC: The Urban Institute Press.

American Public Welfare Association. 1981. *Study of Purchase of Social Services in Selected States.* Washington, DC: American Public Welfare Association.

Bella, Leslie. 1979. "The Provincial Role in the Canadian Welfare State: The Influence of Provincial Social Policy Initiatives on the Design of the Canada Assistance Plan," *Canadian Public Administration* 22(3): 439–452.

Benton, B., T. Field, and R. Millar. 1978. *Social Services—Federal Legislation versus State Implementation.* Washington, DC: The Urban Institute.

Booz-Allen and Hamilton Consulting Firm. 1969. *Purchase of Service—A Study of the Experiences of Three States in Purchase of Service under the Provision of the 1967 Amendments to the Social Security Act.* Washington, DC: U.S. Department of Health, Education, and Welfare.

Canada. Health and Welfare Department, *Part 3 of the Estimates: 1993–1994,* pp. 3–34. Ottawa, ON: Government of Canada.

Conant, Ralph W. and Thomas A. Easton. 1987. "The Entrepreneurial Approach to Privatization," in B.J. Carroll, R.W. Conant, and T.A. Easton (eds.), *Private Means Public Ends: Private Business in Social Service Delivery.* New York: Praeger.

Dyck, Rand. 1976. "The Canada Assistance Plan: The Ultimate in Cooperative Federalism," *Canadian Public Administration* 19(4): 587–602.

Galaway, B. 1978. "PATH: An Agency Operated by Foster Parents," *Child Welfare* 57(10): 667–674.

Gibelman, M. and H. Demone. 1983. "Purchase of Service: Forging Public-Private Partnership in Human Services," *Urban and Social Change Review* 16: 21–26.

Hudson, J., R. Nutter, and B. Galaway. 1994. "Treatment Foster Family Care: Development and Current Status," *International Journal of Family Care* 6(2): 280–296.

Kamerman, Sheila B. and Alfred J. Kahn, eds. 1989. *Privatization and the Welfare State.* Princeton, NJ: Princeton University Press.

Kettner, P.N. and L.L. Martin. 1987. *Purchase-of-Service Contracting.* Beverly Hills, CA: Sage.

Larson, G., J. Allison, and E. Johnston. 1978. "Alberta Parent Counsellors: A Community Treatment Program for Disturbed Youths," *Child Welfare* 57(1): 47–52.

Martin, L.L. 1986. *Purchase-of-Service Contracting for Human Services: An Analysis of State Decision Making.* Unpublished Ph.D. diss., Arizona State University, Tempe.

McCallum, L. 1992. *Residential Redesign Work Plan.* Edmonton, AB: Alberta Family and Social Services.

Mueller, C. 1980. "Five Years Later—A Look at Title XX: The Federal Billion Dollar Social Services Fund," *The Grantsmanship Center News* 8 (Oct./Nov.): 27–68.

Pacific Consultants. 1979. *Title XX Purchase of Service—A Description of States' Service Delivery and Management Practices.* Washington, DC: U.S. Department of Health, Education, and Welfare.

Splane, Richard B. 1985. "Social Welfare Development in Alberta: The Federal-Provincial Interplay," in J. S. Ismael (ed.), *Canadian Social Welfare Policy,* pp. 173–187. Montreal, PQ: Institute of Public Administration of Canada.

U.S. General Accounting Office. 1993. *Foster Care Services to Prevent Out-of-Home Placements are Limited by Funding Barriers.* Washington, DC.

Wedel, K.R. 1974. "Contracting for Public Assistance Social Services," *Public Welfare* 32: 57–62.

8

Government-Sponsored Enterprises as a Credit Allocation Tool in the United States

*Edward J. DeMarco**
Ray C. Rist

Consider this quote from a book by Bosworth, Carron, and Rhyne:

> Federal credit programs are among the least understood areas of government involvement in the economy. In these programs, the government acts much like a bank, raising funds or directing their flow to provide credit on terms it specifies to borrowers it selects. In the sheer volume of the loans there is at least the potential for a substantial impact on the allocation of income and resources within the economy. In several areas—especially housing, education, and agriculture—the loans constitute the principal tool of federal policy. Yet the goals of the programs are often ill-defined and contradictory, and despite the substantial cost to taxpayers, little or no effort has been made to evaluate either the current need for such programs or their effectiveness. (1987: 1)

The authors go on to identify essentially four distinct policy instruments that are used in providing government credit assistance: loan guarantees, direct loans, tax-exempt state and local bonds, and government-sponsored enterprises.[1] The focus of analysis in this chapter will be on the last of these instruments—the government-sponsored enterprises. GSEs differ from other federal credit instruments in that GSEs are privately owned institutions but with charters that limit their activities to a specified public purpose.

The chapter is divided into five sections: the role of GSEs as a policy tool in the United States, the rationale for government intervention in private capital markets, an overview of the creation and evolution of

---

*The authors wish to acknowledge with thanks helpful comments on a previous draft made by James L. Bothwell and Thomas H. Stanton.

each GSE, an assessment of current policy issues regarding GSEs, and an analysis of their effectiveness and current utility as a policy tool. It is our intent to link what we know of GSEs via evaluation efforts to the current thinking on the future of GSEs as a policy tool. In this way, we hope to provide an understanding of GSEs as a rather unique policy tool that has been used on only limited occasions, but with immense financial and political implications.

Government-Sponsored Enterprises in the United States

Overview of GSEs

Between 1916 and 1988, the U.S. government chartered six GSEs. GSEs are privately owned but their federal charter restricts their lending to a particular sector in the economy. Tom Stanton (1992) points out that this mix of private ownership and restricted public charter makes GSEs analogous to mercantile organizations commonplace from the fifteenth to eighteenth centuries in Europe and found today in many Latin and South American countries. Table 8.1 lists the six GSEs and identifies the sector served by each.

TABLE 8.1
An Overview of GSEs
(Dollars in billions)

Name	Created	Year Made Private	Sector Served	Size as of 1990
Farm Credit System	1916	1968	Agriculture	$64
Federal Home Loan Bank System	1932	1951	Housing	$166
Federal National Mortgage Association	1938	1968	Housing	$421
Federal Home Loan Mortgage Association	1970	1970	Housing	$357
Student Loan Marketing Association	1972	1972	Education	$41
Federal Agricultural Mortgage Association	1988	1988	Agriculture/ Rural Housings	N/A

Source: U.S. General Accounting Office 1990, 1991 and Stanton 1991a

As publicly chartered institutions, GSEs have special privileges and associations with the federal government not found other private financial institutions. Each GSE shares most of the following attributes:

- The President appoints some members of the board of directors;
- The U.S. Department of the Treasury has final approval over issuance of debt securities;
- A backstop line of credit with the U.S. Treasury;
- Certain tax exemptions on income as well as tax exemptions on interest income earned by holders of GSE debt securities;
- Exemptions from securities registration requirements with the Securities and Exchange Commission;
- Attributes that add liquidity to a GSE's debt securities and asset-backed securities such as eligibility to serve as collateral for public deposits and no restrictions on the amount of such securities held by an insured depository institution.

Each GSE also has a federal regulator that oversees its safety and soundness. As described below, this oversight has not always been rigorous.

GSEs Fall between Government Corporations and Private Firms

In a lecture at The Johns Hopkins University in April of 1993, Tom Stanton posited that one could position GSEs within a continuum of organizational types as follows:

Private companies—GSEs—Government Corporation—Government Agency

This continuum begins on the left with what we would consider to be traditional private companies that are incorporated and operate within the guidelines of state laws, and are able to conduct any form of business or activity they wish within legal boundaries. They are profit-seeking enterprises that can (and must) adapt and modify their business to changing circumstances and opportunities. They have few protections, but also few constraints.

Close to them, but clearly different, are GSEs. As noted, GSEs can only do what their government charters allow them to do. Thus, they must adopt their business operations to changing economic conditions and circumstances within the confines of their charter. They are restricted to serving one specific economic sector, and may not diversify from that sector into any other without authorization from Congress.

Because of their federal charter, GSEs benefit from having an implicit government backing but their securities lack an explicit "full faith and credit" guarantee of the U.S. government.

Next to GSEs come government corporations. They are expected to be self-sustaining, but carry certain government protections and responsibilities as well as the explicit financial backing of the United States. Three ready examples are the AMTRAK train corporation, the Pension Benefit Guarantee Corporation, and the Tennessee Valley Authority—the former runs a major sector of the American rail system, the second insures certain private sector pension plans, and the latter produces electrical power for a large geographical region. The government corporations are chartered by the government, given a defined purpose that clearly has a public good behind it (ensuring that there is a train system, pensions, and electrical power for the three noted above), and are managed by the government directly rather than being merely subject to government oversight as are GSEs.

At the right end of the continuum are the government agencies. Here one finds the traditional government organization, bureau, department, or office that is directly responsible through a chain of command to the president, the Congress, or both.

As apparent from figure 8.1, several of the GSEs have moved along this continuum. Specifically, several GSEs were once government corporations (either wholly or partially owned by the government). Over time, they changed to complete private ownership but, by retaining other ties to the government through their federal charter, they have not evolved to the end of the continuum occupied by fully private firms.

GSE Ownership and Operations

While all GSEs are privately owned, two are cooperative lending systems where the borrowers are also the GSE's owners. The other four have publicly traded stock. One GSE lends directly to borrowers; the rest lend to, or purchase, guarantee or securitize loans made by other financial institutions.

The Farm Credit System (FCS) and the Federal Home Loan Bank System (FHLBS) are cooperative lending institutions. Borrowers are required to be shareholders. Membership in FCS is voluntary; membership in FHLBS currently is mandatory for most thrift institutions (savings and loans plus savings banks) but is voluntary for commercial banks.[2]

The Federal National Mortgage Association (Fannie Mae), the Federal Home Loan Mortgage Corporation (Freddie Mac), and the Student Loan Marketing Association (Sallie Mae) are owned by private shareholders and their shares trade on the New York Stock Exchange. The Federal Agricultural Mortgage Association (Farmer Mac) has mixed stock ownership consisting of FCS institutions and non-FCS financial institutions.

Each GSE links national and international capital markets with their targeted sector. The GSEs do this by issuing debt securities (notes and bonds) and mortgage-backed securities (debt securities backed by a pool of mortgages). The proceeds are then passed, directly or indirectly, to the targeted borrowers. Of the six GSEs, only FCS lends directly to the targeted borrowers. The other five GSEs are secondary market institutions; that is, they provide financing to other financial institutions (mainly banks, thrifts, and mortgage banks) that in turn lend to homebuyers, farmers, and students.

This financing takes two forms: loans to financial institutions, or acquisition of loans made to targeted borrowers. In the former case, loans made by the GSE are typically secured by the loans made to the targeted borrowers. In the latter case, acquired loans may be held in portfolio by the GSE or sold forward in the capital markets in the form of mortgage-backed securities that carry a guarantee of repayment made by the GSE.

These operations are summarized in figures 8.1–8.3. Figure 8.1 shows the operations of FCS, FHLBS, and Sallie Mae. All three GSEs issue debt securities to investors. FCS, through various distribution networks in the system, lends the money directly to farmers, ranchers, and agricultural cooperatives. Federal Home Loan Banks loan money to banks and thrifts. These loans are secured by mortgages held by banks and thrifts. Sallie Mae does this for student loans held by banks and thrifts. Additionally, Sallie Mae purchases such loans from banks and thrifts and holds them in its own portfolio.

Figure 8.2 shows the operations of Farmer Mac. Farmer Mac issues a guarantee of repayment on a pool of agricultural real estate loans that are sold to investors. Both the private firm that packages the mortgages into the pool, and the mortgages themselves, must meet a set of criteria defined by Farmer Mac. Farmer Mac may also acquire for its own portfolio securities that it has guaranteed and securities guaranteed by the Farmers Home Administration, a government agency.

Finally, figure 8.3 shows the operations of Fannie Mae and Freddie Mac. These GSEs have two basic business operations. They buy mortgages from institutions that originate such loans with home buyers and

FIGURE 8.1
Operations of FCS, FHLBS, and Sallie Mae

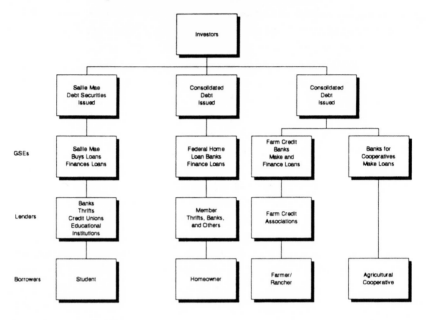

Source: U.S. General Accounting Office 1990

then hold the mortgages in their portfolios. They fund their portfolios by issuing debt securities to capital market investors. They also securitize mortgages. That is, after buying the mortgages from the institution that originated the loan, Fannie Mae and Freddie Mac may then pool such mortgages and sell them to investors as mortgage-backed securities. Essentially, such securities have the payment features of the underlying mortgages but are enhanced by a guarantee of repayment made by the GSE.

FIGURE 8.2
Operations of Farmer Mac

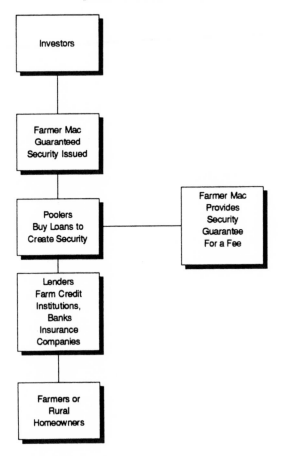

Source: U.S. General Accounting Office 1990

While the GSEs are dominant forces in their respective sectors, their business operations are not unique to GSEs. For example, using Stanton's continuum, the Government National Mortgage Corporation—a government corporation—guarantees securities backed by home mortgages. Investment banks also issue such securities. Lending secured by a pool of loans is also undertaken by both private firms and government corporations.

FIGURE 8.3
Operations of Fannie Mae and Freddie Mac

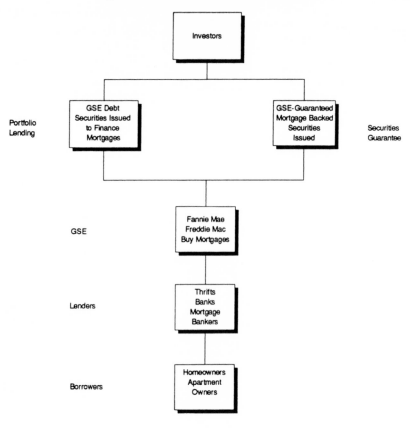

Source: U.S. General Accounting Office 1990

Economic Effects of GSEs

To the extent that GSEs reduce the transactions costs in allocating credit, they improve the efficiency of credit markets. However, to the extent that their operations provide a subsidy to the targeted sectors, they reallocate credit in the economy from where it would otherwise go. This means there is an opportunity cost to GSEs, which is the foregone economic activity that did not receive credit (or received it at different terms) because of the additional credit flowing to the targeted sectors.

While it is beyond the scope of this work to measure the opportunity cost of GSE activities, this is a crucial consideration to keep in mind in analyzing GSEs or any other federal credit programs.[3] While it may appear that GSEs offer a large benefit at little or no cost, the hidden cost is the lost activity from the reallocation of credit resulting from the subsidization of credit delivered to particular borrowers or sectors.

Origins of GSEs as Policy Tools:
The Rationale for Government Intervention

GSEs were designed to correct perceived market failures or limitations in the allocation of credit. In the early part of this century concerns were raised that private lenders were failing to provide sufficient and/or stable credit to certain sectors deemed important for economic growth and well-being. Specifically, access to credit for home buyers and farmers (and later students) was seen as inadequate. In a report on the risks posed by GSEs, the U.S. General Accounting Office (1990) noted that the creation of GSEs was the federal government's response to the perceived failure of private capital markets to properly allocate capital to all sectors of the economy. This failure is generally thought to have occurred for the following reasons:

1. America's banking laws restricted geographic expansion by commercial banks and thrift institutions, thereby contributing to regional differences in credit availability. With interstate and intrastate branching largely prohibited, it was difficult for funds to flow from regions with capital surpluses to regions with capital shortages.
2. Banks' charters placed restrictions on agricultural and home mortgage lending. Furthermore, the nature of agricultural and home mortgage loans was less appealing to banks than commercial loans. This was due to a number of factors including the small sizes, uncertain credit risk, longer payment periods, and heterogenous nature of such loans. That is, banks preferred commercial loans because their short-term and self-liquidating properties made them easier to administer and finance with deposits. Also, student loans lacked any tangible capital to serve as collateral.

GSEs As Instruments for Promoting America's Economic Vision

Geisst (1990) finds the creation of GSEs to be consistent with the federal government's efforts to promote the so-called American dream.

He defines the American dream as a combination of political and economic ideals that embody "the visions of political freedom, home ownership, the accumulation of wealth, and the freedom from want" (p. ix). He finds home ownership to be the primary economic component of the dream, with agriculture representing freedom from want (hunger). He says that education is a recent addition to this vision.

He also finds the structure of GSEs—wedding private market incentives and institutions to those socially desirable sectors—to be a compromise between America's ideological preference for market-driven outcomes and its desire for the government to insure fulfillment of the economic vision inherent in the dream. Thus, the assumption is that the financial markets, left to their own devices, would not allocate credit in a manner consistent with the socially desired allocation. Yet, government too is seen as incapable of efficiently redirecting credit itself and thus it must rely on financial markets and institutions. GSEs, as a policy tool, strike the desired balance. According to Geisst:

> Regardless of the sector of the economy involved, as the vision became more extended, the financial markets began to play a crucial role in the development of the ideal. But their involvement was in keeping with the spirit of market capitalism in that investment risks and returns would still be present. Government and the markets together would find a common ground whereby the good economic life could be achieved. Government's role would be to provide direction and regulation of the markets so that the capital-raising process would not be left solely in the hands of the relative few without constraints on their activities. The markets in turn would provide capital to many sectors of the economy that the government itself was ill-equipped to intervene in for both practical and ideological reasons. (1990:x)

GSEs As a Tool for Promoting Private Interests
Beyond the View of Ongoing Policy Oversight

Whatever their initial merits, Leonard (1986) sees GSEs as an example of extensive government involvement in credit markets that is less discriminate than that described by Geisst. He notes that federal credit programs involve nearly every economic sector, with much of the growth in these programs taking place in the past two decades. He sees in this a pattern of the government working to advance particular interests outside of the ongoing rigor of the congressional appropriations process.

Because GSE activity does not undergo regular review by Congress, the resource allocation decisions implicit in the creation of a GSE do not get regularly tested against new and competing priorities. Since GSEs as a policy tool operate outside the ongoing competition of the budget process, neither the effectiveness nor the appropriateness of the tool is regularly evaluated. As we describe in greater detail below, this results from the tradeoffs present in using GSEs rather than other possible instruments as a credit allocation tool.

History of the GSEs

FCS

The Federal Farm Loan Act of 1916 established the first GSE—the FCS, a cooperative lending system of twelve banks. These twelve regional Federal Land Banks followed the pattern established in 1913 by the Federal Reserve Act, which created twelve reserve banks as regional components of the central bank. However, according to Geisst (1990), the primary model used in shaping the original FCS was the *Landschaft* of Germany, a government-sponsored rural cooperative credit system.[4]

The FCS underwent numerous changes in structure and composition since its creation. During the Depression years, a combination of laws and presidential orders expanded and reorganized FCS to deal with the effects of the Great Depression on the agricultural sector. These steps culminated with an executive order in 1939 that put jurisdiction over FCS in the Department of Agriculture. FCS did not regain its independence until 1953 and did not finish buying back the FCS shares owned by the federal government until 1968.

Bosworth, Carron, and Rhyne (1987) identify three purposes underpinning the FCS: (1) extend credit on terms more suitable for farmers, (2) overcome local credit problems by linking agricultural loans to national credit markets, and (3) reduce the cost of agricultural credit.

FHLBS and Fannie Mae

The FHLBS and Fannie Mae were both responses to crises in housing finance during the Great Depression. The long maturity amortizing mortgages that are standard today were not available in the early 1930s. Most home buyers borrowed short-term—typically using balloon loans—thereby creating a need for frequent refinancing. As the depression progressed, home values dropped, wages and employment fell, and banks and savings and loans needed their loans to be repaid so they could fund the soaring outflow of deposits. In the face of this crisis,

Congress sought to get aid directly to the homebuyer to allow people to keep their homes and restructure their debts.

The Federal Housing Finance Board (1993: 15) points out that discussion of a federal credit facility for home mortgages can be traced back to the 1890s but it took a crisis to put a system into operation. The first response was the FHLBS, created in 1932. While designed to provide support for troubled borrowers, the FHLBS mirrored the structure of the FCS. Twelve regional banks, cooperatively owned by savings and loans, were created. While permitted to lend directly to home owners, only three such loans were made.[5] Instead, the FHLBS provided liquidity to savings and loans, stabilizing their funding base. As with FCS, it allowed for a regional redistribution of credit, equalized borrowing rates, and provided a stable supply of credit. While this succeeded in stabilizing the savings and loan industry, it did not produce the intended result of bringing immediate relief to homeowners struggling with their mortgage debts.[6]

In 1938, Fannie Mae was formed as a government-owned corporation created to deal with financial market problems arising in the depression. By purchasing government-insured mortgages from lenders, Fannie Mae removed the risk that the price and supply of credit used to make such long-term mortgages could change before the mortgages repaid. This had the additional benefit of giving lenders the opportunity to recycle these funds by making still more loans.

Over time, the FHLBS underwent the least change of the three GSEs. The FHLBS completed the repurchase of the federal government's shares in the system in 1951 (Lockwood 1987). At this point, the FHLBS was completely owned by the private sector. It did, however, retain a direct federal tie in that the FHLBS was governed by the board members of the Federal Home Loan Bank Board, a federal agency. Through this connection, some supervisory authority for the savings and loan industry was housed at the individual Federal Home Loan Banks. Congress removed this supervisory authority in 1989.

Fannie Mae's authority to purchase mortgage loans was expanded in 1948 to include the newly created Veterans Administration (VA) mortgage—mortgages to veterans guaranteed by the VA. At this point, Fannie Mae began to play an increasingly important role in housing finance. Legislation in 1954 converted Fannie Mae from a government-owned corporation to a mixed-ownership corporation with preferred stock held by the government and common stock held by mortgage lenders that sold mortgages to Fannie Mae.

Fannie Mae underwent a major transformation in 1968 when it was split into two organizations. One, the Government National Mortgage Association, remained a government corporation and retained primary authority to purchase government-insured mortgages.[7] The other retained the name Fannie Mae and was made a privately owned company with a federal charter to develop a secondary market in home mortgages. In 1970, the last government-owned stock in Fannie Mae was repurchased and Fannie Mae was granted unrestricted authority to purchase conventional mortgage loans (that is, loans not insured through government programs).

The Second-Generation GSEs: Freddie Mac, Sallie Mae, and Farmer Mac

The second generation of GSEs, like the first, was created to overcome perceived deficiencies in how existing institutions were allocating credit. For example, Freddie Mac initially provided thrift institutions the outlet for mortgages that Fannie Mae offered primarily to mortgage banks. Sallie Mae added liquidity to a student loan program created by the government but that was unattractive to lenders because of the illiquidity of student loans.[8] Unlike the original GSEs however, the newer GSEs began as GSEs, not as government-owned corporations. Their initial characteristics reflected the evolution of the original three GSEs from the early 1900s to 1970.

Farmer Mac, established in 1988, is the newest of the GSEs. Its capital is owned by FCS institutions and by commercial lenders to rural areas and to agriculture. Farmer Mac was designed to play a Fannie Mae-like role in developing a secondary market for agricultural mortgages. However, its development has been slow to date.[9]

Rethinking the Role of GSEs

The 1980s saw financial difficulties at Fannie Mae and FCS, and large taxpayer losses from failures of savings and loans. These events, combined with the rapid growth and increasing dominance of the GSEs, have generated three questions. First, how financially safe and sound are GSEs and what risks do they pose to the taxpayer if they again became financially troubled? Second, as financial markets evolve, with new technology and institutions available to service borrowers, how can/should the public purposes of GSEs be modified? Third, under what conditions should new GSEs be introduced?

Safety and Soundness Concerns and Recent Government Oversight

While long operating relatively free from congressional oversight, GSEs have recently been the subject of increased scrutiny. Much of this attention resulted from the financial crises leading to the federal government providing direct financial support to FCS in 1987 and to the deposit insurance fund for the savings and loan industry in the late 1980s and early 1990s. Each GSE has undergone recent modifications to its federal oversight to reduce taxpayer exposure to any losses suffered by a GSE, and a new regulator has been created for Fannie Mae and Freddie Mac.

Financial Difficulties Experienced by GSEs. Financial troubles in GSEs are not new. Individual FCS institutions, and the system as a whole, suffered a number of bouts of financial difficulties, reflecting the economic volatility of the agricultural sector. As noted earlier, such problems led the government to take over the system during the Depression.

By 1987, the collapse of both agricultural land values and interest rates put the financial integrity of the FCS in jeopardy again. If a Farm Credit Bank failed to make its debt payments, the other banks would be jointly liable to make good on the failed bank's obligations. As with all the GSEs, the federal government had no explicit legal responsibility to insure such payments. But with the FCS threatened though, the federal government stepped in. In 1987, Congress made available to FCS up to $4 billion in federally guaranteed bonds.

While less than $2 billion of this authority was actually used, the government's actions here provided clear evidence that the government may step in and support a troubled GSE. Belief that the government would step in again is a large factor in the rates at which some GSEs can borrow from capital markets. Also, investors that believe it is unlikely that the government would allow a GSE to fail are less concerned with the risks undertaken by a GSE than if they believed no government assistance would be forthcoming.

Fannie Mae, like savings and loans that held long-term, fixed-rate mortgages, suffered huge losses in the late 1970s as interest rates rose to unprecedented levels. In 1986 the U.S. Department of Housing and Urban Development reported that Fannie Mae had been insolvent on a market value basis by almost $11 billion in 1981. The department, which was Fannie Mae's federal regulator, took little direct action while Fannie Mae engaged in a risky rapid growth strategy to get out of its difficulties. The move paid off as interest rates fell and Fannie Mae returned to profitability. Yet, had events been less fortuitous, it seems clear that the government would have been reluctant to let Fannie Mae fail. Besides the chilling effect this would have had on the other GSEs, such an action would probably have resulted in significant short-term disruption in mortgage markets and among many savings and loans.

Recent Reviews of the Government's Financial Risk from GSEs

In 1989, Congress took notice of the taxpayers' potential liability to a GSE failure by ordering several federal studies of the GSEs as a group.[10] Generally, these studies found no immediate problems in the GSEs but they all warned of the problems that could arise if a GSE got into serious financial trouble. While the government has no legal responsibility to bail out GSE debtholders should a GSE fail, each study recognized that there were a number of reasons why the government may choose to rescue a failing GSE. Each study offered options or recommendations for improving the government's safety and soundness oversight of the GSEs, concluding that existing oversight was inconsistent at best. Since then, Congress created a new federal regulator for Fannie Mae and Freddie Mac. This regulator is an independent office housed within the Department of Housing and Urban Development.

Difficulties in Redirecting GSEs

Each GSE was created to deal with perceived shortcomings in financial markets. Over time, most of the GSEs have successfully accomplished their original missions in developing or improving credit delivery to targeted segments. Yet, as the original missions are fulfilled, as financial markets develop, and as needs change, how can or should the public purposes of GSEs be updated to keep them relevant? Answers to such questions become greatly complicated by the financial and political power that the GSEs themselves have in encouraging or obstructing any particular change.

Bosworth, Carron, and Rhyne (1987) note that once GSEs successfully link national capital markets with local borrowers, at least some of the rationale for their existence disappears. That is, once such markets are developed, and the risks and returns are understood, then private lenders can and will continue to provide such credit without assistance (or competition) from a GSE.

Somewhat differently, GSEs may be found to improve credit delivery to the originally targeted borrower groups but a different or more narrowly defined borrower group may then be perceived as in need such assistance. For instance, the housing GSEs are generally seen as having improved credit availability for single-family home buyers. But now, there is concern expressed by some that these GSEs do not do enough to ensure credit availability for multifamily mortgages (that is, for apartment buildings and other multifamily occupancy projects). Getting a GSE to expand or reorient its mission to serve a new or narrower group of borrowers is very difficult because of the many interests being served by the status quo.

Existing beneficiaries of a GSE's ongoing operations—whether they are borrowers, depository institutions, bond holders, shareholders, GSE managers, or politicians—may be quite reluctant to see these benefits redirected away from them. Stanton (1991a) notes three aspects to this problem. First, because of these vested interests, Congress may lose the political ability to redirect GSEs to serve the "highest priority public needs" (p. 37). Second, the financial size of most GSEs gives them enormous clout and makes changing their direction difficult. Third, the combination of political and financial power in a GSE may make effective oversight of the GSE's fulfillment of its public mission, as well as effective oversight of its safety and soundness, difficult for the government to accomplish.

Indeed, the GSEs are accomplished political lobbyists. Most have a powerful congressional relations staff or some type of lobbying group to promote their own interests with Congress. Unlike federal agencies, which may not hire lobbyists to represent them before Congress, the GSEs have proven themselves highly capable of marshalling such resources to promote their interests.

The organization of Congress also makes it difficult for the government to address GSEs as a group. As noted above, in 1989 the government began its first major effort to look systematically and collectively at GSEs. Once the various government reports were in, collective action was virtually impossible because the congressional oversight authority for GSEs was dispersed across many committees. This fractured system of oversight hindered Congress from taking a unified approach to dealing with GSEs.

Thus, while GSEs have generally been successful in meeting their original purposes, as times change it is difficult for GSEs to continue meeting new social priorities. Abolishing a GSE once markets are sufficiently developed to be served by fully private entities, or redirecting a GSE to serve segments perceived to be in greatest need is very difficult to accomplish. There is an important lesson here in looking at GSEs as a policy tool. These enterprises owe their existence to the federal government, and they benefit from numerous federal ties. At the same time, they have proven that they can be so powerful that the government loses much of its ability to control or redirect their resources to meet changing priorities.

Creating New GSEs?

An area of current concern in the United States is the provision of credit to small businesses. The recent recession saw many claims that the country was suffering from a "credit crunch"; that is, a shortage in the supply of bank loans to small businesses. Although the evidence that such a shortage exists is mixed at best, recent conditions have led to renewed calls for government action to improve credit availability to small businesses. Among the proposals being put forward are legislative proposals to establish a GSE for small business credit. This GSE essentially would establish a secondary market for small business loans made by banks and other financial institutions.

Among other things, consideration of a new GSE ought to begin with an evaluation of existing credit allocation. Is there an identifiable market failure in credit flowing to the targeted group, either because of some market or regulatory barrier or because of external benefits associated with lending to the targeted group? If so, what are the range of options available for removing or overcoming existing barriers or realizing the external benefits? What are the opportunity costs and possible unintended consequences associated with each option? After undertaking an evaluation like this, if Congress finds that the socially preferred activity cannot obtain sufficient credit through existing institutions, then creation of a GSE ought to be done with consideration of future problems such as those listed in the previous section.

A further lesson can be learned from the newest GSE, Farmer Mac. Created in 1988 at a time when safety and soundness concerns regarding financial institutions were becoming much greater, Farmer Mac has not made meaningful headway toward establishing a secondary market for rural real estate loans. While there are a number of reasons for this, one certainly is that the risk controls put in place to limit taxpayer exposure have left lenders little benefit in pooling loans with a Farmer Mac guarantee.

Analyzing GSEs as Policy Instruments

The issue here is one of assessing the present utility and appropriateness of GSEs as a policy instrument. What are their current strengths and
weaknesses? Is any mechanism or policy tool actually needed? To provide a multidimensional assessment of GSEs, we use the work of Linder
and Peters (1989) where they detail eight attributes of policy instruments.
The question is not one of GSEs' success in responding to the problems
which originally lead to their creation. They have been successful—and
highly profitable besides. Thus, we will stand back from their individual
performances and examine GSEs as a tool of government.

1. Complexity of Operations: GSEs' institutional and organizational
complexity is not especially great if one compares them to other large
financial institutions such as money-center banks. The range of responsibilities for GSEs is limited, the market participants well defined, the
objectives clearly stated, the financial role well understood, and the
different organizations involved all know the rules.

The complexity comes in the degree to which the GSEs have taken
the single area in which they operate—generally the secondary market
for loans and mortgages—and carried the level of sophistication and
financial innovations to a very high level. For example, several GSEs
have introduced innovative but complex ways for managing interest
rate risk that make them pioneers in certain risk management practices.

Program and policy evaluation has a difficult time in assessing innovations, especially those that are constantly changing and adapting to
market forces. It is also the case that judgments about the efficiency
and effectiveness of GSEs as policy instruments are difficult to make
because the continuing changes in financial demands and market forces
mean that the GSEs are moving targets. Retrospective evaluation judgments on GSEs (if even possible) are interesting, but not necessarily
germane to current policy considerations.

There is one other aspect to the complexity of GSEs as a policy tool
that bears mention. Generally, each GSE devotes considerable effort to
managing its relationship with Congress. The GSEs owe their existence to Congress and depend on Congress for charter modifications, as
circumstances and economic conditions change over time. At the same
time, as private firms, the GSEs generally do not want Congress med-
dling with their business operations. For example, a GSE may seek
congressional approval to enter markets that it desires to enter, but it
may be resistant to such actions initiated by Congress. Similarly, GSEs

depend on their ongoing ties to the federal government but may be resistant to meaningful oversight by a federal regulator (Stanton 1991a and 1991b). Therefore, evaluating the impact of the complex relationship between individual GSEs and Congress is difficult. The relations are subtle and managed in a way that does not lead to much public visibility or understanding.

2. Level of Public Visibility: As a policy tool, GSEs have an extremely low level of visibility for the general public. There are few persons outside the financial and banking communities or government who know of GSEs, their roles and responsibilities. The average citizen would have little reason to know any of the GSEs, given that the GSEs operate primarily in the secondary markets. As a result, they receive little press coverage beyond that in the financial sections of newspapers. Television and radio coverage is infrequent. But having said this, it is also the case that the GSEs are such dominant players in their respective markets that they have considerable visibility in financial markets. The current arrangements leave little opportunity for public discourse on GSEs—as well as little opportunity for judgment on their current roles and responsibilities by the public.

3. Adaptability across Uses: The judgement here is based on what arena one defines for GSEs. If it is that of the secondary lending market, then the adaptability is extremely high, as the GSEs have already demonstrated their ability to be effectively used as a tool in this domain over time and across sectors—education, housing, and agriculture specifically. Further, they have been successful in adapting existing financial instruments to generate new products that have kept them extremely competitive in the market place.

But if the arena is, according to Stanton's continuum, either to the left or right of where they are presently, then the adaptability is untested. For the GSEs have not been allowed by their charters to compete across a range of financial markets and with a varying set of organizational and institutional systems. They compete with the private sector, but with a set of unique restrictions and benefits. There is some basis, however, to speculate that the adaptability is rather high, given that three of the original GSEs have gone from essentially the public to the private sector. In the context of the Stanton continuum discussed earlier, they have gone from being government corporations to being GSEs. This they have done with apparently few financial disruptions.

4. Level Of Intrusiveness: Here again the decision on the utility of GSEs as a policy instrument has to be made in the context of how one

defines intrusiveness. If one works with an understanding of intrusiveness of the policy tool to be that of a continuum from little or none on one end (i.e., little evidence of government efforts to generate particular outcomes) to high and forceful on the other (i.e., government-sanctioned coercion, control, or monopolization of an activity or sector), the GSEs fall somewhere in the middle. As a policy tool, they do not carry the formal authority and power given to a federal agency. They must, in the end, survive on the basis of their charters and their ability to be successful in the particular sectors of the financial markets where they operate. They cannot mandate nor legally require the compliance of other actors in the financial marketplace. Except for mandatory membership of savings and loans in the FHLBS, there are no formal requirements, for example, that the primary financial markets have to work with the GSEs.

Yet the GSEs are not without their influence and their ability to dictate the rules of the game within their respective markets. Their charters give them certain protections and financial advantages that have allowed them to become dominant players in their respective areas. For example, Fannie Mae and Freddie Mac have become so influential that the underwriting guidelines they use in determining whether to accept a loan have become, de facto, the underwriting guidelines for much of the single-family mortgage market. That is, many mortgage lenders typically underwrite their mortgage loans according to Fannie Mae or Freddie Mac underwriting guidelines even if they do not intend to sell the loans forward into the secondary market. In this example, their intrusiveness into their particular financial sector is considerable, and dictates the behavior of lending institutions throughout the nation.

5. Relative Costliness: To date, the GSEs have been an almost financially cost-free policy instrument for the federal government. They are in the private sector to make a profit for their shareholders—and this they do nicely. They are also there to facilitate and expand the delivery of credit to their targeted sector, which is what the government created them to do and what it still expects of them. On the surface, it appears to be a win-win situation for everyone involved. However, there are two concerns regarding the cost of GSEs.

First, a concern of many who have looked at GSEs is the issue of their safety and soundness—and the ability of the federal government to adequately conduct the necessary oversight to ensure that GSEs remain just that—safe and sound. The issue is one of reconciling private management with public accountability (Moe and Stanton 1989). The

U.S. General Accounting Office (1990) estimated that by the end of 1989, the total debt and loan guarantees held by the GSEs totaled over $800 billion, an approximately 250 percent increase from 1984. The total current debt issued and loan guarantees made by the GSEs now exceed one trillion dollars.

If a GSE were to run into serious financial difficulty and be on the verge of financial collapse, then the cost to the government could be large—for a GSE and holders of its securities would likely call on the implicit backing of the federal government to bail them out. Whether or not the government did respond with some sort of a bailout, the failure of a GSE would likely result in large losses to other financial institutions and disruptions of credit flows to the sector served by the failed GSE.

Second, focusing just on possible future taxpayer losses from a GSE failure misses the big picture. Economists see the opportunity cost of GSE lending as the immediate cost of their activities. Succinctly, GSEs operate with a government subsidy via reduced borrowing costs and other benefits resulting from their ties to the federal government. The result is the ability of the GSEs to provide credit at a lower rate to targeted borrowers or sectors than would otherwise be the case. The issue for the economist is what would happen in the marketplace without this subsidy. The subsidy generates a flow of dollars into the creation of potentially more mortgages and loans than one would presume to see without the subsidy.

With the funds flowing through GSEs to favored sectors (housing, agriculture, education) the question becomes one of what are the other potential uses of the funds that did not occur because of the distorting influence of the subsidy. If, for example, because of the government subsidy, homeowners were buying larger houses than they otherwise would, what have been the costs of their artificially inflated housing purchase? Did they forego a larger car, a major appliance, or a vacation that otherwise would have been purchased? Perhaps more importantly, did small businesses receive less credit (or receive credit on worse terms) because of the subsidy flowing through GSEs. What did it cost the economy not to have credit extended in these other possible ways?

Stated differently, what have been the distorting influences when the government chooses to subsidize credit in some sectors but not in others. When credit flows to education, housing, and agriculture at the expense of, say, manufacturing, small business, or health care, what are the consequences by sector and for the economy (and society) at large? These are the questions economists would ask, the answers suggesting something of the hidden costs to society of the GSEs, as presently supported by the federal government.

6. Reliance on Market: GSEs exist somewhere between a reliance on the market and a reliance on government. They exist in that middle ground whereby both the market and the government have to be involved and provide the services they do in order for GSEs to accomplish their mission. The profit motive is a powerful driving force for the GSEs, but that profit comes in part because of the very special relation that GSEs have with the government. GSEs were created to overcome certain gaps and imperfections in the marketplace. This they appear to have quite successfully accomplished.

Thus the question arises of whether they still need the special government ties that they presently enjoy. Having cornered a significant share of the secondary market for various types of loans, could the GSEs now be financially self-sustaining and live or die in the marketplace like all other private sector organizations? The question for the analyst of GSEs as a policy tool is that of when should the special relation to the government end and the GSEs become independent private sector organizations, relying on their skill in the marketplace to ensure their survival. A related question in this regard is whether policy tools such as GSEs should be used only in conjunction with a "sunset" provision that mandates a formal review and subsequent decision on whether to sever government support and intervention. As it is, the GSEs are under no timetable or even suggestion of cutting loose from their special relation to government.

7. Chances of Failure: Given the current economic strength of the GSEs, and with the implicit backing of the U.S. government, there is little chance of any GSE failing in the near future. In addition, arguments are made that the GSEs are "too big to fail," implying that the government would have no choice but to step in and rescue any failing GSE simply because the economic repercussions of not intervening are so great. Admittedly, the emphasis here is on the GSE being allowed to fail as opposed to whether, left to its own devices and no government protection, the GSE would or would not survive. As a practical matter, the distinction may be moot. GSEs are widely seen as having the implicit backing of the government, and until such time as their charters are changed, the policy option of allowing them to fail (or their security holders to absorb losses) is unlikely because it could entail substantial political and economic costs.

More importantly, government is not indifferent to the success of a GSE as it is to most private firms. Since the federal government chartered each GSE to serve a public purpose, government not only would not want a GSE to fail, it *wants* GSEs to thrive. Only in this way is the government assured that each GSE will be there to serve their targeted sectors.

Therefore, if the government is expected to be the guarantor of last resort and if the government wants each GSE to remain financially sound in order to fulfill its mission, the government needs to know just how much risk actually exists in each GSE. At present, the quality of its ongoing oversight varies across the GSEs. Thus the government is in the situation of potentially assuming responsibility for the coverage of loans that it has not made, cannot supervise, and is unable to evaluate. It is at this point that the haunting specter of the savings and loan crisis emerges, for this is exactly what the government faced when the savings and loan industry began to collapse (Stanton 1991b).

8. Precision of Targeting: Here one of the key strengths of the GSEs comes to the fore. At the macro level, the charters for the GSEs specify the market within which each GSE shall operate. There is little ambiguity on this point. The clear stipulation of their area of activity and the types of loans they can service allows them to concentrate all their efforts in these particular areas. There is no deflection of effort or interest. In this sense, GSEs are an effective policy instrument.

The precision of targeting with GSEs at the micro level is more ambiguous. The GSEs have, via their underwriting rules and operating procedures, made clear what criteria they use to determine what loans they will buy. That is, through its credit policies, a GSE defines its own targets within the market sector assigned to it through its charter. GSEs also influence changes made to their charters and regulations developed to implement their charters. In this way, the targets at the micro level may become more a reflection of a GSE's pursuit of its own self-interest than the implementation of micro-level targets defined by the government.

Finally, the charters of several GSEs contain additional public purpose objectives for the GSE to meet that go beyond the broad policy objective. For example, the Federal Home Loan Banks have two programs whereby their loans are to be targeted to low- and moderate-income housing projects. Fannie Mae and Freddie Mac also have congressionally mandated requirements for supporting housing finance for low-income borrowers, urban areas, and other under-served segments of the housing market. Preliminary evidence suggests that it is much more difficult to target such goals precisely in the context of a statutory charter for a GSE.

Postscript: Evaluating the GSEs

While the overall intent of this book is to delineate the means and methods of evaluating various policy instruments, it should be apparent from the foregoing that program-evaluation methods would be extremely difficult to apply in a conventional way in assessing GSEs. Their financial magnitude, their political power, and most importantly, their quasi-public/quasi-private status all work against the application of a classical program-evaluation design.

Indeed, one might argue that the further to the left one moves on the Stanton continuum of organizational types discussed earlier, the less applicable are the traditional approaches of program evaluation. We know well here in the United States how to evaluate government programs, agencies, and policy initiatives (i.e., the far right end of the continuum). We are less certain of our craft when it comes to the assessment of government corporations (how does one evaluate a national railroad system?). We would posit that the craft of evaluation is even less well equipped to take on GSEs, let alone the evaluation of private corporations and companies. What has traditionally tended to happen in such instances is the disaggregation of the policy or organization into smaller component parts that are more amenable to traditional evaluation designs. Furthermore, the criteria for evaluating the organizations on the left end of the spectrum are going to increasingly be economic in character, and that moves out of the domain and expertise of most program-evaluation specialists.

The scope of the GSEs and the magnitude of their influence across financial markets is difficult to capture with conventional designs. The recent federal studies of GSEs cited earlier, for example, focused almost exclusively on the "safety and soundness" question. This leaves many other questions unasked and unanswered. But such is the reality of attempting to apply social science methods to the study of large-scale financial institutions.

The resolution of the difficulty in evaluating GSEs with traditional evaluation methods will not happen here. (Could we begin to think of a strategy of socioeconomic evaluation?) We have come directly to the limits of traditional evaluation vis-à-vis this particular policy instrument. Whether and how GSEs can be evaluated is another question. It may be that at this level of complexity, the focus needs to shift, as suggested above, from program evaluation to economics, on the one hand, and policy analysis and organizational design, on the other. It may also have to shift from program evaluation to a more strictly political judgment on the necessary continuation of this particular policy initiative. But it is a question of no small import, for in the interim the U.S. government continues to be seen as the implicit guarantor of the massive financial structures built up by GSEs over many decades. It is an appropriate time to address this issue further.

Notes

1. Loan guarantees are made on loans originated by private financial institutions (typically commercial banks) according to federal underwriting guidelines. Some or all of the default risk is absorbed by the federal government in the form of a guarantee of repayment to the lender. Direct loans are loans made by federal agencies directly to borrowers. Tax-exempt bonds allow state and local governments to raise funds for lending programs where the income earned by the bondholders is exempt from federal income tax. This lowers the cost of funds to the bond issuer, which passes the savings to the borrower, usually in the form of reduced interest rates.
2. Thrift institutions include both savings and loans and savings banks. Before 1989, membership in FHLBS was restricted to thrifts. Savings and loans were required to be FHLBS members but membership was voluntary for most savings banks.
3. Bosworth, Carron, and Rhyne (1987) measure the subsidy inherent in several of the GSEs as well as the subsidy present in other federal credit programs.
4. Geisst states that the development of FCS began in 1912 when President Taft requested U.S. ambassadors to report on how various European countries provided agricultural credit. He adds that the process reversed itself thirty years later when U.S. mortgage agencies became the model used by international and regional credit agencies (p. 105).
5. Federal Housing Finance Board 1993:10.
6. Congress quickly realized that the FHLBS was incapable of providing direct relief to borrowers. A year later, in 1933, it created the Home Owner's Loan Corporation as an entity controlled by the Federal Home Loan Bank Board, the same governing body of the FHLBS. The corporation purchased delinquent mortgages from lenders and then restructured the terms of these debts with delinquent borrowers.
7. A few years later, the Government National Mortgage Association would issue the first security with guaranteed repayment backed by a pool of home mortgages. These became known as mortgage-backed securities and shortly thereafter Fannie Mae and Freddie Mac began issuing similar securities.
8. The federal government created the guaranteed student loan program in 1965. Not unlike government-insured mortgages, the guaranteed student loan put the federal government at risk of loss on student loans made by private lenders. Such loans however, are costly to service because of the complex nature of federal (and state) rules governing their administration and collection and be-

cause the borrowers are highly mobile with no collateral. As a result, Sallie Mae was established in 1972 to enhance the liquidity of the student loan market. By purchasing such loans, and by making advances to lenders secured by student loans, Sallie Mae increases the liquidity in the student loan market, making lenders more willing to make such loans.

9. In 1986, Congress established the College Construction Loan Insurance Association (Connie Lee). Connie Lee is a reinsurer of bonds issued to finance academic facilities. While it has some characteristics of a GSE, it differs in other respects and is not considered a GSE for purposes of this chapter. For more information, see U.S. General Accounting Office 1990.

10. These studies were Congressional Budget Office 1991; Department of the Treasury 1990, 1991; and U.S. General Accounting Office 1990, 1991.

References

Bosworth, Barry P., Andrew S. Carron, and Elisabeth H. Rhyne. 1987. *The Economics of Federal Credit Programs.* Washington, DC: The Brookings Institution.

Geisst, Charles R. 1990. *Visionary Capitalism: Financial Markets and the American Dream in the Twentieth Century.* New York: Praeger.

Leonard, Herman R. 1986. *Checks Unbalanced: The Quiet Side of Public Spending.* New York: Basic Books.

Linder, Stephen H. and B. Guy Peters. 1989. "Instruments of Government: Perceptions and Contexts," *Journal of Public Policy* 9(1): 35–58.

Lockwood, Paul. 1987. *A Guide to the Federal Home Loan Bank System.* Washington, DC: FHLB System Publication Corporation.

Moe, Ronald C. and Thomas H. Stanton. 1989. "Government-Sponsored Enterprises as Federal Instrumentalities: Reconciling Private Management with Public Accountability," *Public Administration Review* (July/Aug.)

Stanton, Thomas H. 1991a. *A State of Risk: Will Government- Sponsored Enterprises Be the Next Financial Crisis?* New York: HarperCollins Publishers.

———. 1991b. "Federal Supervision of Safety and Soundness of Government-Sponsored Enterprises," *The Administrative Law Journal* 5(2): 395–484.

———. 1992. "Taxpayers at Risk: The Moral Hazards of the New Mercantilism." The Institute for Policy Innovation Report No. 116, June.

U.S. Congressional Budget Office. 1991. *Controlling the Risks of Government-Sponsored Enterprises.* April. Washington, DC.

U.S. Department of the Treasury. 1990. *Report of the Secretary of the Treasury on Government-Sponsored Enterprises.* May. Washington, DC.

———. 1991. *Report of the Secretary of the Treasury on Government-Sponsored Enterprises.* April. Washington, DC.

U.S. Federal Housing Finance Board. 1993. *Report on the Structure and Role of the Federal Home Loan Bank System.* Washington, DC: Federal Housing Finance Board, 28 April.

U.S. General Accounting Office. 1990. *Government-Sponsored Enterprises: The Government's Exposure to Risks.* (GAO/GGD-90-97, 15 August). Washington, DC.

———. 1991. *Government-Sponsored Enterprises: A Framework for Limiting the Government's Exposure to Risks.* (GAO/GGD-91-90, 22 May).

9

The Invisible Problem and How to Deal with It: National Policy Styles in Radiation Protection Policy in The Netherlands, England, and Belgium

Maarten J. Arentsen

In this chapter the logic of a national "policy style" is illustrated by the radiation protection policy of three West European countries, The Netherlands, England, and Belgium. Radiation protection policy aims at the protection against the hazards of ionizing radiation. At the beginning of this century, radiation protection developed in Europe and in the United States, as a part of a much larger process of the exploration of the physical forces hidden in nature.

In the three European countries of interest here, the preparation of the Euratom treaty has guided the national formation of a radiation protection policy. Although the Euratom treaty essentially creates national policy for each country, the treaty does allow for national variation in policy style. In this chapter the similarities and differences in radiation protection policy of the three countries will be explored. The main interest is to illustrate the similarities and differences in national policy styles, with special attention to contextual contingencies underlying that logic (see Introduction).

The questions to be answered in this chapter are:

1. To what extent did contextual factors condition the national policy style in radiation protection policy in each of the three countries?
2. What has been the impact of policy evaluation on the national policy style in radiation protection policy in the three countries?

In the Introduction, policy style is defined as "a government's approach to problem-solving and a government's relationship to other actors in the policy-making and the policy-implementation process." The primary aim of policy-making is to develop and choose policy instruments. These instruments are then applied in the policy-implementation process. By applying policy instruments, the implementation process results in policy outcomes. For analytical reasons, a distinction between policy-making and policy implementation may be obvious. To make such a distinction does not deny that policy-making often overlaps into policy-implementation processes in reality.

So in this chapter, the national policy styles for policy-making and policy implementation of radiation protection policy in the three countries will be analyzed separately. First the government's approach in the three countries to the problem of ionizing radiation will be illustrated. Facing the same problem, each country developed national policy instruments to deal with these problems. Choosing policy instruments is here understood to be the policy-making process.

Second, the policy-implementation process is analyzed. The national policy style to apply and to enforce the rules that guide the use of ionizing radiation in each country will be illustrated. In this chapter, the application and the enforcement of legal rules that guide the use of ionizing radiation are understood to be the main activities of the policy-implementation process. Finally, the chapter will end with some concluding remarks about the relationship between policy instruments and national policy styles.

Recognizing the Problem:
The Formation of Radiation Protection Policy

In 1895 the German scientist W.C. Röntgen published an article entitled, "Über eine Neue Art von Strahlen."[1] From that day on Röntgen was a famous man. Not exactly realizing the phenomenon he had discovered, he named it "x-ray." About the same time, Henri Becquerel discovered radioactivity while experimenting with uranium salt. At first, his discovery was overshadowed by Röntgen's. However, both discoveries opened a new, invisible world, previously unknown to mankind. The consequences of both discoveries were soon understood. Scientists all over the world started research programs to explore the new phenomenon and to develop fields of application with, as we know today, tremendous consequences (Wylick 1966; De Ruiter and Van der Sijde 1985).

There are two main types of hazards from nuclear energy: the stochastic hazards, resulting from exposure to a low, continuing dose over many years, and the non-stochastic hazards, resulting from exposure to a high dose during a limited time. The normal use of radioactive substances and x-ray equipment can only result in stochastic hazards. The biological effects of these hazards are based on the physical and chemical reactions of the radiation on the DNA structure. Radiation absorbed in high doses kills biological cells or initiates cell mutations, effects that can have hereditary consequences.

At the time Röntgen and Becquerel made their discoveries, these hazards were not known. However, by applying ionizing radiation, physicians and radiologists discovered these hazards step by step. Their lessons were hard and many of the first scientists paid with their lives for this knowledge. Many of them, not aware of the hazards they were facing, experimented with their own bodies.[2] Trial and error paved the way for radiation protection standards that developed in the first half of this century.

In 1928 a group of scientists formed the International Committee on Radiological Protection (ICRP) to explore the biological effects of ionizing radiation and to develop standards for protection. The foundation of the ICRP was a significant step in the development of a radiation protection policy. The ICRP formulated three basic principles that guided the development of radiation protection.[3] The first states that every use of ionizing radiation has to be legitimated by its usefulness and a lack of alternatives. Second, the individual and collective doses arising from ionizing radiation have to be reduced to levels that are as low as reasonably achievable,[4] taking economic and social factors taken into account. Third, the exposure may never exceed prescribed dose limits, except for medical reasons. In The Netherlands, England, and Belgium, and in many other countries, these principles underlie the national radiation protection policies of today.

About the same time, the United States initiated the *Atoms for Peace* program in Europe, a program aiming at the peaceful application of nuclear power. The French and the Belgians had special interests in this program. France had major interests in nuclear power for strategic and economic reasons (de Gaulle's *Force de Frappe*). The Belgians controlled major supplies of uranium in their colony, the Congo. Both countries were important participants in the Atoms for Peace program. The Dutch joined the Belgians during the negotiations, lacking significant nuclear interests.

Because of these differences in nuclear interests, the three countries took different positions in the preparation of the Euratom treaty, as can be read in a report of the Dutch Health Council (*Gezondheidsraad*) of 2 July 1958. The Dutch participants blamed the French for sending specialists in nuclear reactors, instead of specialists in epidemiology as was agreed upon. The report stated: "It is obvious that France is intending to become the nuclear power in Europe. Because the English and the Americans do not participate, the French are the experts and the opinion leaders" (Report of the Council for Health, 2 July 1958, p. 2, unpublished). The group discussed the implementation of the ICRP standards for health politics. According to the report, the French criticized the standards because these standards directly applied to the reactor types used in France. The Belgians agreed with the French because of their own nuclear interests. Thus, the French dominated the discussion about the epidemiological paragraphs in the Euratom treaty.

At the meeting on 2 July 1958, the Dutch Health council concluded that The Netherlands had only one option: agreement with the French proposals. Rejection of the proposals would have isolated The Netherlands in the discussions. The French were given the opportunity to bring their civil nuclear activities under military interest, thus hiding them from public and international control. At that time the formation of effective protection standards had to account for national nuclear interests.

England took a position comparable to that of Belgium and France. England also had nuclear interests for economic and strategic reasons, but did not participate in the Euratom negotiations because England only joined the European Union a few decades later. In spite of these differences in nuclear interests, the three countries developed quite similar radiation protection policies. These similarities concern radiation protection standards as well as types of oversight policy instruments in the three countries. These standards and instruments result from the similar policy bases in the three countries: the recommendations of the ICRP on radiation protection standards and the Euratom treaty. In each of the three countries the main policy instruments of radiation protection are regulations. Each country developed its own varieties of regulations, as will be illustrated below.

The Netherlands

The first Dutch protection law dates from 1931. This law aimed at the protection against the hazards of x-ray equipment. The law was not implemented because, according to the Dutch Parliament, the law was in conflict with the autonomy of physicians. In 1963 the Dutch Parliament accepted the Nuclear Energy Law (*Kernenergiewet*), a formal law containing regulations for radiation protection. Until then, radiation protection was a part of the formal laws on occupational safety and public health (*Warenwet*).

In the Nuclear Energy Law, the Dutch closely copied the Euratom treaty in which protection standards are subjected to the development of the peaceful application of ionizing radiation.[5] The nuclear part of the law has not been of great importance because The Netherlands lacks an extensive nuclear industry. For that reason the protection part of the law became more important, especially the use of radioactive substances and x-ray equipment.[6]

The major instrument aiming at protection is the general prohibition of possessing radioactive substances or x-ray equipment without a permit. In the Vedung typology, the Dutch instrument is a type of regulation called " a conditional prohibition with permissions." Recently, only some types of radioactive smoke detectors have been excluded from this conditional prohibition. These smoke detectors should meet prescribed technical standards. In The Netherlands, the conditional prohibition with permissions is the main policy instrument in radiation protection.

England

In England the law regulating the use of ionizing radiation dates from 1960. In that year the Radioactive Substances Law was issued. This law addresses the protection of the public health and the environment against the hazards of ionizing radiation. The occupational safety is regulated by the ionizing radiation regulations issued under the Health and Safety at Work Act. In England, public and occupational safety have been regulated separately by two formal documents.

In England the main policy instrument is regulation. The regulation consists of two varieties of the conditional prohibition type, with respect to the potential hazards of the radiation in use. The law differentiates between minor and major uses.[7] The minor use requires that radioactive substances and x-ray equipment must be registered but no permission is necessary. This notification that should precede the actual use of minor substances and equipment is conditioned by standards, issued under the Radioactive Substances Law and the Health and Safety at Work Act. Major uses have to be authorized by government permission that contains standards issued under the Radioactive Substances Act. These same dual standards also apply to the treatment of radioactive waste. The English regulation consists of two varieties of the conditional prohibition type: notification and permission, whereas the Dutch regulation consists only of the permission.

Belgium

As in both other countries, radiation protection in Belgium is also based on a general law, aiming at the protection of the population against the hazards of ionizing radiation. The law contains only formal procedures to apply for a notification or a permission to use ionizing radiation. In Belgium the basic policy instrument is of the regulation type, with some varieties of the conditional prohibition, as in England. However, the Belgians differentiate between four, instead of two, classes of hazards. Each class may be addressed with standards that are issued under the general law.

Class 1 premises are the nuclear sites in Belgium. Class 2 and 3 premises use radioactive substances in open and closed form and x-ray equipment. Class 4 premises use, among others, small x-ray equipment and smoke detectors. The policy instrument for these classes is of the "conditional prohibition with permissions" type. For class 1, 2, and 3 the conditions are specified for each application separately. Class 4 applications have to meet the conditions as stated in a royal announcement, issued under the general law and without intervention of a public authority. Class 1 premises have to be licensed by the central authorities, the minister for labor affairs. Class 2 and class 3 premises have to be licensed by the provincial authorities.

The context of policy formation in the three countries has been quite similar. Although England did not participate in the Euratom negotiations, it agreed to the Euratom treaty when it joined the European Union. Belgium was an important partner in the Atoms for Peace program initiated by the Americans after World War II. Belgium and England developed a nuclear industry that became an important point of reference in the formation of a radiation protection policy. The Dutch lack a nuclear industry comparable with that in England or Belgium.

In spite of these differences in nuclear interests, the three countries have developed national radiation protection policies and have chosen policy instruments that look quite similar. All three countries chose regulatory instruments of the conditional prohibition type, with permissions. Only in The Netherlands are these permissions enacted for each application separately. In England the conditional prohibition with permissions is combined with a less constraining obligation to notify, depending of the type of ionizing radiation in use. In Belgium the regulatory instrument is differentiated in four classes of conditional prohibitions with permissions.

Managing the Problem: The Application and Enforcement of Radiation Protection Regulations

In this section the application and the enforcement of the regulations to use ionizing radiation in The Netherlands, England, and Belgium will be illustrated.[8] The three countries developed similar policy instruments: conditional prohibitions with permissions. The question to deal with here is about similarities and differences in their national policy styles to apply quite similar regulations. National policy style is perceived of as the way in which the regulations are applied and enforced in each of the three countries. First, the institutional setting of the application and the enforcement of the regulation will be explained. Second, the application and the enforcement of the regulation will be analyzed.

Using ionizing radiation, three types of safety standards have to be faced: standards for occupational safety, public health, and environmental protection. The necessity of these standards seems obvious. Workers using ionizing radiation in laboratories or industrial plants should be protected from ionizing hazards. They are the first who might be exposed. The same holds for the protection of the public and the environment. Without protective measures, radioactive substances or radioactive waste might contaminate the environment and expose the public. This may result in stochastic (population) effects.

Occupational safety, public health, and the protection of the environment constitute different policy domains in all three countries. Separate authorities are responsible for each of these public domains. In all three countries these authorities are in some way involved in the application and the enforcement of the radiation protection regulations.

In all three countries, authorities responsible for occupational safety and environmental protection dominate the application and the enforcement of the regulations. Public health authorities only maintain radiation standards for agricultural products, food protection from ionizing radiation, and the like.[9]

Radiation protection specialists are organized in professional groups. Specialized knowledge and professionalism are typical features of the people involved in radiation protection. Radiological workers and protection specialists function as a separate professional group in all three countries. For most employees, starting a career in radiation protection means a lifelong job because of the specialized knowledge in this professional field. Radiation protection specialists are well aware of their own professional status. As will be illustrated below, this professionalism simplifies the application and the enforcement of the regulations in the three countries.

Radiation protection is a highly professional and technical field of public policy. The institutional arrangement of this professionalism differs in the three countries. In The Netherlands the occupational safety part of the protection is a responsibility of the factory inspectorate, part of the Department of Social Affairs. They share the responsibility for radiation protection with the inspectorate for the environment, part of the Department for the Environment. Both organizations grant permits to use ionizing radiation. They prepare the technical specifications for the permits, control whether an applicant is suitable to use ionizing radiation, and prescribe the technical conditions that should be met to get a permit. Officially, the Dutch minister for the environment grants the permits.[10] Both inspectorates are only responsible for granting the use of radioactive substances and x-ray equipment.[11]

In England the institutional setting is about the same as in The Netherlands. Here too, the factory inspectorate and the inspectorate for the environment grant permits and enforce the regulations. In England the factory inspectorate is part of the health and safety executive of the Ministry for Labor Affairs. The inspectorate for the environment has a special organization for radiation protection: Her Majesty's Radiochemical Inspectorate. This specialized organization has two offices: one in London and one in Lancaster in the north of the country. The radiochemical inspectorate authorizes the use of radioactive substances and is also responsible for the safety of the British nuclear sites. The factory inspectorate is not directly involved in granting permits. They concentrate on rule enforcement. They are informed by the radiochemical inspectorate about the places where radioactive substances and x-ray equipment are in use.

In Belgium the institutional setting is different. Permits for class 2 and 3 premises are granted officially by the Belgian provinces. A provincial committee consisting of members of the Ministry of Public

Health, Occupational Safety, and Environmental Protection advises the provinces. Actually, the Belgian factory inspectorate dominates these advisory committees. The inspectorate contacts the applicants and writes the technical specifications for the provinces. The provinces themselves do not have any technical knowledge about using ionizing radiation or protecting against the hazards. The provinces take the technical knowledge from the factory inspectorate. As in The Netherlands and in England, the Belgian factory inspectorate is organized in regions. The factory inspectorate is not involved in the safety of the Belgian nuclear sites. The Belgian inspectorate for the environment is hardly involved in the granting of permits or the enforcement of the regulations for using radioactive substances or x-ray equipment.

In Belgium the institutional context for the enforcement of the regulations is quite straightforward. Every organization using ionizing radiation, whether a dentist using x-ray equipment, or an electricity producer owning a nuclear power plant, has to become a member of a specialized controlling organization. These (private) organizations conduct yearly technical evaluations of the conditions in which the ionizing radiation is used. These specialized organizations have a quite dominant position in the field of radiation protection. They control almost every place in Belgium where ionizing radiation is used. Every user has to pay for the technical evaluations these organizations perform periodically.

Another typical feature of the Belgian institutional setting is a result of the language cleavage in the country. In the organizations involved in radiation protection, the language is often a base for task division, e.g., the specialized organizations operate all over Belgium, but only French-speaking employees operate in the Walloon provinces of Belgium. Only in case of serious incidents is this convention overlooked.

In sum:

1. Radiation protection specialists are organized in professional groups.
2. In each country, radiation protection policy consists of three types of safety topics: occupational safety, public health, and environmental protection. The authorities responsible for occupational safety and environmental protection dominate the enactment and the enforcement of the regulations in The Netherlands and England. In Belgium the factory inspectorate has a dominant position.
3. The institutional context of radiation protection policy differs among the countries. In The Netherlands the arrangement is cooperative. Both inspectorates cooperate in granting permits and enforcing the regulations.

In England the cooperation between the inspectorates is limited as they only share information. In Belgium the cooperation between the organizations involved should be quite intensive (advising committee), but actually, only the factory inspectorate is advising the provinces about the granting of permits. Belgium is the only country in which the control and the enforcement of the regulations are separated.

Now that the institutional context of radiation protection policy has been illustrated, let us look more closely at the actual policy style in each of the three countries. It will be suggested that in spite of differences in institutional context and policy style, policy outcomes and policy effects are quite similar in all three countries. To illustrate this argument, I will first list some of the results in terms of goal attainment of radiation protection policy in the three countries. Second, I will illustrate their policy styles of enacting and enforcing the regulations for using ionizing radiation.

Goal Attainment of Radiation Protection Policy

The goal of radiation protection policy will be attained by using ionizing radiation in compliance with the regulations. The regulations differ with respect to guarantee safety standards. Dose limits is the major indicator of safety standards and compliance with the rules. The dose limits for the vast majority of classified personnel do not exceed the five millisievert a year standard. Data from The Netherlands and England showed that excess dosage sometimes occurs in nuclear premises, industrial laboratories, and as a result of gammagraphical activities. These findings lead to the conclusion that the goal of the radiation protection policy is almost completely attained in the three countries.

Apart from the dose limits, in none of the three countries are the other standards regulating the use of radioactive materials and x-ray equipment fully complied with. It is the record keeping that is most often violated. Rules that have direct consequences for the safety of the users or the environment are rarely violated. The high degree of rule compliance can be explained by the professionalism of the users of ionizing radiation. Dangerous use of ionizing radiation is not in congruence with the standards and status of the professional group. Using ionizing radiation implies compliance with safety standards based on professional knowledge. For the greater part, this professional knowledge coincides with the formal regulations for using ionizing radiation. So in general, the users of ionizing radiation are professionally motivated to comply with the formal regulations. This similarity in compliance orientation appears to have consequences for the policy style in enacting and enforcing the regulations in the three countries.

Policy Style and Application of the Regulations

A professional, motivated target group well aware of the potential hazards of ionizing radiation will comply with regulations that aim at protecting against them, without any resistance. This is especially so when these regulations coincide with professional standards. This happens to be the case in all three countries.

However, the countries differ in their respective policy styles. In England the chemical inspectorate takes quite a pragmatic position in enacting the regulations. Applicants for using ionizing radiation are presumed to have qualified professionals apply for the permit and to use the ionizing radiation with due regard to safety standards. The chemical inspectorate only checks a first application for a permit. Then they want to become acquainted with the new applicant and his organization to control the actual circumstances in which the ionizing radiation is used. They seldom provide technical advice to new applicants. In case of lack of knowledge to apply for a permit, applicants must buy the expertise. The chemical inspectorate only checks the application form against the actual circumstances of the applicant. In case the applicant is already known by the inspectorate, a decision about the permit is only based on the application form.

The radiochemical inspectorate also archives the notifications of using ionizing radiation. A notification is required in these cases where no radioactive waste is produced. Applications for notifications are only controlled administratively. Applicants for notification are not personally visited. So in England the regulations are put into force without close oversight of the applicants. The policy style is quite functional.

The inspectorates in The Netherlands have a somewhat different policy style. For those applying for a permit, the inspectorates act as advisers. Usually they contact the applicant to check the application and to give technical advice with respect to rule compliance. Members of the Dutch inspectorates stress their educative task to socialize the users of ionizing radiation in the professional standards of "the group." Often, members of the factory inspectorate act as "protection missionaries." The Dutch policy style is of an instructive kind.

In Belgium the protection against ionizing radiation and the policy aiming at this end is dominated by specialized organizations. These organizations perform an advisory and supervisory role on the premises where the ionizing radiation is used. For the Belgian inspectorate, this dominant position of the specialized organizations is a reason to enact the regulations in a formalistic policy style. The inspectorate sometimes contacts a permit applicant to check the application. Sometimes these visits result in advising provinces that grant the permits. Usually the specialized organizations are applying for a permit on behalf of an organization. In those cases the inspectorate's advice is based on the application, presuming the specialized organization to be responsible for the reliability of the content of the application form.

Policy Style and Enforcement of the Regulations

The policy style for the enforcement of the regulations is different in each country. In England the policy style is quite functional, as was the style in adopting the regulations. Both inspectorates do not cooperate directly to enforce the regulations but both check on the users of ionizing radiation in a fixed frequency. In England all users of ionizing radiation are visited every three years. If the regulations are violated, both inspectorates allow for improvements without formal prosecutions. Usually, this style of enforcement is effective. However, hard-liners do not get a second chance. If safety standards have not improved, both inspectorates do not hesitate to prosecute. So the policy style of rule enforcement is of a no-nonsense kind.

At the end of the 1980s the inspectorates in The Netherlands did not check on a fixed frequency. Usually, the supervision of compliance with the regulations was combined with an advisory visit for a permit application. In some regions both inspectorates went together for reasons of efficiency. In other regions they paid visits separately. In The Netherlands, users of ionizing radiation have never been prosecuted for violating the regulations. The members of the inspectorate believe that a policy style based on prosecution is not effective; they prefer to offer advice in order to internalize protection standards by radiation users. In their view, this is the only effective way to maintain safety standards. In The Netherlands, the policy style for regulations enforcement is of the instructive kind.

In Belgium there is no policy style of enforcement, because the regulations are not enforced. This is due to the dominant position of the specialized organizations in Belgium. These organizations are given almost full responsibility for all safety standards. Actually, these organizations have only supervisory power and expertise and no power to enforce the regulations. In my investigation of the Belgian radiation protection policy, I found that the specialized organizations do inform the factory inspectorate of violations of the regulations, but this information is often neglected by the inspectorate. To comply with the regulations, the Belgians rely on self-regulating forces.[12] The Belgian policy style of enforcement is of a passive kind.

In summary, it seems that the three countries developed different national policy styles to apply quite similar regulatory instruments. The Dutch developed a policy style of the persuasive type, whereas the policy style of the English is of a pragmatic/functional type. In Belgium the policy style is formalistic and passive in case of enforcement. Now the question is, which factors can explain these differences in policy style between the three countries?

These differences cannot be explained by national characteristics of the radiation protection policy. Earlier it was illustrated that regulation and the safety standards are quite similar in the three countries. In each country, the main policy instrument is of the "conditional prohibition with permissions" type. Only in The Netherlands this kind of policy instrument is treated as a package in combination with advice, information, and persuasion. In both other countries, such a package is less evident.

Another hypothesis for the differences in policy style might be the kind of organizations and individuals using ionizing radiation; Dutch users might need more support to comply with safety standards. However, these differences do not exist. In every country, users of ionizing radiation should be qualified to use ionizing radiation. In England and Belgium this qualification can be hired from outside the organization; in The Netherlands a qualified individual should be an employee of the organization in which the ionizing radiation is used. So the need to advise seems to be more limited in The Netherlands, in comparison with England and Belgium. Nevertheless, the Dutch inspectorates stress their advisory role in enacting and enforcing the regulations. Therefore, lack of expertise in the organizations using ionizing radiation cannot explain the differences in policy style between the countries.

I think two related factors might offer an explanation for the differences in policy style. The first one I call a learning effect of authorities and the second one is about differences in administrative culture in the three countries. In combination, both factors may have resulted in a national policy style in the field of radiation protection policy.

To illustrate the first factor, a few remarks about the use of ionizing radiation are necessary. In the last decades, the use of ionizing radiation has been stabilized. New applications of ionizing radiation are rare, so the actual policy field is quite transparent. In England, ionizing radiation is used in about 5,000 different places, and in The Netherlands in about 2,500 places. The type of radiation in use is limited to some twenty-five different applications. So the policy field is quite transparent, homogeneous, and stable. At the same time, the professional expertise on radiation protection extensively developed, for the greater part initiated by the professional organizations in the three countries. In each country radiological workers are well trained in protection standards and protection specialists are highly professionalized with their own professional standards and codes of practice.

The Dutch authorities did not integrate these developments in their policy style, whereas the English and the Belgians did. In comparison to The Netherlands, the policy style in England and Belgium is much more compatible with the professionalism of radiation users, and more efficient as well. It is my opinion that the English and the Belgians became more adaptive to the growing expertise of radiation users because of their extensive national nuclear industry. The supervision of this industry takes much time and many organizational resources. In England this was expressed by the members of the radiochemical inspectorate. In comparison to nuclear activities, all usage of radioactive substances and x-ray equipment can be labeled as "minor uses." The supervision of this kind of usage should take as few organizational resources as possible. For that reason the inspectorate took a very pragmatic and efficient position to deal with the usage of radioactive substances and x-ray equipment—a pragmatic position that suits the British administrative culture well.

In Belgium, the factory inspectorate is hiding in some way behind the specialized organizations that have a dominant position, while the provincial advisory committees are hiding behind the factory inspectorate. This policy style might be influenced by the specific Belgian administrative culture. Belgium is a divided country right in the middle of an extensive administrative reform. The centralized state has been transformed into a federalist state. During this process that has been going on for many years, authorities seem to wait for each other, in between relying on market forces.

The Dutch lack an extensive nuclear industry. So the professional status of the officials is not "nuclear" oriented. They can only deal with radioactive substances. In their activities the officials act like missionaries or visionaries of protection, a policy style that suits the morality-preaching Dutch administrative culture.

Reflecting on the Problem:
The Role of Evaluation Research in a Technical Field

We now come to the question about the impact of evaluation research. First I will briefly outline the typical features of radiation protection policy and, secondly, I shall discuss the role and impact of evaluation research in radiation protection policy in the three countries.

Our analysis shows that the policy choice in the European Union and in the three countries are primarily problem-driven. Basically, the problem the authorities were facing was of a rather technical character: using ionizing radiation without unintended exposure. The knowledge of the specific features of the three types of radiation (alpha, beta, and gamma radiation) has been the major base of the radiation protection policy of today. In such a problem-driven policy context, the degrees of freedom in policy choice seem rather limited. When facing technical problems, in the end, the logic of policy choice seems to be driven by the technical solutions. Under such circumstances, a policy-formation process may consist of several degrees of freedom, but as time goes by and the problem becomes better known, the freedom to take context-bound decisions will be limited. This is what has happened in radiation protection policy developed in the three countries.

Now what can be the role of policy evaluation in a technologically (problem) driven policy environment such as radiation protection? This question can be answered by looking briefly at the argument Fischer (1980) made in his book *Politics, Values and Public Policy*. Fischer distinguishes four types of evaluation research, two types of the first order and two types of the second order. The first type of evaluation is called *verification*, and is about the congruence of a policy with a certain set of criteria (e.g., goal attainment, effectiveness, and the like). The second type of evaluation is about *validation*, that is, the justification of the situation. This type investigates the situation in order to evaluate whether a criterion fits the situation. These two types of evaluation, Fischer calls first-order evaluation. First-order evaluation does not question the normative bases of a policy, as does second-order evaluation.

Fischer distinguishes two types of second-order evaluation. The first one he calls *vindication* which questions whether values underlying a policy contribute to the dominant society, culture, and provide system support. The second Fischer calls *rational choice*. This is a kind of overall meta-evaluation, assessing the satisfaction of human needs by societal and political structures.

In the case of radiation protection policy, these four types of evaluation all had significance for the policy choice, although in a very different way. In the end, only the first type of evaluation "survived," and is nowadays the main type of evaluation to improve radiation protection standards. The choices made in the past have sometimes been questioned in recent history by suggesting other types of evaluation. A group of American scientists involved in the first nuclear fission warned politicians for the dangers mankind was facing with atomic energy (see De Ruiter and Van der Sijde 1985: 558–567). These warnings can be seen as evaluation of the rational choice type.

In the 1960s and 1970s societal groups and green parties criticized the nuclear industry for the same reason scientists had done years earlier. In the 1970s, the Dutch government initiated a societal discussion on energy scenarios for the future (*brede maatschappelijke discussie*). This discussion was enforced by "no-nukes" groups and left-wing parties in Parliament. The impact of this discussion was rather limited; the planning of new nuclear power plants in The Netherlands proceeded. This planning of new nuclear energy plants only stopped because of the Chernobyl accident and not because of societal resistance (rational choice) against nuclear industry.

By justifying ionizing radiation, the impact of second-order evaluation for policy choice in the field of radiation protection policy, as suggested by Fisher, has been limited. After Röntgen and Becquerel made their discoveries, societies have made decisions that seem to be irrevocable. For that reason, the logic of policy choice in radiation protection is fed only with evaluation research of the first order, especially of the verification type. This type of evaluation has always been rather technical, and has almost always aimed at increasing the reliability of (technical) safety standards. The effectiveness or legitimacy of policy instruments or of policy style has not been evaluated extensively. Radiation protection is dominated by technicians. They think radiation protection policy is about safety standards, standards that should be improved permanently by technological research conducted by technicians, not by policy analysts. Thus the actual impact of social science policy-evaluation research on policy instruments and policy style has been quite limited.[13]

Postscript

In this chapter I have illustrated the policy style of radiation protection policy in The Netherlands, England, and Belgium. Facing the problem of radiation exposure, the countries developed quite similar policy instruments, but differing national policy styles to apply these instruments. The dominant policy instrument in the three countries is of the "conditional prohibition with permissions" type. Only The Netherlands developed a policy style consisting of a package of regulations and information. Economic instruments have no significance at all in radiation protection policy.

Does my study have any significance for the Vedung typology of policy instruments? According to Vedung, policy instruments have two constituent parts: a certain action content and a certain authoritative force. The latter is the main dimension underlying his typology of policy instruments. Authoritative force is about the constraints of instruments on the behavioral alternatives of individuals and organizations, whereas an action content specifies "what to do and how to behave."

Examining the somewhat different national policy styles in the three countries, the question is whether "action content" should be perceived of as a constituent dimension either of a policy instrument or of a policy style. I would suggest that "action content" be seen as an underlying dimension of policy style, rather than that of policy instrument. Disregarding the type of policy instrument, the content of the action manifested in various national policy styles can be more or less constraining as was illustrated by the policy style of radiation protection policy in the three countries. Radiation protection policy illustrates that policy instruments of the same type (regulations), containing similar constraints on behavioral alternatives, can be chosen and applied in different ways, ways that can differ in degree of constraint.

Notes

1. Literal translation: "About a new kind of radiation."
2. In her biography of Marie Curie, Giroud tells about the experiments of Pierre Curie who exposed his arm, on purpose, to radiation to gain more insight into the biological effects of radiation. At the beginning of this century, physicians used their own bodies to tune x-ray equipment.

3. These basic principles still underlie radiation protection policy in the countries of the European Union.
4. The principle of *alara* (as low as reasonably achievable) prescribes that an exposure to ionizing radiation should always be minimized by technical or other measures. The dose limit should not be treated as a quality standard, but as an overall maximum. Under all circumstances, the actual exposure should be reduced as far as possible under the maximum.
5. The Euratom treaty can be regarded as the formal European arrangement of the Atoms for Peace program, initiated by the Americans in the early 1950s.
6. The absorbing, transmitting, tracing, illuminating features of ionizing radiation makes it applicable for many purposes. The medical use for diagnosis and therapy is well known, but ionizing radiation is also used to control industrial processes and to conduct scientific research. Radioactive substances are used as open substances and as equipment in which the radioactive substance is locked up by containment. This containment can be controlled. X-ray equipment is used in the same way and for the same purposes, but is produced by an external energy source (electricity).
7. Radiological laboratories and nuclear sites are perceived as major uses; all other applications of ionizing radiation and x-ray equipment are perceived as minor uses.
8. The content of this paragraph is based on a comparison of the radiation protection policy in The Netherlands, England, and Belgium that I conducted between 1986 and 1991. This research project was guided by a theoretical model based on Simon's concept of bounded rationality and consisted of three major concepts: policy, implementation, and organization. Implementation was perceived of as the application and the enforcement of the regulations to use ionizing radiation. Civil and military applications of nuclear power were, for specific reasons, excluded from the research project.
9. At the time of the Chernobyl accident in 1986, the public health authorities in The Netherlands dominated the management of the crisis. They investigated the contamination of grass, for example, that the Dutch cows were eating at that time. They also inspected the food supply and the food production and ordered the destruction of milk, for example, that exceeded standards of radioactivity.
10. Recently the granting of permits to use ionizing radiation is given to the minister for social affairs.
11. In The Netherlands, nuclear sites are supervised by other organizations and not by the factory inspectorate or the inspectorate for the environment.
12. These self-regulating forces proved to be unreliable. At the end of the 1980s, the Belgian authorities discovered significant irregularities with the treatment of nuclear waste at Mol.
13. As far as I know, my own evaluation research of the Dutch radiation protection policy, conducted between 1985 and 1987, is still unique in the field of radiation protection policy in The Netherlands. The impact of this evaluation has been quite limited, although the evaluation was initiated to improve the effectiveness and efficiency of the policy style. The Dutch National Audit Office, Algemene Rekenkamer, investigated the functioning and efficiency of several Dutch inspectorates, such as the factory inspectorate and the inspectorate for the environment. This study concluded that the functioning of the inspectorates in radiation protection policy was relatively effective and efficient in comparison with the other tasks of the inspectorates (Tweede Kamer 1988–1989, 21 283, no. 12).

References

Arentsen, M.J. 1991. *Policy Organization and Policy Implementation: An Inquiry of the Radiation Protection Policy in The Netherlands, England, and Belgium.* Enschede: University of Twente.

Fischer, F. 1980. *Politics, Values and Public Policy: The Problem of Methodology.* Boulder, CO: University of Colorado.

Ruiter, W. de, and B. van der Sijde. 1985. *The Nuclear Heritage.* Mappel/Amsterdam: Boom.

Simon, H.A. [1947] 1967. Administrative Behaviour. 2d ed. New York: The Free Press.

Tweede Kamer. 1988–1989. *Arbeidsinspectir* (Health and Safety Authority) 21 283, nos. 1-1.

Wylick, R.K. 1966. *Röntgen in The Netherlands.* Utrecht: Hoeijenbos.

10

The Management and Privatization of Korea's Public Enterprises

Nam-Kee Lee

The privatization of public enterprises now appears to be an activity undertaken by governments worldwide. From the countries of the former Soviet Union to the developed industrial democracies of England, France, Japan, Italy, and the United States to those with surging economies such as Mexico, Singapore, China, Brazil, Spain, and Korea, the selling off of public corporations and companies is now accepted as a legitimate and, indeed, necessary function of government. The underlying presumption behind this rush to privatize is the belief that market forces and private-sector incentives will create better economic performance and growth than will retaining these activities and companies in the public sector.

But before moving too far into this discussion, it is important to note that there are basic distinctions in the privatization arena that must at least be noted. Donahue (1989) notes the need to distinguish, in the discussion of privatization, among the following: the selling off of public assets; substituting private workers for an all but identical group of public workers; enlisting private energies to improve the performance of tasks that would remain in some sense public; paying for goods and services privately or publicly; and finally, producing the desired good or the service rendered by a governmental or a nongovernmental organization. The centrality of his point is that the term "privatization" is woefully imprecise. Its use can lead to considerable confusion for there are so many different meanings attached to it. Much the same point has been made by Salamon (1989) and Savas (1987) as well.

In this chapter, the discussion of privatization in Korea will focus on the selling off and transferring of public assets to the private sector (or to be completely precise, to both private- and quasi-private sector organizations). Furthermore, the chapter will address how policy evaluation has come to play such a central role in the management of the many different Korean public enterprises. (For an excellent overview of the current state of policy evaluation in Korea, see Lee 1995).

Before moving into the discussion on Korea, there is one other matter to note. In both the chapter on "Policy Instruments: Typologies and Theories," and in his contributed remarks to the conclusion for this volume, Evert Vedung makes the point forcefully that he does not consider privatization as a policy tool. He refers in both places to privatization as a means of organizational change undertaken by government. The distinction for him is between *tools* and *strategies* of change (on this point, see also Linder and Peters 1989). Privatization fits in the latter category. Such a distinction is acceptable here because of the manner in which Vedung has classified policy tools into only three groups. Were he to have taken a more expansive approach to classifying the tools of government, I am then sure that there would have been a place for privatization to be considered as a policy tool and not as a strategy of organizational change. Indeed, other authors have so indicated in their own discussions of policy tools (cf. Hood 1986; Salamon 1989).

The Role of Public Enterprises in the Korean Economy

In spite of the rapid rate of market liberalization as pursued by the government, the public enterprise sector in Korea is still quite large. In 1994, the total budget for all of Korea's public enterprises combined was 1.82 times greater than the budget for the entire central government.

The public enterprise sector's output accounted for 9.4 percent of Korea's gross domestic product (GDP) in 1990. During the 1970s, an average of 40 percent of the public enterprise sector's share of GDP came from manufacturing. However, the contribution by manufacturing has since been declining, and in 1990 its contribution had fallen to 22.8 percent—about 2.14 percent of GDP.

Public enterprises associated with the social infrastructure, including the areas of power generation, construction, and transportation have, on the other hand, increased their contribution to the public enterprise sector's share of Korea's GDP to about 55 percent, which translates to

TABLE 10.1
Public Enterprises' Share of Gross Domestic Capital

Formation   (Unit: percent)

Sector	1963	1975	1980	1981	1984	1986	1990
Public Enterprises' Share	31.7	33.2	27.6	30.7	20.7	15.6	8.9

about 5.2 percent of GDP. This is an indication as to the increasing importance of Korea's public enterprises in the social infrastructure.

In regards to investment activity, Korean public enterprises' share of domestic capital formation was approximately 30 percent between 1963 and 1981. Although this figure fell to 8.9 percent in 1990, Korea's public enterprises still play a very important role in investment, as can be noted from table 10.1.

The total number of workers employed by the public enterprise sector was 367,946 in 1994. This is only about 1.8 percent of Korea's total work force, thus implying that the public enterprise sector is capital-intensive.

Korea's public enterprises can be categorized into four subgroups according to the type of ownership and the level of autonomy. These four subgroups are as follows:

1. Government Enterprises (GEs) of which there are three in operation in Korea at this time—the Postal Service, the Office of Railroads, and the Office of Supply. These are actual government entities and are regulated in the same manner as other government organizations. These GEs have minimal managerial autonomy.

2. Government-Invested Enterprises (GIEs) are public corporations in which the government owns at least 50 percent of the total capital. All GIEs fall under the jurisdiction of the GIE Management Act, so they are accorded more managerial autonomy than GEs, even though they can be 100 percent owned by the government. GIEs are also subject to government post-performance evaluation standards. Currently, there are twenty-three GIEs operating in Korea. These include four banking institutions, five energy companies, four construction firms, three manufacturing companies, and six public service utilities.

3. Government-Funded Enterprises (GFEs) currently number eight and include the Korea Exchange Bank, the Pohang Iron and Steel Mill Company, and the Korea Import-Export Bank. These are all companies in which the government owns less than 50 percent of the total capital. The role of

the government with respect to management is therefore the same as that of any major shareholder of any publicly traded corporation. However, GFEs are not subject to post-performance evaluation standards.

4. Subsidiaries of Government-Invested Enterprises (SGIEs) are public enterprises owned by the GIEs. The government has no special or direct means of controlling SGIEs (of which there are 106), and the responsibility for their performance evaluations rests with the parent organizations. SGIEs have been created for two purposes: (1) to maximize the efficiency of parent GIEs by specialization; and/or (2) to increase the range of services offered by GIEs.

Brief History of Public Enterprises in Korea

From Independence to 1960

The Korean government established almost all public enterprises during this period by taking over properties which had formerly been owned by the Japanese colonial administration or Japanese businessmen. GEs formerly operated by the Japanese colonial administration—which controlled the railroads, postal service, telecommunications, and monopolies—had been taken over, and other major enterprises owned by the colonial administration or Japanese businessmen had been transformed into GIEs.

Public enterprises were not only the economic backbone of production, employment, and investment, but also the major engine for achiev-

TABLE 10.2
Status of Korea's Public Enterprises
(as of March 1994)

Type	Number of Companies	Number of Employees	1994 Budget (Unit: US$ [millions])
GEs	3	73,481	5,228
GIEs	23	75,776	59,737
GFEs	8	41,188	14,289
SGIEs	106	77,501	18,972
Total	140	367,946	98,226

Exchange Rate: Won
800 equals US$ 1.00

ing political goals, that is, the industrial rehabilitation following the mass destruction of the country during the Korean War.

The 1960s

Public enterprises became a major engine of economic development in accordance with the implementation of the First and Second Five-Year Economic Development Plans during the 1960s.

At the initial stage of economic development, the central government had no choice but to intervene, through public enterprises, in the development of major industries and the social infrastructure. Only the government was in a position to marshal the tremendous resources necessary for development as the private sector was not yet able to proceed with development on its own.

In the 1960s, many GIEs as well as GFEs were established. Enormous investments for the establishment of public enterprises were made possible by the introduction of foreign capital loans as domestic capital resources were not available.

During the late 1960s, concerns increased greatly in regards to the management performance of public enterprises that had been established through foreign capital loans. This was mainly in consideration of the repayment of the principle and interest. In order to improve management efficiency, the privatization of public enterprises was pursued instead of leaving the enterprises in the public sector and introducing a proper performance-evaluation system. Privatization was encouraged by the growth of the private sector, which had become capable of taking over public enterprises with the expansion of the national economy.

The privatized public enterprises began to record profits within only a few years. Their improvement in profit-and-loss balances was thought by many to illustrate the superior management efficiency of the private sector in relation to that of the public sector.

1970–1983

During this period, many GIEs were established. The government also created subsidiaries of GIEs (the SGIEs) by allowing GIEs to invest in the private sector, thereby indirectly allowing the government to carry out national industrial policy more effectively. (For a careful assessment of the Korean public enterprise system during this period, see Song 1986.)

The first performance evaluation system for GIEs was introduced in 1968. The supervising minister decided the management performance target for each GIE at the beginning of the calendar year and evaluated its performance by February of the next year. However, under this system it was rather difficult to measure management performance because the management target was only based on the size of the budget, and the impact of the system was somewhat nominal because there was no compensation based on the results of the performance evaluation.

In order to rectify these problems, the government established the GIE Administration Act of 1973, the purpose of which was to effectively control the GIEs. The act specifically defined GIEs as companies in which the government held more than 50 percent of the total equity. The government began its efforts to administer GIEs systematically in order to improve their management performance.

The new performance evaluation system was applied beginning in 1973 as follows (see Song 1986: 29–50).

First, the performance evaluation was conducted twice each year. Second, a diverse set of evaluation criteria were established. The enterprises were evaluated according to standards which were decided on the basis of past performance. Bonuses ranging from 50 percent to 200 percent of basic salaries were provided to individuals working for GIEs based on the results of the evaluations. And finally, the responsibilities for evaluation were transferred from the Supervising Ministry to the Economic Planning Board (EPB), the government ministry responsible for social and economic development planning.

1984 to Present

Since 1984, many subsidiaries of GIEs were established in order to promote specialization and secure managerial autonomy. In early 1985, many commercial banks and the Korea Oil Company were privatized because of the relatively rapid growth of the private sector. The most important outcome of this period, however, was the complete reformation of the management system of GIEs. From the late 1970s to the early 1980s, the inefficiency of GIEs was clear in spite of governmental efforts to rationalize management. The call to limit governmental interference in the management of GIEs became greater both as their management became more complex and as they rapidly grew. In this period, every GIE was controlled by the government through a host of laws and regulations such as the GIE Administration Act and the GIE Budget and Accounting Act.

The budget of GIEs had to be approved by the president after examination by the Cabinet Council and concerned ministries. The majority of the executives of GIEs were recruited from outside of the companies and were selected for political considerations rather than for managerial professionalism. Those executive directors appointed for political considerations were in most cases not equipped with detailed knowledge of the company in question, and few of them had vested interests in the development of the companies. This led to the weakened management efficiency of GIEs as well as to the demoralization of the employees.

Repeated audits by different government organizations such as the Board of Audit and Inspection, the Supervising Ministry, and the Ministry of Finance resulted in repetition and the inevitable waste of time and manpower. Furthermore, the conservative nature of the management dampened any efforts at organizational creativity of GIEs. The government guidelines of various government organizations were not only overlapping and duplicating, but also contradicting among themselves. Such situations resulted in the waste of time on the part of the government and were a source of inefficiency on the part of GIEs.

The post-performance evaluation system was implemented in such a way as to be almost completely without internal constraints and controls. As but one example, nearly all GIE employees received the maximum bonus allowable—200 percent. The system therefore did not provide proper incentives for improving efficiency.

In order to improve efficiency, the government carried out reforms of the GIEs' management system. The major objectives of the reforms were guaranteeing managerial autonomy and the application of the new performance evaluation system to oversee management.

Korea's New GIE Management System

Reform of the GIEs' Regulation System

Prior to 1983, all GIEs were subject to a host of laws and regulations. Those that were imposed on individual companies, such as the GIE Budget and Accounts Act, the GIE Administration Act, the Board of Audit and Inspection Act, the Procurement Fund Act, and other directives had a significant impact on business activities in Korea.

The GIE Management Act, enacted in 1984, repealed both the GIE Budget and Account Act and the GIE Administration Act, thus changing the way in which GIEs were governed. The GIE Management Act increased managerial autonomy while conversely reducing the degree of control possessed by the government over management. This act also introduced the performance evaluation system in order to give the GIEs a more self-governing role. What follows is a short description of the key aspects of this new performance evaluation system.

Improvement of the Board of Director's System. In the past, the GIE board of directors were the standing bodies of the organization which performed policy-making functions and had administrative responsibilities. However, according to the new system, every board member including the chairman now served on a non-standing basis. The membership of the board was restructured to include a diverse set of individuals who were to remain outside of the GIE. These people included delegates from the government, consumer representatives, professors, and specialists in the areas concerned. Accordingly, direction from the government and the diverse opinions from the interested parties were now all considered together in the GIE policy-making decisions.

Guarantee of Managerial Autonomy. The new system has granted managers of the GIEs greater autonomy in making decisions pertaining to budgeting, personnel, procurement, and so forth. Personnel decisions, especially appointments of senior executive officers which used to be made by the government via the Supervising Ministry, are now made by people within the organization. Requisitioning supplies from the Office of Supply has become voluntary instead of compulsory, and audits have been simplified so that only the Board of Audit and Inspection may audit the GIEs. Furthermore, the GIEs' budget had previously been determined by the cabinet, the president, the Supervising Ministry, and the EPB. Now the GIE's budget is prepared according to common government guidelines and requires only the approval of its board of directors.

The Management Evaluation Council. The Management Evaluation Council has been created to serve as a top policy-making organization in government in order to operate new management systems. The Management Evaluation Council formulates important policies for the GIEs on such matters as guidelines for preparing management objectives, performance evaluations, incentive bonuses, and so forth. The council is chaired by the minister of the EPB and consists of eight ministers who supervise GIEs and three private commissioners who have appropriate knowledge and experience.

The Introduction of the Performance Evaluation System. The performance evaluation system was introduced in order to guarantee a GIE's accountability. Under this system, the GIEs are given performance evaluation criteria at the end of the calendar year. These performance evaluation criteria outline the GIE's goals for the coming year. Evaluations are then conducted in March of the next year, that is, fifteen months after the goals were first given to the GIEs. The past year's management performance report is submitted by 20 March, and the Management Evaluation Council determines the results of the performance evaluation by 20 June.

In order to ensure the fairness of the evaluation, the Economic Planning Board organizes a yearly ad-hoc management evaluation task force. This task force establishes the evaluation criteria and subsequently evaluates the performance of the GIEs. The local management evaluation task force consists of thirty to forty users and includes accountants, professors, researchers, and relevant specialists.

Each GIE's incentive bonus is determined according to the results of the performance evaluation. The government honors the GIEs that perform well and may propose the removal of managers of those GIEs that perform poorly.

Impact of Korea's New GIE Management System

Since the introduction of Korea's new Management System in 1984, the evaluated performance of the GIEs has improved. Table 10.3 shows the average performance evaluation scores from 1984 to 1993. Given a standardized target grade of 87.5, the average performance evaluation was quite good as the actual average has been around 90. This seems a clear indication that the average performance of the GIEs during this period was much better than originally expected.

Another simple indicator of the performance improvement is the reduction in the budget deficits incurred by GIEs. The number of enterprises operating with budget deficits and the size of the deficits have been substantially reduced since the introduction of the new system as shown in table 10.4.

TABLE 10.3
Average Realized Performance Scores of GIEs

1984	1985	1986	1987	1988	1989	1990	1991	1992	1993
90.4	90.2	90.3	90.4	90.2	90.3	90.0	89.6	89.6	89.4

Source: Economic Planning Board, Government of Korea

TABLE 10.4
Number of GIEs Incurring Budget Deficits and their Size

	1983	1984	1985	1986	1987	1988	1989	1990	1991	1992
Number	5	1	–	1	4	2	2	2	2	2
Size of Deficit (mil. won)	35,911	530	–	963	9,605	26,600	15,638	24,284	15,638	6,547

Source: Economic Planning Board, Government of Korea

This has been a desirable change for the management of public enterprises.

The Privatization of Korea's Public Enterprises

During the 1980s, with the trends toward internationalization and liberalization, the Korean government committed itself to realigning Korea's social and economic systems according to free-market principles in order to strengthen the economy. It was believed that the best way to increase efficiency is through privatization and competition. Privatized firms provide employee incentive systems, ultimately saving on production costs, and thus improving their own financial structure. In this context, the privatization of public enterprises was encouraged.

There are basically three criteria used by the Korean government in deciding whether or not to privatize a particular public enterprise. The first is the level of public interest for the goods and services produced by the target enterprise. If public interest is considered more of an important issue than efficiency, privatization should not be enforced. The second criterion is the scale of capital of the public enterprise. Those public enterprises that require exorbitant amounts of capital cannot be undertaken by private enterprise. The last criterion is the profitability of the public enterprise. If there is no reason to believe that the target enterprise will be profitable in the future, then there will, of course, be no demand for the company's stock.

Privatization involves large-scale selling off of government shares to a broad spectrum of the population. There are four reasons why the government wants to sell its shares of public enterprises to the public.

The first reason is to form a national consensus and build a commitment to sustaining economic development. This can be done by increasing the level of participation by the general public in privatized public enterprises. Second, such a sale will also help reduce the disparities in income distribution by spreading economic benefits to low-income laborers who have contributed to the nation's economic growth; it will also help raise the morale of the employees of the privatized enterprises, with the purpose of resolving long-standing labor disputes. Third is the protection of "key" industries from being owned by a few people. The final reason is to stabilize the rapid development of the stock market by increasing the number of stockholders.

With this in mind, the Korean government decided to plan for the privatization of eleven GIEs and GFEs. Five of these enterprises are designated for complete privatization and six enterprises, including the Korea Electric Power Corporation and the Korea Telecommunications Authority, have been selected for partial privatization because of their importance to the national economy. The government will continue to hold more than 50 percent of the shares of these six enterprises.

According to this schedule, the Pohang Iron and Steel Company sold 34.1 percent of its shares to the public in May of 1988, the Korea Electric Power Company sold 21 percent of its stock in August of 1989, and the Korean Stock Exchange was completely privatized in February of 1988.

With the exception of the three companies mentioned above, the plan for the sale of the stocks (except those of the Korea Telecommunications Authority, which sold 15 percent of its stock in October 1993 and May 1994) has not yet been implemented. This is because the Korean stock market has not yet fully recovered from a severe slump which began in 1990. The stocks of these public enterprises will be sold when the market begins to recover and when the government believes that it will have no adverse effects on this recovery.

The stock market has rebounded since 1993, and the government proceeded accordingly. In 1994, the Citizen's National Bank and the Foreign Exchange Bank were divested to the private sector. The National Textbook Company was also privatized in 1994. In addition, 59 of a total of 106 GIE subsidiaries will be privatized during the next few years (see table 10.5 below.) These subsidiaries have achieved their objectives and have limited relations with their mother companies. Some subsidiaries of GIEs which are competing in the private sector will also be privatized. In addition, the government also has plans to sell shares in a number of other GIEs in the coming years. Table 10.6 reports on this timetable.

In order to provide more detail on how these present initiatives to privatize the GEs and the GIEs are proceeding, the following three cases are discussed as examples.

Case No. 1: The Conversion of the
Korean Telecommunications Authority

The Korean Telecommunications Authority (KTA) was transformed from a GE into a GIE on January 1, 1982. This conversion was performed in order to guarantee managerial autonomy and flexibility, thereby increasing efficiency and reducing bureaucracy. This conversion was the initial approach to the privatization of KTA. After the stabilization of KTA's GIE status, the government will privatize it. The conversion has not been made earlier because the telecommunications industry is of vital importance to the public interest. Additionally, the employees preferred to retain the status of "government official." However, the recent technological advances in the world's telecommunications industry have forced Korea to reevaluate its position on holding back from changing KTA from a GIE into a truly private sector company.

Shortly after its conversion, KTA became successful in many areas. Firstly, sales volume increased by 328 percent, up from 962 billion won (US$ 1.2 billion) in 1982 to 4.12 trillion won (US$ 5.15 billion) in 1991, while profit increased 258 percent from 133 billion won (US$ 166 million) to 476 billion won (US$ 595 million). Outlays for research and development (R&D) had concurrently been increased from 16 billion won (US$ 20 million) to 165 billion won (US$ 206 million). In addition, KTA is planning to hire more research personnel and to increase its outlays for R&D to 6 percent of total revenue by 2001, up from 4 percent in 1991. Researchers accounted for 1.5 percent of KTA's work force in 1991, but they will account for 5 percent of KTA's work force by 2001.

There has been a significant increase in the quality of services offered by KTA since its conversion to a GIE. Telephone-switching capacity has increased 290 percent from 4.5 million to 17.5 million connections, and the number of subscribers has increased 257 percent from 13.2 million to 40.2 million. The yearly "breakdown rate" dramatically decreased between 1982 and 1991, from 69.4 minutes per line to 2.3. Finally, the cost of services has been reduced on numerous occasions within the past ten years. In 1990 alone, charges for domestic long-distance calls had been cut 10 percent and charges for overseas

TABLE 10.5
Current Privatization Schedule
(Firms Selected for Privatization)
(Total Privatization)

Firms	Government Holdings Before (percent)	Primary Services or Products	Method Employed
Korea Stock Exchange[1]	65.2	Regulation of securities, sales, review of new stock offerings	Sold to member firms
National Textbook Co., Ltd.	50.0	Publishing and supplying of elementary and middle school textbooks	Public tender offer
Foreign Exchange Bank	2.5[2]	Deals in foreign exchange	Public tender offer
Korea Appraisal Board	49.4	Appraisal of bank collateral and firms' assets	Sold to current stockholders
Korea Technology Development Corporation	20.8	Providing credit, credit guarantees, and loans for technology development	Sold to current stockholders

[1]This firm was completely privatized in February 1988.
[2]The remaining 97.5 percent is held by the Bank of Korea.

long-distance calls had been cut by 8.4 percent as well. Overseas long-distance charges were cut by an additional 7 percent in 1993.

KTA has also made impressive progress in the area of technology development. Recently, KTA installed electronic domestic long-distance lines and completed the "great-sphere telephone automation," thereby eliminating on-line congestion. In addition, KTA plans to establish the "real-time" system throughout the entire country. "Great-sphere telephone automation" is the name given for the first stage of the Integrated Service Digital Network (ISDN). KTA has also met with great success in developing the Time Division Exchange (TDX).

TABLE 10.6
Partial Privatization
(By selling shares to the public)

Firms	Government Holdings Before (percent)	Primary Services or Products	Government Shares after Privatization
Korea Tobacco & Ginseng Corporation	100.0	Production and distribution of tobacco and ginseng	51 percent
Korean Electric Power Corporation[1]	100.0	Electrical source development and electricity generation	51 percent
Korea Tele-communications Authority	100.0	Telegram and telephone facility, development and maintenance	51 percent
Pohang Iron and Steel Company[2]	69.1	Production of steel	35 percent
Citizens National Bank	72.6	Promotes household savings and expands financing for small enterprises and low-income groups	51 percent
Small and Medium Industry Bank	99.9	Providing credit guarantees, loans, and discounts to small and medium sized industries	51 percent

[1]In August 1989, 21 percent of this firm was privatized.
[2]In May 1989, 34.1 percent of this firm was privatized.

Since 1982, KTA has accomplished great feats in R&D and customer service which is a direct result of greater managerial autonomy and efficiency arising from its transformation from a GE to a GIE.

The official view of the Korean government has, since the early 1980s, been and continues to be that the best way to increase efficiency is by the gradual movement towards privatization and competition; thus the

Korean government decided to sell off 49 percent of KTA's assets. In accordance with the privatization process, some government regulations were eliminated in order to speed up the process of privatization. Government regulation in the telecommunications area necessitated a permit for business activity, and this created an informal entry barrier. These regulations were qualified via the revision of the Electricity Business Act in December 1989. Even though these regulations were designed to cure market failures, many generated economic inefficiencies.

Currently, competition is encouraged in the mobile telecommunications business, the data telecommunications industry, and in the overseas long-distance telephone market. In 1992, a second overseas long-distance telephone company, Dacom, began competing directly with KTA.

Privatization has mainly been effected through the sale of assets, either by public-tender offers or people's share with fixed prices. The primary purchasers of this stock were employees, individual investors, and firms.

In order to effectively cope with the change that will occur in the competitive climate caused by the restructuring of the telecommunications market, KTA will implement an innovative internal management scheme, thus creating a modern information technology industry. Now that the mobile and data communications operations have been privatized, KTA will be the final company to be privatized in the entire telecommunications sector.

Case No. 2: The Privatization of the Korean
Tobacco and Ginseng Corporation

The Korean Tobacco and Ginseng Corporation (KT&G) was converted from a GE to a GIE in April 1987. KT&G was successful not only in management related affairs, but also in boosting the morale of its employees.

KT&G posted healthy gains in several areas. KT&G's sales volume increased from 1.52 trillion won (US$ 1.90 billion) in 1987 to 2.36 trillion won (US$ 2.95 billion) in 1991. Since 1987, three new brands of cigarettes have been introduced to meet consumer demand, and they have obtained a significant share of the cigarette market in Korea. KT&G also managed to nearly double its productivity during this time from 4,701 pieces per man-hour to 8,171 pieces. Additionally, the distribution system has been improved, and KT&G is now able to reach even the most inaccessible communities.

Other improvements in customer service included the creation of a consumer protection office for engaging in troubleshooting activities as well as the placement of a greater number of vending machines across the entire nation. To improve the quality of their products, KT&G has implemented quality-control and employee-suggestion systems.

In regards to their ginseng division, sales volume has increased 352 percent, from 8 billion won in 1987 to 37 billion won in 1991. The increase in sales volume was a direct result of new product development and increased sales promotion.

In addition, KT&G has increased its outlays for R&D from 0.98 percent of sales revenue to 1.37 percent. Through this increase, KT&G has been able to develop a high-density composite fertilizer which reduced the cost of cultivating tobacco. The benefits of ginseng have also been researched by KT&G who discovered that the root improves the function of the liver, acts as an anti-carcinogen, and decreases cholesterol levels.

Soon after the initial stage of privatization (conversion from a GE to a GIE), KT&G was reorganized in order to improve sales potential and to prepare itself for a change in management. The work force was reduced from 11,465 in 1986 to 9,200 in 1991 as a result of improvements in automation and efficiency. In addition, KT&G improved its personnel system and adopted an ability-based employment program in order to boost morale. When needed, KT&G hires service companies to assist in simple labor tasks such as maintenance, cleaning, and so forth.

The installation of a computer system has also played a big part in KT&G's improvement in efficiency. KT&G was the first of Korea's public enterprises to adopt the POS and bar code system. After 1986, the Korean tobacco market was flung open to foreign competition; hence KT&G had to improve the quality of its products and its productivity in a very short time.

Even after its initial conversion, KT&G still contributes 42.7 percent more to the government's finances than it did in 1986; specifically, 1.9 trillion won (US$ 2.4 billion) in 1991, up from 1.1 trillion won (US$ 1.4 billion) in 1986. This increase in revenue can be attributed to the larger sales volume arising from improved efficiency of the GIE.

Although KT&G has benefitted immensely from conversion to a GIE, some inefficiencies in management will persist until KT&G becomes fully privatized. In the meantime, as in the cases of KTA and the Korean Electric Power Company (KEPCO), the government will sell a large portion of its share of stock to the public in order to further increase efficiency.

Case No. 3: The Privatization of the Korean National Railroad

The Korean National Railroad (KNR) which is still a GE will be converted to a GIE in 1995. The railroad industry is gaining more attention because of problematic traffic congestion on the nation's highways and air pollution caused by such congestion. The railroad industry is going to be reorganized in order to accommodate an expected increase in the number of railroad passengers.

Korea is considering embarking on a high-speed train project in the very near future with France's TGV. Current conditions have pushed this project as well as the entire transformation of KNR to the forefront of domestic issues.

KNR recorded a deficit of 12.6 billion won (US$ 15.7 million) between 1987 and 1991. Such a deficit is a tremendous burden on the government's finances and is another reason to reform KNR. Not unlike KTA and KT&G, KNR is expected to become a profitable company soon after completing managerial reorganization. As in the case of other GEs, KNR will first become a GIE, and then, in the long run, become completely privatized.

Conclusion: The Korean Experience

The major objective of Korea's program of privatization is the increased efficiency of public enterprises. With this in mind, the government has taken action in several different ways. Each public enterprise being unique, the government has dealt with each one differently, with priority placed on the public interest.

Complete privatization has been prescribed for some public enterprises while transformation from GEs to GIEs has been prescribed for others. Conversion from a GE to a GIE has sometimes been done to specifically increase efficiency, as was the case for both KTA and KT&G. But becoming a GIE is not the final objective: These GIEs will eventually be completely privatized. In order to encourage efficiency while enterprises are still GIEs, the government has introduced the GIE evaluation system and the associated system of performance bonuses.

In 1984, the government passed the Government-Invested Enterprise Act as one means of guaranteeing the autonomy of public enterprises.

The act did manage to achieve positive results, but problems still persist, especially with respect to management systems and the ability to respond quickly in a rapidly changing technological environment. The results of the past twenty years strongly suggest, though, that privatization appears to be the most effective way to increase efficiency within the policy restraints of the Korean system of governance.

Privatization has also been pursued in an effort to more evenly distribute wealth. The personal wealth of individuals who previously never had the opportunity to invest has been increased as result of the government's offering of shares at discount prices. Investors with lower-than-average incomes are now eligible to become shareholders in Korea's most important companies.

Lastly, selling off government-held shares in various GEs and GIEs increases the government's budget revenue. This extra revenue may be spent on the social infrastructure or on social welfare programs. For these key reasons, Korea will continue to pursue its program of privatization in the future.

References

Donahue, John D. 1989. *The Privatization Decision: Public Ends, Private Means.* New York: Basic Books.

Hood, Christopher C. 1986. *The Tools of Government.* Chatham, NJ: Chatham House Publishers.

Lee, Yoon-Shik. 1995. "A State of the Art of Public Policy Evaluation in Korea," paper presented to the IIAS Working Group on Policy and Program Evaluation (May). Department of Public Administration, Soong Sil University, Seoul, Korea.

Linder, Stephen and B. Guy Peters. 1989. "Instruments of Government: Perceptions and Contexts," *Journal of Public Policy* 9: 35–58.

Salamon, Lester M., ed. 1989. *Beyond Privatization: The Tools of Government Action.* Washington, DC: The Urban Institute Press.

Savas, E.S. 1987. *Privatization: The Key to Better Government.* Chatham, NJ: Chatham House Publishers.

Song, Dae-Hee. 1986. "Performance Evaluation of Korean Public Enterprises: Policy, Practice, and Experience." Working Paper no. 8601 (October), Korea Development Institute, Seoul.

11

Conclusions: Policy Instruments Types, Packages, Choices, and Evaluation

Marie-Louise Bemelmans-Videc and Evert Vedung

This book set out to offer its reader insights into the process of policy instrument choice and the role assigned to and actually played by evaluation in this process. To that purpose, there were basically three questions that needed to be answered:

1. Is there a general *typology* of policy instruments, of sufficient theoretical and empirical value, that helps discern the crucial characteristics of policy instruments and of the choice between them?
2. Given a formulated normative theory of policy instrument choice that stipulated central *criteria* of "good governance": What were the apparent considerations in our case studies that led to a certain choice? And closely related to that question: What was the role of *evaluation* in influencing the choice process? What evaluation criteria did actually play a role in legitimizing choice?
3. Does the comparative public policy approach and the concept of *policy style*, either nation- or sector-bound (the *context*), help to explain choices made?

The Policy Instruments Typology

A necessary requisite for the successful application of the policy-instruments approach to evaluation is that a fruitful and preferably parsimonious scheme of policy instruments be available. The present volume has been guided by a classification of policy tools into regulatory, economic, and informational instruments, spelled out in Evert Vedung's introduction. His discourse on public policy instruments is a discourse on political power. His typology is consequently based on the authoritative force or degree of constraint involved in the governance effort. It links the choice on this crucial characteristic to a nation's (or, indeed, sector's) dominant ideological position with regard to the degree of intervention in societal processes, and therefore to general political and administrative strategies.

The typology has proven to be fruitful in analyzing and explaining actual practice in the case studies presented in this book. However, our investigation has also lead to new specifications/variations within the general types.

While being elementary types, the three categories of policy instruments—the stick, the carrot, and the sermon for short—contain numerous internal variations. One such variation is that all three of them may be phrased either in the affirmative or in the negative. This is illustrated in figure 11.1.

Three Archetypes

In the next few sections, we will discuss the three archetypes one by one, then penetrate the notion that they may come in packages, and after that develop the idea that instruments can be joined to organizational forms.

Regulation Instruments

Donald Lemaire explores the formation, application, evaluation, and efficiency of regulatory tools. Among other things, the author argues

FIGURE 11.1
Three Archetypes of Policy Instruments
with Affirmative and Negative Variants

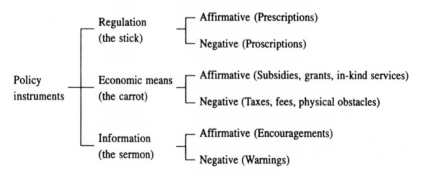

that the selection of government tools are largely determined by the nature of the policy area. He further observes a case where regulation is used to regulate regulation, as when the Canadian government instituted a policy that directs federal departments and agencies on how and when to use regulation. The stated objective of the policy is to ensure that use of the government's regulatory powers results in the greatest net benefit to Canadians. Departments and agencies are required to justify the need for regulation; weigh the benefits of the regulations against their cost; establish the framework needed to implement regulatory programs, that is, compliance and enforcement policies, management systems, and resources; determine the relevance, success, and cost-effectiveness of existing regulatory programs; and provide for an open regulatory process.

For existing regulatory programs and for substantive new or amended regulations, departments and agencies must demonstrate that: (1) a problem or risk exists, government intervention is justified, and regulation is the best alternative; (2) Canadians have been consulted and have had an opportunity to participate in developing or modifying regulatory programs; (3) the benefits of regulation outweigh the costs, and the regulatory program is structured to maximize the gains to beneficiaries in relation to the costs to Canadian governments, business, and individuals; (4) steps have been taken to ensure that the regulatory activity impedes Canada's competitiveness as little as possible; (5) the regulatory burden on Canadians has been minimized through such methods as cooperation with other governments; and (6) systems are in place to manage regulatory resources effectively, that is, that compliance policies are articulated as appropriate, and that resources have been approved and are adequate to discharge enforcement responsibilities effectively. In policy-instruments language, this is undoubtedly regulation of regulation, or more properly regulation for the adoption of other regulations. In public management terms, it is a case of process-oriented management, that is, the government attempts to direct the managerial processes of its departments and agencies instead of directing their outputs and outcomes.

Another interesting case study of the regulation type of policy instrument is Arentsen's study of radiation protection policy in The Netherlands, England, and Belgium. All three countries choose to regulate conditional prohibition trough permissions, however, implementing it in different ways, which resulted in different degrees of constraint. More will be said about this case when we discuss policy styles.

Economic Instruments

Economic tools of government are penetrated from various angles in the book. Particularly intricate types and patterns of economic instruments are discussed in the DeMarco and Rist chapter on U.S. semi-private lending organizations (ch. 8). In this context, we shall deliberate only on two basic forms: (1) subsidies and (2) contracting-out.

A *subsidy*, according to Frans L. Leeuw, is an economic policy instrument predicated on the conditional transfer of funds by government to, or for the benefit of, another party for the purpose of influencing that party's behavior with a view to achieving some level of activity or provision. Subsidies are financial incentives expended on the condition that the receivers undertake some activity that the government deems desirable or important.

While enjoying widespread popularity, subsidies are characterized by a number of difficulties. Leeuw notes that recipients may receive a subsidy although they have decided to undertake the stipulated action anyway without any subsidy. In this case of free riding, subsidizing is unnecessary and wasteful. Another problem is benefit snatching. Subsidies intended to provide benefit to consumers turn out to be a benefit for the producers. Producers may indicate that the costs of making some good will increase and subsequently prompt the government to increase the subsidy level. Had there been no subsidy increase, the increase in production costs may not have taken place.

Assessments of positive and negative aspects of subsidies are based mostly on investigations focusing on particular subsidies in specific policy sectors. To remedy this narrowness, the Dutch National Audit Office conducted a government-wide empirical investigation of subsidies dealing with questions like: (1) How many subsidies in which functional policy fields were issued by The Netherlands government? (2) What information did the government possess with regard to the goal-directedness, implementation, and ex-post evaluation of these subsidies? and (3) Were there differences between types of subsidies, on the one hand, and coverage by ex-post evaluations on the other? The questions were explicitly based on a theoretical framework in which the distinction between processes to be controlled in society and governmental control processes is central. The latter were analyzed in a systems-theory fashion, according to which governmental control processes are goal-directed processes that must be controlled by a number of *other* processes—processes of metacontrol as it were—enabling the controllers to collect data, perform measurements, and make necessary adjustments. The whole analysis was performed in an institution-free manner, in that no attention was paid to the impact of social, political, geographical, and other environmental factors that can and probably will have an influence on the management of subsidies.

The grand survey found 722 programs that were classified as subsidy programs. The findings of the survey include: (1) with respect to more than 80 percent of the 281 subsidies sufficiently large to be of evaluative interest, no evaluation criteria were formulated before they were enacted; (2) for all 722 programs, no valid information on implementation costs were available; (3) of the 410 subsidies where the benefits of an ex-post evaluation may be larger than the costs of performing it, it was found that 268 had not been evaluated, and (4) only 40 out of 718 subsidies (6 percent) were covered by both ex-ante and ex-post evaluations.

At the end of chapter 3, Leeuw posits that the findings of the survey suggest some new, intriguing research questions of an explanatory character. These questions include the consequences and costs of what Leeuw calls the "chains of subsidies": that unintended effects of certain subsidization are to be reduced through other subsidies. An example provided by the author is the long-term subsidization of the tobacco industry in Western countries while new subsidies are issued to finance anti-smoking information campaigns. Leeuw's observation ought to be emphasized. The issue of unintended and unanticipated side effects is a crucial one in policy-instruments research and evaluation, a point made several times in this book.

Contracting-out has become an increasingly popular economic instrument of improving the efficiency of government services. According to Joe Hudson, Richard Nutter, and Burt Galaway in chapter 7, contracting-out is a type of economic policy instrument that amounts to a decision by government to buy from private agencies rather than make or deliver goods and services itself. In turn, a government's policy decision to use the contracting-out instrument leads to a series of general decisions which are delineated in the chapter. The chapter also provides a carefully crafted list of tasks that are carried out in specific contracting-out situations.

The rationale for contracting-out include the following considerations: (1) to reduce the cost of services and improve effectiveness; (2) to provide government social workers with more choice of service providers and types of services; (3) to increase consumer choice; and (4) to reduce, or at least not increase, the size of public bureaucracy. All of these might be used as value criteria in ex-post as well as ex-ante evaluations of contracting-out arrangements. An especially interesting section of the chapter is where the authors expound on the fuzziness of some of these rationales and attempt to provide detailed specifications of them.

The efficiency argument for increased government contracting with private firms is based upon the idea of competitive bidding for public contracts. In contrast, it is the absence of competition in the public sector and of the concomitant pressures for keeping costs down, as well as the near impossibility of putting public agencies out of business, that prompts the conclusion that the lowest private bid is likely to be less than the cost of public supply. The efficiency argument also rests upon the assumptions that the costs of production are known by the bidders and the production plan proposed will be implemented, and that the goods and services requested by the government can be unambiguously specified. If these conditions are not met, it may become necessary to intervene in the contractual relationship after the contract has been let, which may create high transaction costs and undermine the efficiency of the arrangement.

With respect to evaluation, the authors put much stress on the different stakeholder perspectives involved. Each level of authority—federal, state, or provincial; county or regional; and officials from private agencies—may serve as evaluation users. Therefore, the initial questions to resolve in planning an evaluation of a contracted service are: Who are the primary clients for the study; what are their perspectives on the program; and what are their evaluation questions? The authors advocate that several perspectives should be taken into account. They also seem to adhere to what may be called the "North American stakeholder model," according to which the evaluation is performed by evaluators, who contact the stakeholders to get their perspectives and carry out the evaluation independently of them. The "Swedish stakeholder model" incorporated in the Swedish public policy commission system would be different: the stakeholders themselves, or rather their representatives, would serve on the team and actually carry out the evaluation (see Vedung 1996). In addition, the authors rightfully emphasize the necessity of making explicit the factors that explain why certain results are produced. In other words, in order to be practical and useful, evaluations should be theoretical and try to explain failures and successes. Kurt Lewin's famous dictum comes to mind: "there is no more practical thing than a good theory."

Information Instruments

Chapter 4 by Frans van der Doelen and Evert Vedung defines information instruments as government-directed attempts at influencing people through transfer of knowledge, communication of reasoned argument, and moral suasion. Why are information programs chosen as policy instruments? Several hypotheses are suggested: because universal compliance is not necessary; because public interest coincides with user interest; in paternalistic contexts; as a response to sudden crises; in situations of difficult bureaucratic oversight and of message drought, and when there is no counterinformation; and to legitimate a future resort to more intruding policy instruments. In addition to these rationales, the symbolic function of information programs is heavily stressed; often they are used to provide a token appearance of concern.

The authors argue in chapter 4 that information programs are more in need of evaluation than regulatory and economic programs, because they do not contain an automatic feedback mechanism. Economic programs are implemented in a bureaucratic setting with written records. For a grants program, for example, it is possible to get a general overview of the number of users, because applications are stored and often extra information concerning the characteristics of the applicants is available in the documents. To an even larger extent, the same goes with regulation. For instance, officially recorded violations of traffic security acts give some general feedback concerning the way the instrument is dealt with by society. Unlike economic and regulatory policy tools, mass-mediated government campaigns do not automatically generate knowledge about the number of listeners, viewers, or receivers and the way they generally respond. And it is these forms of information efforts that are often used, because they are relatively cheap and easy to launch.

The case for proper evaluation of information programs is worth pondering. The practice, though, is that especially this type of policy instrument lacks a firm evaluation culture. A review by the Dutch National Audit Office of approximately seventy national information programs gives some noteworthy results. As far as there were good evaluations available, it appeared that information had little impact. Information efforts by government produced knowledge changes ranging from 6 to 18 percent, attitude changes ranging from 0 to 12 percent, and behavioral modifications in a range from 0 to 13 percent. The budgeting of the information efforts was not transparent, the target groups were too large and amorphous, some information programs weakened the effect of others, and the impacts in general were very hard to track and assess.

A striking feature in this review is that most evaluations of information activities concern knowledge effects. Little evaluation pertains to attitude changes and almost no research at all is directed at changes of behavior. Also typical is that pilot evaluations of any kind before the full program is launched are rare. The policy instrument with very hard-to-detect effects seems to have a weak evaluation culture. How is this paradox to be explained?

The reaction of the Dutch ministries to the report provides some clues. The minister of justice, for example, emphasized that firm evaluation of this inexpensive policy instrument would cost more than the use of the instrument itself. Second, they noticed that information campaigns are often resorted to in crisis situations, because of their flexibility and the relative absence of bureaucratic red tape. In such situations it is inappropriate to arrange a good pilot evaluation before the full program is inaugurated. The relative inexpensiveness and adaptability of information programs thus contributes to a weak evaluation culture.

In their comprehensive review of 100 campaigns from the viewpoint of effectiveness, capacity to undermine the democratic relationship between citizens and government, and, particularly interesting, their political appeal, Weiss and Tschirhart conclude:

> Policy instruments with the capacity for effective intervention, which are politically feasible to use in a wide variety of circumstances, and with positive consequences for democracy and citizenship, are scarce indeed. P[ublic] i[nformation] c[ampaign]s do not deliver on all three counts every time; but the remarkable thing is that they are capable of delivering on all three counts. These positive conclusions do not negate the concerns and risks we have discussed. But they do make a case for including public information campaigns in the relatively short list of important instruments available in the policy design repertoire. (1994: 104)

Sometimes, government communication efforts—like other policy-instruments programs (Sieber 1981)—create perverse impacts. An unexpected boomerang effect is recorded in the history of forest fire protection campaigns by the Dutch government. After 1985, the Dutch government stopped with radio and television spots that warned against forest fires in the summer. The television spots showed someone carelessly dropping a cigarette in a wood or leaving bottles, after which a huge fire and scared running deer were shown. One reason for stopping the campaign was that immediately after the broadcasting, sudden fires occurred and several forests were burnt. Forest managers suggested that the spots drew the attention of pyromaniacs. Fires with unknown causes were probably deliberately set by malicious people, who reacted exactly contrary to the central intention of the campaign. Recent research into the effectiveness of government information campaigns on environmental issues again not only reveal disappointing but also opposite effects (Tertoolen and Kreveld 1995).

Energy conservation is one of the most exemplary policy areas in which information programs play a considerable, even dominant role. A comparison of the Dutch and Swedish energy conservation policies after the 1973 oil crisis shows some striking similarities. In both countries, energy conservation policies may be regarded as massive information efforts coupled with generous economic incentives. Swedish and Dutch authorities have denounced sticks and relied upon a package of sermons and carrots to bring people in line with national energy goals. What is the rationale behind this ample use of information?

In both countries the instrumental contribution of information programs to the ambitious energy conservation targets is significant but modest, due to the programs' voluntary character. But the information programs have a strong symbolic or token political function as well. In both countries, energy conservation is of crucial importance from an energy viewpoint because of the popular opposition to nuclear power. From a party strategy viewpoint, the information programs are highly visible and give the idea that government has undertaken massive efforts to stimulate energy conservation. When, after a long time, this policy does not solve the energy problem, the popular resistance against nuclear power may have faded away. Old plants may continue to operate and new plants can be built to provide a supply-side solution to the energy problem. Information programs, having symbolic or token political functions, legitimize rather than effectuate policies on the short term.

Packaging of Policy Instruments

Public policy instruments come in packages rather than in isolation. It has been a major thrust of this book to articulate something worthwhile about instrument packaging. What kinds of packages are there? Vertical, horizontal, and chronological packaging of instruments will be discussed. In vertical packaging, one instrument is directed at the implementation of another whereas in horizontal packaging two or more policy instruments or subtypes of the major policy instruments are directed at the same targets. Chronological packaging implies a certain time order in the selection among diverse policy tools.

Finally, we shall also address combinations of organization and instruments.

Our normative theory of good governance stipulates various criteria for instrument choice, criteria which represent values that often compete or conflict. In this light, the idea of combining instruments is the consequence of the search for optimum solutions, illustrated most clearly in horizontal packaging but also in chronological sequencing of policy instruments.

Vertical Packaging

Vertical packaging is predicated on the notion that the government uses several layers of actors to reach the final addressees, where higher-level actors are supposed to exert influence over lower-level actors through the use of policy instruments. In this view, policy instruments are employed by the government toward its own agencies, by its agencies toward some intermediary agency, by this intermediary agency toward another intermediary agency, and by the latter toward the final addressees. The general idea of policy-instruments use at various vertical levels of governance is illustrated in figure 11.2. It is important to stress that the model is intended neither as a depiction of empirical realities, nor as a normative ideal. It is intended as a Weberian ideal-type, as a heuristic tool for analysis.

FIGURE 11.2
Vertical Packaging of Policy Instruments

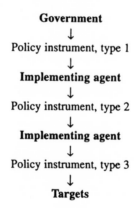

Government
↓
Policy instrument, type 1
↓
Implementing agent
↓
Policy instrument, type 2
↓
Implementing agent
↓
Policy instrument, type 3
↓
Targets

Figure 11.2 suggests three vertical levels of policy instruments use, but it could, of course, be two, four, five, and even more.

All across the industrialized world, regulation is used to regulate the government's own regulatory processes. A Canadian example of this type of vertical packaging of regulation to regulation is the one already mentioned, provided by Lemaire. The Canadian government has introduced a regulatory policy to force itself to review its own approach for selecting regulations. This regulatory policy directs federal departments and agencies on how and when to use regulation. Regulation, Lemaire argues, is the only policy tool in Canada that is subject to regulation.

Lemaire also provides an example of the regulation of information which is widely used all over the industrialized world, namely *mandatory labeling* (Hadden 1986, Bardach and Kagan 1982). The particular Canadian consumer-protection legislation implies truth in advertising and in packaging. The latter case is an example of regulation to force producers and distributors to provide information to the consumers. We may also maintain that governments direct a regulatory measure toward producers and sellers of goods and services in order to provide the consumers with information that enables them to make enlightened and rational decisions. This vertical packaging of regulation and information is depicted in figure 11.3.

Regulation can also be vertically packaged with economic instruments. *Price regulation* is a paradigm case of this mixture. Only the name tells us that price regulation is a regulatory instrument. Since producers, distributors, and sellers are obligated to follow the price directives issued by government, price regulations are regulatory. But

FIGURE 11.3
Vertical Packaging of Regulation to Information

Government
↓
Prescription to put on labels
(Policy instrument: Regulation)
↓
Sellers (Implementing agents)
↓
Labels
(Policy instrument: Information)
↓
Consumers (Targets)

FIGURE 11.4
Price Controls as a Package of Regulatory and Economic Instruments

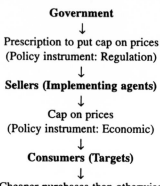

Government
↓
Prescription to put cap on prices
(Policy instrument: Regulation)
↓
Sellers (Implementing agents)
↓
Cap on prices
(Policy instrument: Economic)
↓
Consumers (Targets)
↓
Cheaper purchases than otherwise
(Circumstance to be influenced)

the instrumental purpose of price regulations is to influence the consumers by setting a cap on prices. This means that they are economic instruments as well. The consumers will pay the regulated price that will be (usually) lower than the unregulated market price would be. In other words, consumers are offered a material asset in order to be better off. But the method used to accomplish this is through regulation of producers and distributors. This vertical joining of regulation to economic incentives is sketched in figure 11.4.

In the cases so far provided, regulation is used to vertically control other instruments. But economic instruments and information can also be employed to govern other instruments. In the present context, our review will be confined to situations in which economic instruments are used to control others. An example of the economic-regulatory type of packaging, although this is not represented in the present book, is *government procurement* of goods and service, a kind of contracting-out as it were.

In his book *Regulation and Its Alternatives*, Alan Stone (1982: 126) tells a story that can illustrate this vertical packaging of economic instruments with regulation. In July 1980, U.S. Secretary of Labor Ray Marshall, told the Firestone Tire and Rubber Company that it could no longer contract with the U.S. government. The Secretary's decision was based on an executive order that prohibited government contractors from engaging in racial and sexual discrimination. Whether it was a fair de-

FIGURE 11.5
Vertical Packaging of Economic Instruments in the Canadian-
United States Contracting-Out Case

Government
↓
Contracting-out
(Policy instrument: Economic in cash, i.e., money with strings)
↓
Service agencies (Implementing agents)
↓
Contracting with foster parents
(Policy instrument: Economic in cash, i.e., money with strings)
↓
Foster parents (Implementing agents)
↓
Service
(Policy instrument: Economic in kind)
↓
Children (Targets)

cision or not is open to discussion. According to Stone, all the company had done was to hire a lower proportion of minorities and women than the quota established by the U.S. Labor Department. No discrimination charges against Firestone were made or proved. But the U.S. Labor Department reasoned that racial and sexual discrimination is rarely obvious and that failure to meet government quotas, however rigid, without some justification was convincing proof of this inequitable practice.

Directed procurement—in this particular case, withdrawal of procurement contracts—was used as a policy instrument involving the taking away of future material benefits, in other words as an economic means of government. But the interesting thing is that it was used to enforce particular regulatory standards—quotas. An economic instrument was vertically packaged with a regulatory one.

An interesting case of vertical packaging of economic instruments to economic instruments is provided by Joe Hudson et al. Their case is illustrated in figure 11.5.

First the service is contracted out to service agencies implying that cash money is disbursed on certain provisos. Second, the service agencies enter into contracts with foster parents, which also implies that cash money is disbursed on certain provisos. Finally, the foster parents

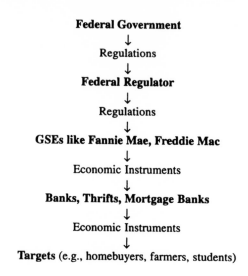

FIGURE 11.6
Four-tiered Vertical Packaging of Policy Instruments in the U.S. GSEs Case

Federal Government
↓
Regulations
↓
Federal Regulator
↓
Regulations
↓
GSEs like Fannie Mae, Freddie Mac
↓
Economic Instruments
↓
Banks, Thrifts, Mortgage Banks
↓
Economic Instruments
↓
Targets (e.g., homebuyers, farmers, students)

provide family treatment care for the eligible children, where the service in policy-instruments language must be regarded an economic policy tool in kind.

Another case of economic-to-economic instruments packaging is described by DeMarco and Rist. Most of the government-sponsored enterprises that they analyze in their chapter are "secondary market" institutions. They provide financing (economic instruments) to other financing institutions like banks, thrifts, and mortgage banks, that in turn lend money (economic instruments) to homebuyers, farmers, and students. Actually the packaging reasoning can be pushed even further. Since the GSEs are also controlled by federal regulations concerning, for instance, the composition of their board of directors and the area where they are allowed to be active, we get the regulations-economic instruments-economic instruments combination. A simple illustration is provided in figure 11.6.

There seems to be no end to human inventiveness as far as vertical packaging of policy instruments is concerned.

Horizontal Packaging

In horizontal packaging, two or more policy instruments are directed simultaneously at the same agent. For instance, an agent may be forced to do something but in order to facilitate his compliance the government may also offer financial help and advice.

Frans van der Doelen's chapter on the give-and-take strategy (ch. 5) ends with a policy-instruments doctrine, which seems to involve horizontal packaging of affirmative and negative variants of the same major type of policy instrument. It is horizontal because both types of instruments are directed simultaneously at the same target population and the one is not used to entice some implementing agent to act toward the target group, as in vertical packaging. The author argues forcefully that stimulative and repressive variants of the communicative, economic, and regulatory models should be combined into comprehensive policies, because the stimulative instruments legitimate and create support for the intervention whereas repressive instruments effectuate the intervention and produce results. The author further maintains that an accepted stimulative policy does not bring the objectives any closer to realization, and a strong repressive policy arouses so much resistance that it frustrates the implementation and scarcely produces the desired effects. Therefore an appropriate (horizontal) package of stimulation and repression will influence the feasibility of a policy. He concludes: "It is therefore a package which can barely be missed in practice."

This advice has been repeated in recent research, for example, in the field of environmental subsidies, with low effectiveness in influencing environmental decision making by private companies. Combinations of judicial, economic, and communicative instruments appear to be more effective (Vermeulen 1993).

Chronological Sequencing of Policy Instruments

The third major type of policy-instruments packaging to be dealt with here, chronological sequencing, implies a certain time order in the selection among diverse policy tools. For instance, first information is used, after some time economic means, and finally, after some more time, regulation.

Also in chapter 5, van der Doelen notes that policy instruments are sometimes employed in sequence in such a way as to suggest increasing degrees of constraint, for example, from information transfer through economic incentives to directives. Reference is made to the three-Es strategy: education, engineering, and enforcement. The idea is that over time a policy problem is tackled in three different ways: first by the provision of information (education), subsequently by the application of selective incentives (engineering), and lastly by the establishment of rules and regulation (enforcement). The underlying notion is that in solving social problems the authorities apply tools of increasing strength in successive stages.

In Evert Vedung's chapter on policy instruments (ch. 1), the similar time-sequencing suggestion by Doern and Wilson (1974: 339, Doern and Phidd 1983: 128ff.) is mentioned. According to these authors, "politicians have a strong tendency to respond to policy issues (any issue) by moving successively from the least coercive governing instrument to the most coercive." The idea is that over time a policy problem is tackled in three different ways: first by the provision of information such as uttering a broad statement of intent, subsequently by the application of selective incentives, and lastly by the establishment of regulations accompanied by the threat of sanction. Again, the underlying notion is that in solving social problems the authorities employ instruments of increasing strength in successive stages.

Why are policy instruments applied in this particular order of increasing constraint? First of all, the prevalence of this pattern is far from established; more conscious research on policy-instruments adoption is needed. In spite of scant evidence, two explanations are advanced in the book. One reason is concerned with the promotion of the legitimacy of and public confidence in the intervention. The least coercive instrument is introduced first, in order to gradually weaken the resistance of certain groups of individuals and adjust them to government intervention in the area. After some time, the authorities feel entitled to regulate the matters definitively by employing their most powerful instrument. If people then protest, the government may reply that more lenient tools have been employed but to no avail.

A certain preference of order among the instruments may also be deduced from a liberal political philosophy. The first principle of classic liberals is to avoid government intervention altogether. But if government intervention is deemed necessary, they would ideally adhere to a minimal-constraint principle. Minimal constraint means to visit on the populace the least possible amount of "trouble, vexation, and oppression" as Adam Smith put it (Hood 1986: 190ff.). The minimal-constraint principle would dictate that lower-constraint instruments such as moral suasion and financial incentives be preferred to higher-constraint instruments like regulation, where all else is equal (Doern and Phidd 1983: 112).

Combining Policy Instruments and Organizations

While a case can be made for the *logical* separation of organizational arrangements and policy instruments proper, the two can be combined in various ways. Organization and instruments can be *practically* combined into so many packages as to defeat all efforts at typification.

In recent literature, the importance of the organizational setting for the functioning of policy instruments is stressed more and more. Arentsen, for instance, emphasizes the need for linking public policy and organization theory. No doubt, organizing, reorganizing, and deorganizing are crucial tenets of every administrative policy. Governments constantly change their organizations to cover new issue-areas, ensure public confidence, and increase functional effectiveness. Organization is necessary for the provision of regulatory, economic, and informational policy instruments. Policy instruments cannot be applied if there is no government organization or government mercenary to do the job. Without proper organizations, government information campaigns, grant programs, or regulatory regimes cannot be implemented. The way implementation is organized obviously influences the impact and legitimacy of policy instruments.

The joining of instruments to organizational matters is best illustrated by the classical and recent political debates on socialization and privatization. A maximum meaning of privatization is transformation of the ownership of an activity from the public to the private sector. The opposite is socialization, implying that the ownership of an activity is transferred from the private to the public. A less radical meaning is the partial or full transformation of the operation of an activity—but not the ownership—from the public to the private, and vice versa (for a good overview of the discussion of the "when" and "how" of privatization and of the choice of organization—for-profit or non-profit—see Gormley 1994).

As can be inferred from Nam-Kee Lee's contribution on Korea's public enterprises (ch. 10), policy instruments and organization can be combined in two ways. First, government enterprises must work under certain conditions, determined by central authorities. These conditions may be expressed in rules and directives which are policy instruments of a regulatory character, stipulating the processes through which the enterprises should be managed. They constitute a kind of process-oriented management on behalf of the government toward the enterprises. They contain directives concerning, for instance, the composition of the board of directors of the enterprises, who should appoint senior executive officers, the guidelines within which the board can manage the enterprise, who should decide about the budget, how their procurement function should be carried out, and how the enterprises should be audited and evaluated. In cases where the enterprises are funded via the government budget, economic instruments are also involved. Second, the enterprises themselves also apply policy instruments toward the public. Sometimes these instruments are of a regulatory character, for instance in the case of the Korea Stock Exchange, which issues regulations concerning sales of securities and shares. In most cases, however, they seem to be of an economic character either in kind or in cash. For instance, the provision of elementary and middle school textbooks (National Textbook Company, in-kind economic instrument), the provision of credit guarantees and loans for technology development (Korea Technology Development Corporation, in-cash economic instrument), the production and distribution of electricity (Korea Electric Power Corporation, in-kind), and the production and distribution of ginseng (Korea Tobacco and Ginseng Corporation, in-kind) are all instruments that are economic in character.

Nam-Kee Lee also intimates that the history of the Korean public enterprises has taken the form of an inverted "U." After 1945 the Korean government established a considerable amount of public enterprises by taking over property formerly owned by the Japanese colonial administration or by Japanese private businessmen. The public enterprises constituted the economic backbone of the country and were, in the 1960s, the major engine for achieving the political goal of industrial rehabilitation following the incredible mass destruction of the Korean War. Around 1970 there was a growing concern about the performance of the public enterprises. From this time onwards, it seems that organizational reform of the public enterprises in Korea has been undertaken primarily to improve the working of the services provided to the public. It has also proceeded according to a certain ordered pattern. First, some management reforms have been implemented, such as the first performance evaluation system followed by the 1984 performance evaluation reform. Nam-Kee Lee describes how the latter system has worked. The evaluations proper are carried out by an annual ad-hoc management evaluation task force, which establishes evaluation criteria and carry out the evaluation. The ad-hoc form is chosen to ensure evaluative fairness. The task force is composed of "accountants, professors, researchers, and concerned specialists." The results of the evaluation are connected to the incentive bonus issue. The author argues that the new evaluation system has resulted in substantial performance improvement of the enterprises. In a second step, the operational form of the enterprises are changed into a less government-directed and more private-operated form. Lastly, the enterprises are fully privatized.

An illustration of a different instruments-organization-instruments combination is provided in the contribution by Edward J. DeMarco and Ray C. Rist on government-sponsored enterprises as credit allocation tools in the United States (ch. 8). Contrary to Korean public enterprises, U.S. GSEs are privately owned organizations but with federal charters that regulate their use of economic instruments to a specified public purpose. On a scale ranging from private companies via government corporations to government agencies, the GSEs occupy a place between private companies and government corporations.

Like the Korean corporations, some internal processes of the six U.S. GSEs are controlled by regulatory instruments. For instance, there are rules concerning who should appoint members to the board of directors. In addition, they are subsidized by the federal government, that is, the government uses economic instruments toward them. There are also regulations concerning how they should use their major economic subsidization instruments either directly toward the public or indirectly via other financing organizations—for example, a prescription that the U.S. Department of the Treasury has the final approval over issuance of debt securities, and a prescription that each of them is restricted to serving one specific economic sector such as farming. Toward the public or toward other financing institutions, the GSEs use a variety of economic policy instruments.

DeMarco and Rist advance interesting arguments on the evaluation of complex organizational/institutional arrangements like GSEs. For instance, some GSEs have introduced intricate, innovative ways for managing interest-rate risk that make them pioneers in certain risk management practices. Innovations always create problems for goal-achievement evaluators, because by definition they cannot be foreseen and included among the initial program goals. Yet it is crucial that innovations and other unforeseen and unexpected effects be taken into account in evaluations. Another unintended effect of the GSEs are the distorting influences and hidden costs to society when the government chooses to subsidize credit in some sectors but not in others. In general, the authors emphasize that evaluators are not very well equipped to make overall assessments of large and complex phenomena like GSEs, because they are used to desegregating policies and organizations into smaller component parts that are more amenable to traditional evaluation designs. Their observation raises the larger general issue of how to evaluate, not singular programs, but comprehensive policies covering entire policy sectors like energy, land use, and environment. This is a question often raised by elected and appointed officials alike but on which there is no good answer.

In the paragraphs above we have not only discussed the numerous internal variations and external combinations of instruments, but also indicated the role of evaluation in instrument choice. In the next paragraph we reflect on the implicit or explicit evaluation criteria in choice processes.

Evaluation Criteria and the Choice of Policy Instruments

What criteria should, and actually will, lead politicians and administrators in their choice of instruments? To answer this question, we have introduced four central criteria of "good governance" against which choice may be legitimized. These criteria will, of necessity, also be central to the evaluation criteria that play a role in research relevant for policy design, more specifically for policy-instruments choice.

Much discussion of policy instruments, and part of our case studies seem to reflect this, rests on a view of public policy- making as an exercise in the logic of efficient choice and in particular as an exercise in economizing. Classical administrative theory has for a long time been preoccupied with substantive efficiency in the adoption of policy instruments. In admitting that ends are politically contested and value-driven, classical theory treats them both as externally given and embraced in the sense that it is assumed that the actors really want to achieve them. Provided ends are given, the selection of instruments is considered a neutral, even scientific enterprise. Since instruments should be chosen for efficiency, the choice of the most efficient means to attain a given end can in principle be ascertained in an objective fashion by resorting to scientific procedures. Decisions on policy instruments are seen as choices of means in goal-directed problem-solving processes.

The proper role of administrative theory is, given politically or socially decided goals, or even assuming that some goals are worthwhile, to determine, through the use of best empirical methodology and social theory available, the most efficient means to reach the indicated goals.

Since the goals are assumed to have been set by extra-scientific sources, the administrative theorist can pursue fact-finding about means in a purely value-neutral and objective fashion (Fischer 1990). Popper's words comes to mind: "Piecemeal social engineering resembles physical engineering in regarding the *ends* as beyond the province of technology" (1957: 3). Associations also go to Herbert Simon: "the adaptation of means to ends is the only element of the decisional problem that has a factual solution" (1976: 184, 45ff.).

This presentation does not hold true any more; the value-laden character of instrument choice, the status of the instrument as "sub-objective" in a policy (or "intervention") theory is fully recognized. The dominant role of the efficiency criterion of good governance has for some decades now been compensated by the political and legal approaches in public administration theory, stressing values of democracy ("responsiveness") and of legality (including principles of proper process like motivation and equity). As we have argued earlier, these central criteria of evaluation will in actual practice often represent mutually incompatible objectives. These dilemmas at the heart of the choice process were illustrated amply by the packaging formulas described above. Actual prioritization will be greatly determined by national or sectoral policy styles, which are embedded in the political and administrative culture and ensuing strategies. We therefore conclude that in most cases high level instrument choice is also governed by other considerations than effectiveness and efficiency.

In line with the argument that evaluation can be used conceptually, politically, and ritually (Shadish, Cook, and Leviton 1991), it is worthwhile to also discuss the symbolic or political uses of policy instruments. The examples are there in our case material.

First of all, in political life it is common that the instruments are politically controversial while the stated goals are unanimously embraced. The reason for this is that stated goals sometimes are intended to fulfill other functions than indicating targets to be achieved. They are used for symbolic reasons to agitate and garner support and to legitimize the instruments chosen to some audience. In the symbolic and legitimizing perspective, stated goals are used to bring support to the basic issue at stake, a particular choice of means. In the partisan perspective, instruments are chosen because they further politically strategic ends. Instruments are selected to promote the power of the instigators. For instance, instrument choice is made to bolster the strength and power of the party, usually in order to win the next election, or keep the party united, or enable coalition building. In the network perspective, instruments are inaugurated for the purpose of building or strengthening organizations in the hope that they will provide valuable support in the long run. A bureaucratic agency is built up and given instruments not in order to be immediately efficient in the substantive area, but to provide political support in the long run. Consequently, in political life, policy instruments may be embraced although they have little instrumental, substantive significance for the attainment of immediate policy goals.

Sometimes instruments are controversial or preferred for direct ideological reasons. Fees to permit pollution, for instance, have been opposed for a long time by environmentalists and left-wing parties with reference to deep-seated ethical concerns. It would be ethically wrong to allow polluters to buy themselves free to pollute our common amenities. Pro-growth lobbies and center-to-right parties on the other hand have tended to favor economic instruments for environmental protection, with reference to efficiency considerations.

Let us now look at the intended or assigned role of ex-ante and ex-post evaluation in the case studies presented in this volume and of the apparent or presumed evaluation criteria.

The *practice of evaluation* fluctuates quite impressively: in some cases, like the Canadian regulation-of-regulation example, it has acquired an explicit status; in The Netherlands, ex-ante and ex-post evaluations cover 30 to 50 percent of subsidies (measured in total sums involved), while information policies in The Netherlands and, to a lesser extent, Sweden lack "a firm evaluation culture." In the case of the U.S. policies with regard to GSE's, the innovative and complex character of the arrangements pose serious evaluation problems; in the case of contacting-out (Canada and the United States) and the radiation protection policy, evaluation practice is quite limited. In all cases, the authors argue for the need of (increased) evaluation, not only for the obvious reasons (such as the need to test effectiveness, e.g., of a combination of instruments), but also with reference to lack of automatic feedback mechanisms (as in information campaigns), the negative-unintended and even perverse effects registered and the normative requirement of involving stakeholders in the review of the program's success.

As for *evaluation criteria*: in the cases presented, effectiveness and efficiency clearly dominate. However, there are also interesting examples of additional criteria of participatory democracy and requirements related to "due process" criteria, like in Canada's regulation policy. Sometimes, the criteria are really more pragmatic than principal in nature, as in information campaigns, or technically defined (however as such meant to enlarge effectiveness) as in the case of the radiation protection policy. Missing criteria are most intriguing, like in the case of the Dutch subsidies, where most often (ex-ante) evaluation criteria were not formulated, indicating a lack of reflection on the relation between the subsidy and the intended goals.

It is obvious, that generalization on this point would require larger numbers of case studies. However, we are confident that the cases presented give a reasonably good overview of the varying rationales for evaluation and for instrument choice.

The Context Variable: Policy Style in Nation and Sector

Does "politics determine policy" or, rather, will "policy determine politics" (Freeman 1985)? Is a policy style, as the outcome of a nation's systemic characteristics, culture, and structure, of decisive influence on the choice of instruments, or rather the very nature of sectorial problems? This volume offers two cases that may provide indicative answers.

Arentsen (ch. 9) argues that The Netherlands, the United Kingdom, and Belgium have basically chosen to institute the same policy instruments in their radiation protection policy, but have adopted different policy styles in the implementation of these identical instruments. In policy-instruments language, all three have adopted a regulatory approach, or more specifically, regulations of the conditional-prohibition-with-permissions type. There is a general prohibition of possessing radioactive substances or x-ray equipment without a permit. Admittedly, there are some differences within this general orientation. The Dutch regulation applies to all users. In England, minor users do not need a permit but they must comply with an obligation to notify the authorities and register the use. In Belgium, the users are divided into two groups with different conditions for permits. Yet all in all, Arentsen argues, the adopted policies look very similar.

While the goal of the radiation protection policies is almost completely attained in all three countries—the dose limits are hardly ever exceeded—the policy styles in the implementation of the instruments are very different among them. The Dutch developed a policy style which the author calls instructive, meaning that the public authorities contact the permit applicants to advice and educate them. The policy style of the English is of a functional type. The authorities maintain some distance from the applicants. If violations are discovered, the authorities allow for improvements. Yet hardliners do not get a second opportunity—they are prosecuted. In Belgium, the policy style is formalistic and passive in case of enforcement. Most things are relegated to specialized professional organizations. The Belgians rely on self-regulating forces.

Which factors can explain the differences in policy style between the three countries in their implementation of the same regulatory instruments? Arentsen asserts that the answer lies in the policy area. The English and the Belgians controlling the agencies give priority to the extensive nuclear industry in both countries, resulting in less controlling attention to the users of radioactive substances. This strategy is legitimated by the professionalism of the users of radioactive substances, although the English have adopted this professionalism more effectively in their controlling strategy than the Belgians. The Dutch, on the other hand, lack a nuclear industry with strong professions; this explains why the governmental authorities themselves take on a more active, educational, and advisory role. They can only concentrate on the users of radioactive substances, although the professionalism of the Dutch users is not less than that of the English and the Belgian ones. As a result, the Dutch users seem to be patronized by the Dutch controlling agencies.

The other comparative study of the same policy sector is offered by Vedung's and van den Doelen's chapter on energy conservation policy in Sweden and The Netherlands (ch. 4). Both governments denounced "sticks" and relied upon a package of sermons and carrots instead. In the view of the authors, with support of empirical material, these are not—of necessity—the most effective instruments; energy price setting most probably is. The authors stress the symbolic use of these instruments. In speculating on the reasons for both countries to choose similar packages of instruments, the "policy (sector) determines politics" hypothesis seems to offer the most probable explanation.

A Final Note

Policy instruments fascinate, since they are the tools through which governmental authorities wield their power. We have offered analytical tools and empirical material that we hope do offer the promised enlightening structuring of the field. We have explored individual types of instrument as well as their vertical, horizontal, chronological, and organizational packaging. We have given an overview of the roles played by evaluation and of the evaluation criteria deemed important in the choice of instruments. The evidence of a comparative nature was limited to two interesting cases. As we argued in the Introduction, the international dimension in public policy choice is in need of further exploration given the increasing internationalization of the public domain. Obviously, this offers a challenging and also most difficult invitation to the classic finale of any policy research book: the request for more research.

References

Bardach, E. and R.A. Kagan. 1982. *Going by the Book: The Problem of Regulatory Unreasonableness*. Philadelphia: Temple University Press.

Doern, G.B. and R.W. Phidd. 1983. *Canadian Public Policy: Ideas, Structure, Process*. Toronto: Methuen.

Doern, G. B. and V.S. Wilson, eds. 1974. *Issues in Canadian Public Policy*. Toronto: Macmillan of Canada.

Fischer, F. 1990. *Technology and the Politics of Expertise*. Newbury Park, CA: Sage.

Freeman, G.P. 1985. "National Styles and Policy Sectors: Explaining Structured Variation," *Journal of Public Policy* 5(4): 467–496.

Gormley, W.T., Jr. 1994–5. "Privatization Revisited," in *Policy Studies Review* 13(3/4): 215–234.

Hadden, S. 1986. *Read the Label: Reducing Risk by Providing Information*. Boulder, CO: Westview.

Hood, C.C. 1983. *The Tools of Government*. London: Macmillan.

Popper, Karl R. 1957. *The Poverty of Historicism*. London: Routledge & Kegan Paul.

Shadish, W.R., Jr., T.D. Cook, and Laura C. Leviton. 1991. *Foundations of Program Evaluation: Theory and Practice*. London: Sage.

Simon, H.A. 1976. *Administrative Behavior: A Study of Decision- Making Processes in Administrative Organizations*. 3d ed. London: Collier-Macmillan.

Sieber, S.D. 1981. *Fatal Remedies: The Ironies of Social Intervention*. New York: Plenum Press.

Stone, A. 1982. *Regulation and Its Alternatives*. Washington, DC: Congressional Quarterly Press.

Tertoolen, G. and D. van Kreveld. 1995. "Ineffectiviteit en schadelijke bijwerkingen van voorlichting: Overheidscampagnes ter discussie," *Beleid en Maatschappij* 5: 296–303.

Vedung, E. 1996. *Public Policy and Program Evaluation*. New Brunswick, NJ: Transaction Publishers.

Vermeulen, W.J.V. 1993. "Milieusubsidies: pacificerend, maar weinig effectief," *Openbare Uitgaven* 3: 171–181.

Weiss, J.A. and M. Tschirhart. 1994. "Public Information Campaigns as Policy Instruments," *Journal of Policy Analysis and Management* 13(1): 82–119.

Contributors

Maarten J. Arentsen is vice-director of the Center for Clean Technology and Environmental Policy of Twente University, The Netherlands. Dr. Arentsen's research focuses on regulatory policies for energy and environment as illustrated by his publications, which include *Radiation Policy in The Netherlands* (1988), his dissertation on *Policy Organization and Policy Implementation; An Inquiry into Radiation Protection Policy in The Netherlands, England and Belgium* (1991) and recently (1996) *Economic Organization and Liberalization of the Electricity Industry* (with R. Künneke).

Marie-Louise Bemelmans-Videc is professor of Public Administration at the University of Nijmegen, The Netherlands, and Advisor to the Netherlands Court of Audit in The Hague. Her professional interests and publications are in the theory and practice of public administration in general and in auditing and evaluation in particular. She is a founder of the European Evaluation Society and associate editor for Evaluation Studies for *Knowledge and Policy: he International Journal of Knowledge Transfer* (Rutgers University, USA).

Edward J. DeMarco holds a Ph.D. in economics from the University of Maryland. he has had a number of appointments in both the legislative and executive branches of the United States government. His recent appointments include the United States General Accounting Office, The Federal Reserve Board, and currently, the United States Treasury.

Burt Galaway is a professor at the University of Manitoba, Winnipeg.

Joe Hudson is a professor in the faculty of social work, University of Calgary in Alberta. Dr. Hudson previously served as the audit principal in the Office of the Auditor General of Canada, responsible for examining federal government initiatives in program evaluation and performance measurement.

Nam-Kee Lee is vice chairman, Economic Planning Board of the Fair Trade Commission of Korea.

Frans L. Leeuw is currently professor and director of the Humanities and Social Sciences Department, Netherlands Open University as well as professor of evaluation research, Department of Sociology, Utrecht University, The Netherlands. Earlier he was affiliated with the Netherlands Court of Audit (1987–1996), Leiden University (1978–1987) and Utrecht University (1974–1978). He is vice president of the European Evaluation Society.

Donald Lemaire is general counsel, Department of Justice Canada, Ottawa, since 1993. Previously he served as evaluation analyst, Employment and Immigration, Canada 1982–1984, evaluation analyst, Correctional Service of Canada, 1984–1986, coordinator, Program Evaluation, Social Sciences and Humanities Research Council 1986–1988, and evaluation analyst, Program Branch, Office of the Comptroller General of Canada 1990–1993.

Ray C. Rist is the evaluation advisor to the Economic Development Institute of The World Bank. He is also the administrator of the World Bank scholarship programs. Dr. Rist has prior appointments in both universities and the United States government. He has authored or edited twenty-two books and written more than 110 articles. He has guest lectured in more than forty countries and served as a consultant to many national and international organizations.

Frans C.J. van der Doelen is presently a senior policy advisor at the Ministry of Justice, The Netherlands. Dr. van der Doelen earned his Ph.D. (1989) with a thesis on *Policy Instruments and Energy Conservation; the Implementation and Effects of Information Campaigns and Subsidies in Dutch Industrial Energy Conservation Policy, 1977–1987.* He held positions at the Faculty of Public Administration of Twente

University, the Netherlands Court of Audit and the Ministry of Justice. He is widely published on public administration and policy evaluation.

Evert Vedung is professor of political science in Uppsala University's Institute for Housing Research (Gävle) and Department of Government (Uppsala), Sweden, and associate professor in the Department of Public Administration, Åbo Academy University, Finland. He has also been a visiting scholar and professor at universities in Austria, Denmark, Korea, Norway, Poland, and the United States. Besides housing and planning, Evert Vedung's research interests include policies for land use, nuclear energy and energy conservation, global environmental policy for the protection of the ozone layer, implementation and evaluation, local government, political language, and the comparative method. His book *Public Policy and Program Evaluation* was recently published by Transaction.

Index

About the Editors

Marie-Louise Bemelmens-Videc is professor of public administration at the University of Nijmegen, The Netherlands, and advisor to the Netherlands Court of Audit in The Hague. Her professional interests include the theory and practice of public administration in general and of auditing and evaluation in particular. She was a senior Fulbright fellow in the United States in 1988. She is a founder of the European Evaluation Society and associate editor for evaluation studies for *Knowledge and Policy; The International Journal of Knowledge Transfer* (Rutgers University, N.J.).

Ray C. Rist is the evaluation advisor to the Economic Development Institute of The World Bank. He is also the Administrator of the World Bank scholarship programs. Dr. Rist has prior appointments in both universities and the United States government. He has authored or edited twenty-two books and written more than 110 articles. He has guest lectured in more than forty countries and served as a consultant to many national and international organizations. Dr. Rist received his Ph.D. in sociology from Washington University (St. Louis, Mo.) in 1970.

Evert Vedung is professor of political science in Uppsala University's Institute for Housing Research (Gävle) and Department of Government (Uppsala), Sweden, and associate professor of public administration in the Department of Public Administration, Åbo Academy University, Finland. He has also held a special position on evaluation research in the Swedish Research Council for the Humanities and the Social Sciences.

CPSIA information can be obtained at www.ICGtesting.com
Printed in the USA
BVOW031258120612

292438BV00001B/3/P

9 780765 805461